Three Minutes a Day

VOLUME 5 4

THREE MINUTES A DAY
VOLUME 54

Tony Rossi
Editor-in-Chief

The Christophers
5 Hanover Square
New York, NY 10004

www.christophers.org

Scriptural quotations in this publication are from the Revised Standard Version Bible, Catholic Edition, copyright 1965 and 1966 by the Division of Christian Education of the National Council of Churches of Christ in the U.S.A. and the New Revised Standard Version Bible, Catholic Edition, copyright 1989 by the Division of Christian Education of the National Council of Churches of Christ in the U.S.A. and used by permission.

Our founder, Father James Keller, M.M., chose the following prayer attributed to St. Francis of Assisi as the Prayer of The Christophers because it represents the potential for good that God instilled in each of us.

Lord, make me an instrument of Your peace.
Where there is hatred, let me sow love;
where there is injury, pardon;
where there is doubt, faith;
where there is despair, hope;
where there is darkness, light;
and where there is sadness, joy.

O Divine Master, grant that I may not so much seek
to be consoled as to console;
to be understood as to understand;
to be loved as to love.
For it is in giving that we receive;
it is in pardoning that we are pardoned;
and it is in dying that we are born to eternal life.
Amen.

PRAYER OF ST. FRANCIS
(ADOPTED AS THE PRAYER OF THE CHRISTOPHERS)

The Christophers warmly thank
all our friends, sponsors and supporters
who have made this 54th volume of
Three Minutes a Day possible.

Contributing Writers

Tony Rossi

Sarah E. Holinski

Joan Bromfield

Paul McAvoy

Mariann Hughes

Melissa Kuch

Garan Santicola

Dear Friend,

We are pleased to present volume 54 of our *Three Minutes a Day* series. Within these pages, you will find inspiring readings for each day of 2020. This is a very special year because it marks the 75th anniversary of the founding of The Christophers!

Father James Keller, M.M., started The Christophers in 1945 with the expressed intention of spreading a message of hope and reminding all people that they have a special mission in life that God intends for no one else but them. Over the years, The Christophers' message has touched countless lives. There are no dues, or meetings, or formal obligations associated with being a Christopher. Our organization is not inward looking; we are outward looking. Christopher means "Christ-bearer," and to be a Christopher all one need do is allow Christ to enter your heart. Then, remain committed to sharing His love with everyone you encounter.

Our *Three Minutes a Day* series is designed to support your daily mission by providing a few short moments of reflection on how God works in our world. We hope these readings inspire you to know that God is at work in your life and in the lives of your friends, loved ones, and all those you encounter. That awareness can change how you react to certain situations and help you to cooperate more fully with the workings of the Holy Spirit.

Christ said, "Take My yoke upon you, and learn from Me; for I am gentle and humble in heart, and you will find rest for your souls. For My yoke is easy and My burden is light" (Matthew 11:29-30). When we see our role as one of cooperating with the daily miracles of grace that God effects in the world, it lightens our burdens and helps us to find harmony in life. We hope this book brings you peace and kindles fires of inspiration to light your journey to true and lasting joy.

Mary Ellen Robinson, Vice President
Father Edward M. Dougherty, M.M., Board of Directors
Father Dennis W. Cleary, M.M.

Reach Out in the New Year, Part One

After reading about a study that showed loneliness in the United States had reached epidemic proportions, Elizabeth Manneh felt that God was challenging her to improve the lives of others as her New Year's resolution. Writing on the website *Busted Halo,* she shared some of her ideas:

■ "Be observant. It's easy to miss signs of loneliness, so keep an eye out for those on the fringes who might benefit from words of welcome, a friendly conversation, or a kind gesture."

■ "Give your time. Maybe somebody you know is struggling with a stressful job, coping with a personal crisis, or lives alone and doesn't feel like going out without a companion. Offer to take them for a much-needed night out."

■ "Taking someone to medical appointments is another way to give your time. A few years ago, my mother needed regular hospital treatments every day for three weeks, and the hospital was over 25 miles away. Her church made up a rotation of people who drove her there, chatted with her while she waited, and brought her home afterwards. She felt very loved."

More tomorrow...

Bear one another's burdens. (Galatians 6:2)

Make me sensitive to the loneliness of others, Lord.

Reach Out in the New Year, Part Two

Here are more of Elizabeth Manneh's New Year's resolutions (via *BustedHalo.com*) to help ease the loneliness of others:

- "Carry yourself with kindness. Treating others with a positive attitude can make a huge difference in someone's day. Smile and say hello to the supermarket cashier, the bank teller, or the senior citizen in line for the bus."

- "Put your skills to good use. When I was a single parent, I dreaded facing household maintenance or repair jobs, and was overjoyed when our neighbor offered to fix our gas fireplace when the switch got stuck. For some, even a small job like repairing a leaky faucet is a task that can seem mountainous, but it's easy for the handy DIY enthusiast. Think about what needs you might be able to meet in your community."

- "Send a handwritten card. Snail mail is not dead!…Why not dust off your pen and write a good old-fashioned letter? Many older people struggle with modern technology, but will keep and reread a letter over and over again."

Turn to me and be gracious to me, for I am lonely and afflicted. (Psalm 25:16)

Teach me to be of service to others, Jesus.

It Was a God Thing

Jamario Howard, JaMychol Baker, and Tae Knight were waiting for their order at Brad's Bar-B-Que in Oxford, Alabama, when Jamario noticed an elderly woman sitting by herself. He wondered if she might be lonely, so he went over, began chatting with her, and learned her name was Eleanor Baker.

Eleanor told Jamario a little about her life, including that she was a widow, and tomorrow would have been her 60th wedding anniversary. The young man knew he couldn't leave this lady by herself, so he invited her to join him and his friends for dinner. She did, and they had a wonderful evening together.

When Jamario posted a picture of their group on Facebook, the story went viral. Eleanor told *CBS News* that she considers the evening "a God thing. I think God sent me there."

Jamario added, "I used to say when I was younger, and I still say today, I want to change the world somehow. And I don't know how. I'm not rich. I'm not famous…But we can show the world it's alright to be kind. And then, before long, maybe the world will be a much better place."

If we love one another, God lives in us, and His love is perfected in us. (1 John 4:12)

Help me show the world "it's alright to be kind," Lord.

A Flight Attendant with a Servant's Heart

Vicki Heath had met thousands of passengers during her years as a flight attendant for Southwest Airlines, but there was something special about Tracy Sharp, a 35-year-old woman with Down syndrome, who was flying back home to Sacramento with her parents. After engaging the family in conversation, Vicki learned that Tracy's dream was to work as a flight attendant.

Vicki stayed in touch with the Sharps, and several weeks later called them with the offer to have Tracy serve as her assistant on a flight from Sacramento to Seattle. Tracy was thrilled!

Her parents joined her on the trip and relished watching their daughter interact with passengers and hand out food and drinks. As reported by *Woman's World* magazine, "At the end of the flight, all the passengers applauded their wonderful flight attendant, and Tracy boasted a 100-watt smile."

Vicki concluded, "I will never know why God chose me to befriend Tracy, but He did. I've learned it doesn't take much to make somebody happy...and it brings you amazing joy, too!"

She opens her mouth with wisdom, and the teaching of kindness is on her tongue. (Proverbs 31:26)

Lead me to bring joy to someone today, Father.

Business Owner Offers Second Chances

George Vorel of Carnegie, Pennsylvania, is a successful business owner who operates industrial steel plants. The work is dangerous and requires precision. Perhaps that's why many are shocked to hear that Vorel has hired, and continues to hire, former drug addicts who are in recovery.

He told his story in *Guideposts*, focusing on his family's experience with addiction and his personal conversion. Vorel's daughter was in and out of trouble and rehab, struggling to stay clean. One day, he heard a preacher on the radio talking about St. Paul's letter to the Romans and about being conformed to God's will. Vorel began to pray and came to see that the best role he could play in his daughter's life was to love her, no matter what.

Eventually she was successful with her recovery, and Vorel saw what a difference that made. Like his experience drawing closer to God, recovery was a second chance at a new life. Vorel decided to do everything he could to give that same second chance to others, and he began by welcoming job applicants who were in recovery.

Blessed are the merciful, for they will receive mercy. (Matthew 5:7)

Jesus, may I reflect Your mercy to those in my life.

"Why Don't You Just Trust in God?"

Anthony Hopkins is one of the world's most celebrated actors of stage and screen. From his portrayals of chilling psychopaths to reserved English authors, he brings a passion and intensity to his roles. That intensity worked against him in his earlier years, though, leading him towards alcoholism.

When he was in his late 30s, Hopkins knew he had to stop drinking. He was attending AA meetings when a woman asked a question that changed his life: "Why don't you just trust in God?" From then on, the self-described atheist began to think about God. Whether it was grace or desperation, he turned to God. His desire to drink left him, never to return.

Hopkins has continued to hold on to faith in his life. He speaks charitably about his former cohort of atheists, but also muses, "I wonder about some of them: why are they protesting so much? How are they so sure of what is out there? And who am I to refute the beliefs of so many great philosophers and martyrs all the way down the years?"

The kingdom of heaven is like a merchant in search of fine pearls; on finding one pearl of great value, he...sold all that he had and bought it. (Matthew 13:45-46)

Your promises, Lord, are worth more than earthly glory.

Light in Winter's Darkness

On a frigid January evening, author Mary DeTurris Poust, tired after a long workday, arrived home to take her dog out for a walk. Her mood was as dark as the night sky until she noticed "white twinkling lights on the neighbor's trees and the sight of a family gathering around a dinner table through a brightly backlit window...I was suddenly overwhelmed by the beauty of everyday life in an artistic creation right outside my front door."

DeTurris Poust returned home with a new perspective: "With the holidays behind us and a lot more winter ahead, it can be easy to get bogged down in the darkness and drudgery...Our minds are already counting the days to spring and sunshine."

"What if, instead, we basked in the density of winter darkness, settled in for the season, and focused instead on the flashes of light and color and warmth that are even more brilliant than usual because of the stark contrast to the world around us?...Simple joys hidden in plain sight can make all the difference, if we can learn to stay in—and appreciate—the now of our lives."

Be transformed by the renewing of your minds, so that you may discern what is the will of God. (Romans 12:2)

Open my eyes to the lights in the darkness, Lord.

Honor Servants

While volunteering at a nursing home, 27-year-old Beth Regan noticed the beautiful relationship between World War II veteran Bob Graham and his wife, Rosie.

"He brushed her hair every morning," Regan told *CBS News*. "He'd hold a mirror in front of her and tell her every day how beautiful she was. When she was unable to hold utensils, every day Bob would feed her first before he ate himself."

When Rosie passed away, Regan continued to visit Bob. Then, two years later, at age 97, he passed away as well. Worried that few people would attend his funeral, Regan used social media to invite people to honor this amazing man at St. Elizabeth Ann Seton Church in Westchester County, New York.

What happened next stunned her. Hundreds of people showed up to give him a hero's funeral, complete with a police motorcade, a pipe and drum corps, and over 200 military veterans, police, and firefighters from all over New York. Regan said, "I'm overwhelmed with emotion and support. The outpouring of love is incredible."

The greatest among you will be your servant. (Matthew 23:11)

Lord, may we honor those who have served.

God's Divine Appointment

Foster parenting is close to *Hallmark Channel* actress Jen Lilley's heart because she and her husband Jason are foster parents themselves. In fact, they adopted the son they had fostered for two years, and also took in his little brother.

Lilley recalled that, initially, she was hoping for a child that was elementary school age, particularly the 8-year-old girl she and Jason had been mentoring. But that plan didn't go through, so the agency asked them to take in a four-month-old boy with special needs. Lilley felt reluctant to do so, but ultimately agreed. She now calls it "God's divine appointment."

She said on *Christopher Closeup,* "That process ever since has been the most rewarding, emotionally stretching, and spiritually stretching journey of my life. I would do it again, 100 times over, and I hope to foster until I die."

Parenting has also deepened Lilley's love and appreciation for her husband. She explained, "If you already have a good marriage, I highly suggest throwing kids in the mix because it opens up your heart on a whole different level."

Whoever welcomes one such child in My name welcomes Me. (Mark 9:37)

Open couples to the idea of foster parenting, Jesus.

Destigmatizing Mental Illness

Twenty-five years ago, Deacon Tom Lambert from the Archdiocese of Chicago learned that his oldest daughter was suffering from a mental illness. When he and his wife looked to the Church for mental health resources, they found nothing, so they decided to do something.

Deacon Lambert helped found a local commission and national Catholic council on mental illness. He told *U.S. Catholic*, "One in four people deal with a mental illness in any given year. For one in 22 people, that illness is persistent and chronic. These people are in our pews, in our neighborhoods, and in our families...yet we don't talk about mental health.

"Because mental illness is so stigmatizing, people feel they're going through this alone. Showing them that there are those who accept them for who they are and what they're going through and love them for who they are is the ultimate spiritual gift we can bring. One of the most healing things we can do as people of faith is to listen to others, hear what they're going through, and meet their spiritual needs."

Since you are eager for spiritual gifts, strive to excel in them for building up the church. (1 Corinthians 14:12)

Divine Physician, grant strength and healing to those struggling with mental illness.

Wrong Number Spawns Beautiful Friendship

Though Callie Hall was a young adult, she felt devastated when she heard her parents were getting a divorce. Little did she know that a wrong number from a stranger would help her through that difficult time.

One day, Callie got a phone call from an unknown number, so she let it go to voicemail. It was from a woman named Grandmamma Margaret, who mistook Callie's number for her grandson Barry's. Callie called her back to explain she had the wrong number, but Grandmamma Margaret kept calling.

"It brought me joy to see that number come up on the phone because of the amount of love and joy she had," Callie recalled to *Southern Living*.

Soon, Grandmamma Margaret was leaving messages not for Barry, but for Callie herself. These phone calls quickly blossomed into a friendship, so the older woman invited Callie to visit her home in Columbia, South Carolina.

Callie said that Grandmamma Margaret was just as lovely in person and she is "beyond blessed this sweet lady called the wrong number."

You shall also love the stranger.
(Deuteronomy 10:19)

Jesus, I trust You'll help guide me in difficult times.

Ulster Project Finds Common Ground

When the opportunity presented itself for Melinda Leonard to bring a chapter of the Ulster Project to Louisville, Kentucky, she took it without hesitation. She had experienced the project years before while living in Tennessee, and understood its ability to build bridges between people of different religions.

The Ulster Project brings both Catholic and Protestant teens from Northern Ireland to live with families in specific places in the United States for one month stays, during which time they engage in activities for the purposes of finding common ground.

The host families always have a teenager of the same age, so the experience becomes a dynamic intersection of people from various backgrounds working to understand how to live in harmony with one another.

In an interview with *The Record* newspaper, Leonard said, "My hope is that we get to the end of the program and these teens will have been informed and encouraged that they possess the skills to be effective leaders and peacemakers, and that they can make a difference in their communities and in the world."

Those who love God must love their brothers and sisters also. (1 John 4:21)

Lord, help me to build bridges between people.

Inside a Vegetative State

People who suffer severe brain traumas are sometimes left in persistent vegetative states in which they may move their eyes, but otherwise show no signs of awareness or communication ability. They can't even follow the generic "squeeze my hand" command by which doctors evaluate consciousness. Medical personnel are therefore left uncertain if the patient is completely unaware or if they are trapped inside their bodies.

However, neuroscientist Adrian Owen has now devised a pioneering technique to talk with people in vegetative states. The website *FreeThink* states, "Using fMRIs, neuroscientists discovered that there are distinct patterns in brain activity when healthy, conscious people think about doing different things—say, playing tennis vs. walking through their house.

"Owen put vegetative patients inside an fMRI and asked them to respond to yes or no questions by imagining one activity or the other. He found...that around 20% of the patients he scanned were actually aware of their surroundings—and thanks to his technique, able to communicate for the first time."

He has filled them with skill to do every kind of work. (Exodus 35:35)

Guide humanity toward healing and hope, Creator.

Snow Angels Help Dialysis Patient

Natalie Blair feared the winter weather forecast. As a dialysis patient, a huge snowstorm could be a matter of life or death. To her relief, four high school seniors came to her rescue and shoveled a path so that she could reach her dialysis treatment on time.

When high school student Patrick Lanigan heard the forecast for eight inches of snow in his New Jersey community, he knew he needed to do something to ensure that his neighbor, Blair, could reach her dialysis treatment.

As reported by *CNN*, Lanigan, along with three other Parsippany High School seniors, helped shovel Blair's pathway at 4:30 a.m. the following morning. The pathway was cleared in 30 minutes and Blair was able to get to her treatment on time.

The students' act of kindness was captured by a photo and shared on social media by Lanigan's father, Peter, who called the four high school students "Snow Angels." And that is exactly what they were by helping a neighbor in need.

You have shown me great kindness in saving my life. (Genesis 19:19)

Loving God, may I put my neighbors' needs before my own.

The World's Oldest Barber

Does doing what you love keep you young? Ask 108-year-old Anthony Mancinelli.

After 95 years in the barber business and cutting three generations of hair, the Italian immigrant and New Windsor, New York resident has been named the "world's oldest barber" by the *Guinness Book of World Records*.

In 1919, Mancinelli emigrated to New York with his family from Naples, Italy. To help his family financially, he decided to learn the barber trade when he was 12 years old. He opened his own shop seven years later, and now—more than nine decades later—he still loves what he's doing.

He is asked by even his doctor what is the secret to his long life? "Only one man knows the secret," Mancinelli told *Guideposts*. "The Man above...I tried never to do anything wrong, so maybe the Man above is rewarding me with long life."

Mancinelli still has no retirement plans and hopes to keep doing what he loves until the Lord takes him.

And I shall dwell in the house of the Lord my whole life long. (Psalm 23:6)

Lord, help me to live each blessed day to its fullest.

The Right Attitude

Eddie Luisi has worked in television for most of his life, most notably as "stage manager to the stars" on ABC's *Good Morning America,* but also as director of The Christophers' old television show. While giving a talk to students at Keokuk High School in Iowa, he shared one secret to his successful career: an excellent work ethic.

As an example, he recalled one of his first jobs in TV that started at 6:30 a.m. Luisi noticed that the producers "were coming in tired and cranky, so I got there at six in the morning and had some of the work done when they arrived." His bosses noticed his commitment, positive attitude, and hard work, so when an opportunity for a promotion came up, he got it.

Luisi advised the students to approach their lives and careers in the same way. He said, "I've done the news, weather, sports...whatever they needed. I learned from every job, every experience, and I always treated everybody with kindness. Every person on earth should be treated with kindness."

Whatever your task, put yourselves into it, as done for the Lord. (Colossians 3:23)

Lord, instill me with initiative and a positive attitude.

The Blessing of a Pothole

Paramedics in Gretna, Nebraska, were racing a 59-year-old man to the hospital because his heart was beating 200 times a minute. He would need an electric shock to return his heart to its normal rhythm, but the hospital was 20 minutes away.

Suddenly, the ambulance hit a tremendous pothole that delivered such a jolt to the vehicle that the man's heart rhythm returned to normal! One doctor explained that this kind of occurrence is extremely rare, but it can happen—and a man's life may have been saved in the process.

In life, it's easy to get distracted by the pursuit of money or comfort or power. As a result, we might lose track of what's most important. Then, we hit a metaphorical pothole—an unexpected occurrence or piece of news—that shocks us back to reality, restoring our natural rhythm.

Try to live in a way that you don't need potholes to remind you how precious your health, your loved ones, and all God's blessings are.

Let the words of my mouth and the meditation of my heart be acceptable to You, O Lord, my rock and my redeemer. (Psalm 19:14)

Guide my steps to live according to Your will, Father.

A Robbery's Unexpected Outcome

In 1996, 18-year-old Danny Givens and some friends entered a St. Paul, Minnesota VFW hall intent on robbing everyone there. Givens shot off a bullet right away to make sure people knew he meant business. But he hadn't counted on armed, off-duty police Sergeant Art Blakey being there. The two exchanged fire, with each one being shot in the stomach.

When Sgt. Blakey's daughter Brooke arrived at the hospital, her father's first words to her were, "I'm fine, is he OK?" She couldn't believe that her dad was so concerned about the criminal who had shot him. But that's who Blakey was.

He asked the judge for leniency when Givens was sentenced, and he visited Givens' mother during the 12 years he was in jail. Givens told *KARE-TV*, "I was in prison the whole time knowing this gentleman had nothing but love for me."

Givens became a Christian in prison, and when he returned home after his release, Blakey was there. Blakey hugged Givens and said, "I'm so proud of you. I love you. I forgive you." The two men remained friends until Blakey's death in 2018.

God proves His love for us in that while we still were sinners Christ died for us. (Romans 5:8)

Teach me to practice Christ-like love, Divine Savior.

The Friendship Houses

In Durham, North Carolina, something unique is happening in North Street Neighborhood, where "people with and without disabilities... flourish in a shared life of welcome, belonging, and mutuality, with Jesus at the center."

Specifically, the Friendship Houses allow graduate students at Duke Divinity School to live with someone who has a disability. The results have been a grace for everyone involved.

Amy Papinchak has a developmental disorder, which results in intellectual disability. Before moving to North Street, she felt alone. But once she joined this special community—and especially after she became best friends with a young woman named Avery Bond—Amy's life and spirit thrived!

Amy and Avery act like lifelong, loving sisters. Avery's husband Zach, who also took part in this project, told *ABC News' Local-ish,* "Slowing down and allowing yourself...to be in friendship with people with disabilities is a hidden treasure we're missing out on in our busy lives. Maybe just slow down and get to know one person who's different than you."

A true friend sticks closer than one's nearest kin. (Proverbs 18:24)

May I be welcoming to someone with special needs, Lord.

MLK on Loving Your Enemies

The Rev. Dr. Martin Luther King Jr. pursued civil rights for African Americans in a peaceful way because he took to heart Jesus' call to "love your enemies." In one sermon, quoted in the book *A Knock at Midnight*, he shared his thoughts on the subject:

"There is a final reason, I think, that Jesus says, 'Love your enemies.' It is this: that love has within it a redemptive power. And there is a power there that eventually transforms individuals. Just keep being friendly to that person. Just keep loving them, and they can't stand it too long.

"Oh, they react in many ways in the beginning. They react with guilt feelings, and sometimes they'll hate you a little more at that transition period, but just keep loving them. And by the power of your love they will break down under the load. That's love, you see. It is redemptive, and this is why Jesus says love. There's something about love that builds up and is creative. There is something about hate that tears down and is destructive. So love your enemies."

Love your enemies and pray for those who persecute you, so that you may be children of your Father in heaven. (Matthew 5:44)

Strengthen my ability to love my enemies, Jesus.

A Chief Gets Stuck in the Snow

Kansas City Chiefs' guard Jeff Allen was prepared to play the Indianapolis Colts in a 2019 playoff game. What he wasn't ready for was the storm that led to his BMW getting stuck in the snow, preventing him from driving to that game.

Thankfully, a man named Dave was driving his truck down the road and spotted Allen's car (though he had no idea who the NFL player was). Dave towed Allen up the hill, allowing him to drive away on his own.

In all the rush and excitement, Allen forgot to get Dave's full name and contact information, so he took to Twitter the next day asking for help tracking him down and noting that he "drove a 97 or 98 Black Suburban." Sure enough, social media came through with an answer, connecting Allen with Dave Cochran, a homeless man who lives in his truck with his girlfriend and dog.

In gratitude for his help, Allen gave Dave free tickets to the AFC Championship Game. In addition, a local repair shop replaced three missing windows in Dave's truck for free. Dave was thrilled to receive these unexpected kindnesses in return for his own good deed.

Let us not grow weary in doing what is right, for we will reap at harvest time. (Galatians 6:9)

May I give, expecting nothing in return, Father.

The Gift of Life

In 1973, 18-year-old Margaret Teece discovered she was pregnant. She knew she would carry the child to term, but also realized that she didn't have the capability to raise a baby, especially with the child's father deployed overseas.

The *North Texas Catholic* reports, "Margaret went to Birthright, a pregnancy resource center, who then brought her to Catholic Charities. With the support of a woman from adoption services, she told her parents about the pregnancy."

After the baby was born, Margaret placed her daughter, who she named Carole, up for adoption. Eventually, Margaret went on to get married and have three sons. But she always thought about Carole.

In 2017, Carole had her DNA tested through *Ancestry.com* and learned that Margaret was her birth mother. The two connected and now have a loving relationship. Carole said, "[My mother] chose life for me when many others in her shoes might not have. I have always felt so incredibly blessed because of her selfless act... Now, God has given me this most amazing gift by allowing me to finally know and love her."

Choose life. (Deuteronomy 30:19)

Make our culture more open-minded toward adoption, Lord.

225 Miles for a Special Delivery

Rich Morgan and his wife, Julie, used to live in Battle Creek, Michigan, where their favorite pizza place was "Steve's Pizza." Though they've moved several times in the last 25 years, they still considered Steve's the gold standard.

The couple planned to travel from their current home in Indianapolis back to Steve's, but had to go to the hospital instead. They discovered that Rich's cancer had worsened, and he didn't have much time to live. He was moved to hospice care.

A relative of the Morgans called Steve's Pizza, hoping they could send a note to Rich to brighten up a trying time for him. They did one better. Manager Dalton Shaffer, the grandson of the original Steve, found out what Rich's favorite pizza was and drove 225 miles to deliver it.

Within four hours, Dalton arrived at the hospice with a pepperoni and mushroom pizza for Rich and Julie. The family was overwhelmed with gratitude, but Dalton said he was happy to do it and that they were in his prayers. Rich's family put out a message on Facebook thanking Dalton for "the epic pizza delivery and the unbelievable kindness of a stranger."

**Clothe yourselves with compassion.
(Colossians 3:12)**

May I sing Your praise with acts of compassion, Jesus!

How to Predict a Snowstorm

You can tell when a snowstorm is coming by looking for natural weather signs, wrote William E. Osgood in *Wintering in Snow Country*. Here are some things to watch for:

- A red sky at sunrise that changes quickly to lemon yellow.
- A halo around the sun or moon, caused by snow crystals in the atmosphere.
- The hunger of birds. Birds know snow is on the way and they try to eat all they can before it starts falling.
- A shivery cold feeling. This is caused by the high humidity that usually precedes a storm.
- Sounds. They carry very distinctly and can be heard long distances just before a storm.

Jesus once told people that they could read the signs of an approaching storm in the sky, but could not understand the signs of the times. He reminded them that each of us is accountable for the way we live our lives. So remember to love both God and neighbor each and every day.

You know how to interpret the appearance of the sky, but you cannot interpret the signs of the time. (Matthew 16:3)

Give us insight into Your ways, Father.

"You Need Food? I'll Give You Food"

One Saturday evening, Jitendra "Jay" Singh, owner of a 7-Eleven in Toledo, Ohio, was informed by one of his clerks that a possible shoplifter was wandering around the store. From the surveillance cameras in his office, Singh witnessed a young man stuffing several snack items into his pockets.

Jay confronted the teenager and asked him why he was stealing. The teen admitted it was because he and his brother were hungry. Jay recounted to *CBS News*, "I said, 'You need food? I'll give you food. That's not a problem.'"

Cedric Bishop, another customer in the store, then saw Jay fill a bag with more substantial hot food items and give it to the boy, free of charge. Bishop was so moved by Jay's kindness to the youngster that he posted this story to his social media account, where it received an overwhelmingly positive response.

"It's basically our Indian culture that if you give food to a hungry person," Jay humbly concludes, "that's considered like God will bless you for that."

I was hungry and you gave Me food.
(Matthew 25:35)

Father, whenever possible, may we respond with kindness.

The Will to Learn

Joseph Wallace grew up poor and struggling in Manhattan. At age 17, he dropped out of school, barely able to read at a second grade level. He explained: "When you're a kid and you don't have decent clothes, you don't want to go to school."

Wallace took a job in the garment district, pushing trolleys through the streets. With perseverance and hard work, he managed to establish his own dry-cleaning business and made it a success. But he still could not read or write.

So Wallace decided to do something about it. He found a teacher willing to give him private lessons, and he started studying. He finally began to master reading and writing at the age of 42.

It is never too late to learn. God gives us the power to better ourselves, to grow, to acquire new skills no matter our age or condition. But it takes patience and determination. What area of your life needs a fresh decision to turn it around?

Learn where there is wisdom, where there is strength, where there is understanding. (Baruch 3:14)

Lord, don't let past failures or shame hold me back from pursuing a worthwhile goal. Give me the courage to move in the right direction.

Prayer of Gratitude

This is a story about how an American flyer developed a philosophy of life while in a German prisoner-of-war camp during World War II.

When Lt. Robert H. Doolan's plane was shot down over Holland, he was arrested and placed in solitary confinement for one month. Finally, he was sent to a POW camp where he lost 40 pounds.

Despite the hardships he faced, he wrote the following prayer in prison: "O Lord, let me remember: That every day I awaken is a beautiful day. That there is always someone worse off than I who needs my help. That there is no such thing as bad food. That prayer will accomplish miracles. Let these simple facts be my guide through life."

That attitude helped him pull through. If you're facing small or large challenges in your life, consider saying Lt. Doolan's prayer. Maybe it can help you pull through, too.

My steps have held fast to Your paths...I call upon You, for You will answer me, O God. (Psalm 17:5,6)

I have tried to walk in Your way, God. Help me in times of trouble.

Three Wishes for Ruby's Residents

What are three things in the world you wish you could have? That's the question a fifth-grader asked nursing home residents near her hometown of Harrison, Arkansas. Their answers not only surprised her, but prompted her to help grant their wishes.

When Ruby Kate Chitsey visited the nursing home where her mother worked in 2018, she asked residents what they wished for. To her surprise, many of them lacked simple luxuries to make them happy: pants that fit, food from outside the nursing home, a working phone in their room since they were lonely.

Ruby became emotional at their responses and, with her mother's help, started a GoFundMe page called "Three Wishes for Ruby's Residents." The youngster raised nearly $70,000 to grant these residents, and many more in other nursing homes, their wishes.

"They weren't new cars or a million dollars [they wanted]," Ruby told *CNN*. "They were very simple things that you could just go in Walmart and get—and that's what we do."

Blessed are the pure in heart, for they will see God. (Matthew 5:8)

Help me, Lord, to share the simple luxuries in my life.

Making Peace in an Angry World

In *The New York Times*, columnist David Brooks noted that angry disagreement has become widespread in American culture today. He offered several thoughts on pursuing a better way.

- **"Your narrative will never win.** In many intractable conflicts...each side wants the other to...admit it was wrong the whole time. This will never happen...Find a new narrative."

- **"Agree on something.** If you're in the middle of an intractable disagreement, find some preliminary thing you can agree on so you can at least take a step into a world of shared reality."

- **"Gratitude.** People who are good at relationships are always scanning the scene for things they can thank somebody for."

- **"Reject either/or.** The human mind has a tendency to reduce problems to either we do this or we do that...There are usually many more options neither side has imagined yet."

- **"Presume the good.** Any disagreement will go better if you assume the other person has good intentions."

Put away from you all bitterness and wrath and anger...and be kind to one another. (Ephesians 4:31-32)

Teach me to be a peacemaker, Messiah.

Sadie to the Rescue!

It was 3:30 p.m. on a Wednesday, and 11-year-old pit bull Sadie was a dog on a mission. Her owner, Serena Costello, was not home, but Sadie's sharp nose had sniffed out a gas leak in the house. After trying unsuccessfully to break out through the front door, the tenacious pit bull somehow managed to open the back sliding door and began racing down her block, relentlessly barking in alarm.

Someone called the New York Tuckahoe Police Department, believing her to be a runaway dog. When the cops came and tried to catch her, however, Sadie eluded them, forcing them to chase her all the way back to her home. "When they [police] went to investigate," Lawrence Rotta of the police department told *CBS2*, "they noticed an odor of gas emanating from the doorway."

The police notified the fire department and electric company, and the gas was turned off. A potentially deadly crisis was averted—all thanks to one plucky and persistent dog. "You saved us," Costello crooned to Sadie, as she gave her beloved pet a grateful hug.

Who teaches us more than the animals?
(Job 35:11)

Abba, bless our pets, faithful companions and protectors of us all.

She'd Make Time for Fun

At the age of 85, Nadine Stair of Louisville, Kentucky, reflected on her life in *Family Circle* magazine and noted how she would change things if she had another go round. She said:

"I'd dare to make more mistakes next time. I'd relax, I would limber up...I would take fewer things seriously. I would take more chances. I would climb more mountains and swim more rivers...I would perhaps have more actual troubles, but I'd have fewer imaginary ones.

"You see, I'm one of those people who live sensibly and sanely hour after hour, day after day. Oh, I've had my moments, and if I had it to do over again, I'd have more of them...Just moments, one after another, instead of living so many years ahead of each day...

"I would start barefoot earlier in the spring and stay that way later in the fall...I would ride more merry-go-rounds. I would pick more daisies."

Each of us only has one life to live. Make the most of each new day while you have the chance.

Teach us to count our days that we may gain a wise heart. (Psalm 90:12)

Help me, Father, to worship You in joy.

An Educator for the Ages

Born in Plum, Texas, in 1885, Clara Belle Williams had a love for learning. As she got older, she pursued higher education at Prairie View Normal and Independent College, graduating as valedictorian in 1908. But not everything came easy for Williams. The reason: she was African American.

While teaching at Booker T. Washington Elementary School in Las Cruces, New Mexico, Williams began taking courses at New Mexico College of Agriculture & Mechanic Arts (NMCA&MA). Because she was black, many of her professors wouldn't allow her to sit in their classrooms with the white students. Williams was forced to stand in the hallway and take notes from there. But she refused to let racism hold her back.

Williams earned her Bachelor's Degree in English in 1937, becoming NMCA&MA's first black graduate. She remained a lifelong learner and educator—and her three sons all graduated college with medical degrees. Clara Belle Williams lived to the age of 108, leaving behind a legacy that continues to be admired today.

[Mortals] look on the outward appearance, but the Lord looks on the heart. (1 Samuel 16:7)

Guide and heal the victims of racism, Lord.

The Heart of Perfection, Part One

"Any time our faith becomes more about criticizing others—or even criticizing ourselves—rather than leaning on and loving Jesus, we're in trouble." That's an insight that Colleen Carroll Campbell gleaned about herself—and society in general—when she began reflecting on her own perfectionist nature.

The author had always prided herself on doing her jobs flawlessly. But when she became a mother, the level of perfection she demanded from herself became emotionally and spiritually draining—and impossible to live up to.

Colleen looked to her Catholic faith for answers, specifically to the saints she had admired for their perfectionism. She discovered that these holy men and women were actually recovering perfectionists, who had followed a new path after gaining divine spiritual insights.

In addition, Colleen learned that an obsession with flawlessness is rooted in the idea that we can earn God's love instead of simply receiving it as the gift and grace that it is. More of Colleen's story tomorrow...

My grace is sufficient for you, for power is made perfect in weakness. (2 Corinthians 12:9)

Teach me to be less critical of myself and others, Jesus.

The Heart of Perfection, Part Two

As a result of her experiences, Colleen Carroll Campbell wrote a book called *The Heart of Perfection: How the Saints Taught Me to Trade My Dream of Perfect for God's.*

In it, she addresses Jesus' mandate "Be perfect as your heavenly father is perfect." During a *Christopher Closeup* interview, Colleen said, "I did struggle a lot with that. I thought the universal call to holiness meant that...anything short of flawlessness is something to beat yourself up about."

Eventually, Colleen found new truths about God in the parable of the Prodigal Son. She notes that serious Christians often have trouble seeing themselves as the prodigal son because we think we're holier than him. But in reality, we all fall short of pleasing God at times, and we are all in need of His mercy.

"When you begin to embrace that," said Colleen, "you're no longer imposing this intense standard on yourself [because] you realize that's not what God is asking of you. He's not asking for flawlessness. He's asking more and more for surrender."

More of Colleen's story tomorrow...

While he was still far off, his father saw him and was filled with compassion. (Luke 15:20)

Move me beyond the damaging effects of perfectionism, Jesus.

The Heart of Perfection, Part Three

One of the recovering perfectionists that Colleen Carroll Campbell admires is St. Jane de Chantal, a widow with four young children. She dealt with numerous challenges, including difficult in-laws. Colleen said, "Jane was intense...She was skimping on sleep...She was trying to pray around the clock. Meanwhile, everything was falling apart around her."

Then Jane met Francis de Sales, who dispelled Jane's notion that God wanted her to do everything perfectly and drive herself harder and harder. Colleen noted that Francis taught her, "Be gentle with the child who interrupts you. Decide not to gossip about those in-laws who drive you crazy...Be patient with everyone, but above all with yourself."

Colleen concluded, "When Jane internalized this advice, she not only became more patient with herself, but it trickled down. She became more patient with the in-laws, the kids... She grew into this paragon of gentleness...It's amazing what grace can do in the life of any perfectionist if we open our hearts to God's dream of perfect for us rather than our own."

The patient in spirit are better than the proud in spirit. (Ecclesiastes 7:8)

Increase my patience with myself and others, Holy Spirit.

Good Things Will Happen to You

A young Pakistani woman with special needs took part in the 2019 Special Olympics in Abu Dhabi. She shared her backstory with the website *Humans of New York,* revealing that she was bullied and called "idiot" as a child because she was different.

"I felt like jumping out the window," she said. "I didn't want to eat. I became so weak that my mom would feed me with her own hands...I had an imaginary friend named Amanda. She was a fairy...She was very pretty. She had a beautiful crown. She'd make me laugh, and encourage me, and tell me not to be sad. She'd say, 'Good things will happen to you.'"

At age 14, this young woman went to a swim meet with her mother, but was too scared to jump in the pool. An older woman named Ronak approached her, then gave her a hug that made her feel genuinely loved. Ronak told her, "Please, join Special Olympics. It will change your life." The young woman took Ronak up on her offer and made real friends for the first time in her life. Her imaginary friend Amanda never returned.

Come in, my daughter, and welcome.
(Tobit 11:17)

May I never belittle anyone for being different, Lord. Help me welcome those with special needs.

A Trailblazer's Vision

The doctor gave 19-year-old Willie O'Ree the bad news bluntly: the retina in his right eye was shattered and he would be blind for life, never able to play hockey again.

It was 1955, and O'Ree was with Canada's Junior League Kitchener Canucks. A puck had struck him in the right eye because helmets and face shields were not yet a part of the game.

O'Ree felt devastated at first, but soon realized he could still see perfectly out of his left eye. As reported by Tony Paige in New York's *Daily News,* O'Ree made adjustments when he was on the ice so he could see what was going on. When a professional team eventually invited him to join because he was such a good player, he didn't volunteer the information about his right-eye-blindness—and the team never asked.

O'Ree went on to play 21 years of professional hockey and, as an African Canadian who became the NHL's first black player, came to be known as the Jackie Robinson of hockey. When he talks to kids today, he offers his life as proof that goals can be achieved despite tremendous challenges.

I will lead the blind by a road they do not know. (Isaiah 42:16)

Help me overcome my challenges, Lord.

Because One Person Cared

In the harsh winter of 1954, Abbé Henri Pierre, a Capuchin monk who had been a hero of the French Resistance, mobilized the entire government and people of France to do something for the poor and homeless who were dying in the streets.

Abbé Pierre called for the creation of shelters to help those without homes—and many people responded. He helped build 8,000 low-rent apartments in the Paris area. He founded 52 self-sustaining communes in France and helped 100 others throughout the world.

The initiative was called the "Emmaus movement" after the New Testament town near which two disciples met the risen Christ. The homes were supported by people selling scrap paper and repairing and selling broken furniture and appliances.

The Emmaus motto is, "Give instant help to those nearest and in need. Show them how to help themselves. Afterward, let them help others."

Thousands received decent housing, food and jobs because one man saw a need and began to fill it.

Trust in the Lord, and do good. (Psalm 37:3)

Grant us a greater measure of courage, Jesus, to follow You with trusting hearts.

Sick Days to Support a Life

When Alabama high school teacher David Green ran out of sick days to help care for his infant daughter, a group of teachers performed an incredibly selfless act: they donated their sick days to him.

In early 2019, David and his wife, Megan, faced a parent's worst nightmare. They found out their 10-month-old daughter, Kinsley, had leukemia. With Kinsley fighting for her life, the couple was inundated with hospital bills and frequent doctor visits. After David used his last sick day, Megan called on the generosity of others so that her husband could continue to have time with their daughter.

"Kinsley is the biggest daddy's girl and needs him to be here as often as he can," Megan wrote in a post, as reported by *Lightworkers.com,* "so she would be so thankful for any donated days so she can spend time with her Daddy."

Alabama teachers answered the call and generously donated 100 sick days to David. One such teacher, Anna Kachelman, told *WHNT-TV,* "This was a real physical way that we could help him and his family."

For everything there is a season, and a time for every matter under heaven. (Ecclesiastes 3:1)

Dear Lord, help me answer the call to give the gift of time.

A Dedicated Leader

In the spring of 2019, the University of Notre Dame bestowed the Laetare Medal on Norman Francis, the longtime president of Xavier University of Louisiana, the only historically black Catholic university in the Western Hemisphere.

A civil rights leader and pioneer in Catholic higher education, Francis was the first African American president at Xavier, a school founded by Saint Katharine Drexel. He accepted the post in 1968 and retired last year at the age of 83.

"I did not build Xavier. I was part of Katharine Drexel's mission to provide a quality education for all," he said.

In a statement reported by *Crux*, Notre Dame President Father John Jenkins said, "For more than 50 years, Dr. Francis has been at the center of civil rights advocacy by leveraging the power of Catholic higher education. In bestowing the Laetare Medal upon him, Notre Dame recognizes his leadership in the fight for social justice through educational empowerment."

How much better to get wisdom than gold! To get understanding is to be chosen rather than silver. (Judges 5:12)

Lord, make us leaders who extend opportunity to all.

A Teacher's Heroism

Angela McQueen is a high school teacher in Mattoon, Illinois, who experienced an educator's worst nightmare. While walking around on cafeteria duty, she noticed a student close to her pull out a handgun.

Without hesitating, she sprang into action, grabbing the shooter's hand and trying to direct his gun up to the ceiling. After wrestling him to the ground, another teacher jumped in to help subdue him, but not before two students were injured by gunshots. Luckily, all survived.

McQueen told the newspaper *The Pantograph*, "It's the mama-bear instinct. I don't have kids of my own, but these are still 'my' kids. You're not going to do this to my kids."

After the event, McQueen went outside to console the students who had run screaming from the cafeteria. Her only concern was for her students, even more than for her own safety. Local police credit her actions with helping avert a terrible outcome. To the school and student's families, she is a hero.

No one has greater love than this, to lay down one's life for one's friends. (John 15:13)

Lord God, help me honor and be grateful for those who protect the innocent.

Eye Can Write

Twelve-year-old Jonathan Bryan of Wiltshire, England, was born with severe cerebral palsy. He cannot speak, and relies on oxygen and a feeding tube.

His parents, Chantal and Christopher, were told that because of his severe condition, he would be "unteachable" and that he would never be able to communicate. They didn't take that answer as the final word, though. In a recent story published on *Lightworkers*, they shared their journey.

Chantal developed a technique where Jonathan could spell out words by pointing to an alphabet card with his eyes. Jonathan has done more than communicate his daily thoughts this way: he's written a 192-page memoir: *Eye Can Write*.

Archbishop of Canterbury Justin Welby recently met Jonathan and was struck by the conversation. He tweeted, "In Jonathan I met a fellow disciple of Christ. He profoundly knows the love and grace of God...He speaks with more conviction and joy of the hope of resurrected life with Christ than I have witnessed for years."

When you give a banquet, invite the poor, the crippled, the lame, and the blind. (Luke 14:13)

You are closest to those who are suffering, Lord.

Should I Pop the Question?

Romantic infatuation has little to do with true love, in the opinion of Ray Short, a sociologist who taught a marriage course at the University of Wisconsin. True love just doesn't happen magically, he said, in advising students to make sure they're really in love before marrying. He offered these checkpoints to identify infatuation:

- Thinking the other person is faultless.
- Loss of interest when separated by time or distance.
- Frequent quarrels.
- Impatience with the other's family or friends.

"If you ask yourself about a relationship before you go ahead," said Short, a married father of five, "it may keep you from saying 'I do' and then later saying you don't."

There are no infallible signs that a marriage will or will not work. But a willingness to give and receive love wholeheartedly, an unselfish spirit, is a good indication that true love is really there.

And the two shall become one. (Mark 10:8)

Lord, grant couples the wisdom to ask the right questions before they marry.

Baker Delivers Unexpected Valentines

Lisa Cotoggio of Queens, New York, is a baker who owns Grandma's Cheesecake Sandwiches, a company that sells cheesecake treats online. For Valentine's Day in 2018, she decided to bake 150 heart-shaped pastries for the homeless people she encounters around New York City.

Cotoggio told her story to the *NET-TV* series *Currents* and credited her Catholic faith and education with being an inspiration. "They teach you, in Catholic school, to be caring and humble and to help the less fortunate," she said.

From Long Island to Manhattan, Cotoggio handed out her mini-cheesecakes on the streets and in shelters. "I don't have my own Valentine, and I figured a lot of homeless people didn't have [one] either; so I thought maybe I could be everyone's Valentine this year and make some people feel better," she said.

The recipients got more than a delicious dessert; they got the important message that someone cares for them. Michael Lopuch, a guest at a soup kitchen, said, "She's blessed for doing it, and I'm blessed for receiving it."

Go therefore into the main streets, and invite everyone you find to the wedding banquet. (Matthew 22:9)

Lord, help me to spread more love this Valentine's Day—and every day.

The "Secret" to Staying Married

On the occasion of her parents' 50th wedding anniversary, nurse Katie Duke revealed on Instagram that they are often asked what their secret is to staying married. This is what her mom and dad had to say:

"There is no such thing as one secret thing that makes a marriage last. It's a constant effort of forgiveness and love, a consistent dedicated friendship, an open mind, loyalty and faith, the ability to learn from life's lessons, and letting go of past things that can keep you from growing together.

"Along these years, we've learned lessons about the world, about each other, and about ourselves. You see, it's so easy for people to give up, and we never expected this to be a walk in the park, but after 50 years, every moment was worthwhile. So, at the end of the day, there is no 'one thing' that works.

"Find someone who is loyal and loves every aspect of you, even the annoying nuances, find someone who can balance making you laugh and taking you seriously, find someone you do not want to live without, and make a decision to grow together."

Above all, maintain constant love for one another. (1 Peter 4:8)

Give married couples the wisdom and grace to grow together, Lord.

The Power of Gratitude

Gratitude can be a powerful force. The act of thanking someone for a kindness, or a job well done, can give glory to God, who should be the ultimate source of our gratitude.

Writer Shemaiah Gonzalez recently reflected on gratitude in a piece on *Busted Halo*. She wrote about the powerful gospel account of the 10 lepers who were healed, but only one came running back to Jesus to thank Him. Our Lord appreciated the thanks, and sent the man on his way with a blessing for his faith.

In our everyday lives, the opportunities for gratitude are endless. Those who teach us, who serve us meals, who fix our cars and our plumbing problems, and hundreds of other ordinary tasks all could be boosted by a simple thanks.

By cultivating this attitude, Gonzalez points out, we become more open to the miracles that surround us. She writes, "As I start to thank God for His mercies in my life, I see more answers to prayers: a new friend, someone's healing, a found solution...God's blessings become even more apparent. All we have to do is say, 'Thank You!'"

With gratitude in your hearts sing psalms, hymns, and spiritual songs to God. (Colossians 3:16)

Thank You, Lord, for this day, and all the good in my life.

Ask If He Wants to Help You

Jordan Taylor of Baton Rouge, Louisiana, was just doing his job stocking shelves at a grocery store when he noticed he had an audience. Jack Edwards, a 17-year-old with autism, was mesmerized by Taylor's stocking of the juice and milk in the refrigerator section.

Rather than be put off by the unusual attention, Taylor engaged him. He told *CNN*, "Something in the back of my mind was just like, 'Ask if he wants to help you.'"

Taylor and Edwards stocked shelves together for half an hour, carefully and methodically, with Taylor showing Edwards where each item went. Sid Edwards, Jack's father, said, "It was a big deal. When you go to a grocery store with an autistic kid… people don't understand. They're not very accepting. Somehow this young man reached my son."

Taylor's kindness created a beautiful memory for Edwards, whose father captured it on video. His Facebook post went viral, allowing tens of thousands of people to view this one act of kindness that lit up a boy's day.

Wine and music gladden the heart, but the love of friends is better than either. (Sirach 40:20)

May I be a friend to somebody today and share Your love, Jesus.

Magnificent Miles Finds a Home, Part One

Lonnie Snyder's wife kept trying to persuade him to expand their family through adoption, even though they were both pushing 40 and had two teenagers already. Sometimes she would even show him pictures from an organization called Rainbow Kids, which featured orphans with special needs. But Lonnie just wasn't interested in taking on this new responsibility.

As he told *Humans of New York,* "One day in 2015, we had an outside speaker visit our office. He talked about his child with Down syndrome. And my heart was completely changed. I went home and told my wife the story. I was crying. She was crying. And I think both of us knew what was going to happen.

"A few days later she forwarded me an email from Rainbow Kids. The title was 'Magnificent Miles.' He was living in a Taiwanese orphanage. Just a beautiful little boy. Fifteen months old. Fluffy hair. And all alone. We knew it was our son."

More of the story tomorrow…

A new heart I will give you, and a new spirit I will put within you. (Ezekiel 36:26)

Open husbands and wives to the idea of foster parenting and adoption, Heavenly Father.

Magnificent Miles Finds a Home, Part Two

Lonnie soon learned that applying for an international adoption was "a nightmare." There were so many hoops to jump through. And the cost was $32,000. But he and his wife already viewed Miles as their son, so they weren't going to give up. It took 14 months to complete the process, but in 2017, they traveled to Taiwan to pick Miles up from the orphanage and bring him home.

In 2019, Lonnie told *Humans of New York,* "[Miles is] four years old now. He runs to me every time I open the door...Even though he can't express himself, he's amazingly empathetic. He's drawn to people who look alone. There are meltdowns. And there are days when I feel like I'm not qualified for any of this. But on the days you don't think you can get through it—you don't realize that you're getting through it. And in the end, you're getting more than you ever give.

"Recently my wife started sending me pictures of other children, but I always said 'no.' Until I saw Miles' little sister for the first time. She's from the same orphanage. Her name is Maddie. We submitted our papers three weeks ago."

You have been the helper of the orphan. (Psalm 10:14)

Lead children with special needs to loving homes, Holy Spirit.

Back on the Job — and Glad

Work was the essence of a good life to 81-year-old Harry Sandborn, a retired railroad dispatcher who became a teller for Chase Manhattan Bank.

Sandborn was one of over 100 retirement-age people employed by the bank in a special work program for the elderly begun in 1953. Called "per diems," they worked as often as five days a week or as little as two or three times a year. Evaluation reports on the "per diems" were always very high.

Explained one 75-year-old worker, "I was bored doing nothing. Now I feel like a model in a 'before-and-after' ad. I believe that older workers are more reliable; we were brought up different, we're more responsible."

Not every retired person can—or wants to—go back to work. But all deserve an opportunity to make their special contribution. Why not, with God's help, reach out to one older person you know and make his or her life a little more fulfilling?

**In old age they still produce fruit.
(Psalm 92:14)**

Father, may we show respect and love for older persons.

A Good Deed Each Day

Breanne Zolfo of Crown Point, Indiana, owns a small coffee shop, *Café Fresco,* through which she helps her community practice good deeds.

As reported on the *Today Show,* it all started six years ago. When the shop wasn't busy, Breanne would write inspirational quotes on the cups she would give to her customers. That proved popular, so she began writing suggestions for good deeds on the insides of sleeves of coffee. She encouraged customers to donate to homeless shelters or charities, and take a photo of themselves doing it. In exchange, she would give them a free cup of coffee.

Also in the shop is a special tip jar, where the money raised goes to help someone local with a surprise good deed. Once, Breanne bought a bike for a homeless man with the money. He returned years later to explain what a difference that made in his life.

"We planted a small seed in Crown Point, Indiana, and now people are spreading our mission to other cities and states. When we have other people helping us, that's when we can do it everywhere," Zolfo said.

He satisfies the thirsty, and the hungry He fills with good things. (Psalm 107:9)

Lord, help me to do a good deed for someone today.

The Hero in Us All

When cab driver David Glascock saw smoke pouring from a building, he jumped from his cab, entered the structure, and alerted the residents.

Stumbling through smoke and darkness in the two-story Los Angeles apartment house, he succeeded in evacuating 35 persons. "I ran up to the first door and banged on it and shouted 'Fire!'" he explained. "Then I did the same thing down the line."

When firemen arrived, they were able to remove the remaining tenants from the building, none of whom was seriously injured.

Heroism takes many forms—a cabbie saving fire victims, a mother watching a sick child during a long night's vigil, a caretaker in a nursing home treating residents with compassion.

God has given you a spark of greatness, too. Don't wait for the "big moment." Instead, start now to respond more fully and courageously in your responsibilities toward family, job, and community.

Get up, so that I may send you on your way. (1 Samuel 9:26)

Jesus, help us to imitate Your unflagging courage in carrying out the Father's will.

Elbowing Aside Unkindness

When former Detroit Piston's basketball star Joe Dumars was fined twice for shoving and elbowing other players many years ago, his reaction was typical for him. He said, "As I look back on both incidents, I see that I could have avoided them. And my wife scolded me about them, too."

Respected as one of the league's most gentlemanly players, Dumars was quick to add, "Don't take my kindness for weakness."

Real kindness is never weak. Instead, it requires strength to act generously or to restrain ourselves when we feel like lashing out. Each of us has opportunities every day to be kind.

But why go to the trouble? Just remind yourself of how much it meant to you the last time somebody bothered to treat you with kindness.

Support your faith with goodness, and goodness with...mutual affection, and mutual affection with love. (2 Peter 1:5,7)

God, help me make the choice to act with kindness.

Bullied Boy's Birthday Redo

One Tuesday morning, Grand Rapids Police Officer Austin Lynema saw a little boy running down the block after a school bus. On pulling over and asking the boy if he needed help, Officer Lynema learned that the youngster's name was Thomas Daniel, he had missed his bus, and his mother didn't have a car to drive him to school.

The policeman offered Thomas a lift, which he accepted. During the car ride, Thomas confessed that it was his ninth birthday, and he was having a party later. He was afraid no one would show up because he was bullied by his classmates, so he invited Officer Lynema to his party. The policeman accepted.

Unfortunately, Thomas's worst fears were realized, and Officer Lynema was his only guest that night. The next day, Lynema and a few other officers took matters into their own hands, and threw Daniel an unforgettable "birthday redo."

"No kid should get bullied," the Grand Rapids Police Department Facebook page posted about the second party, along with pictures from the event. "Next year, Thomas Daniel, make sure you drop us that invite...We wouldn't want to miss it!"

**You shall love your neighbor as yourself.
(Mark 12:31)**

God, comfort and strengthen victims of bullying.

Give Up Worry for Lent, Part One

Gary Zimak absolutely LOVED eating sweets. So for many years, he decided to give them up for Lent as a sacrifice for God. Though he stuck to his commitment, he came to realize that the spiritual benefits were lacking.

During a *Christopher Closeup* interview, Gary said, "Several weeks into Lent, the focus shifted and I lost sight of why I was doing it. All I kept thinking was: Two weeks until cake! I would literally be standing at the convenience store drooling over doughnuts...It took me a while to [ask]: is this helping me grow spiritually?"

Gary suspected that other people might be having the same results with their Lenten sacrifices, so he wrote a book based on his own experiences with debilitating worry and anxiety. It's called *Give Up Worry for Lent*.

Gary said, "People are stressed out about the state of the world, their finances, their health. It is such a powerful open door to lead people to Jesus. They're looking for relief, and He's the relief they're looking for, even though they don't realize it."

Do not worry about anything, but...let your requests be made known to God. (Philippians 4:6)

I bring my worries to You today, Jesus. Help me.

Give Up Worry for Lent, Part Two

In *Give Up Worry For Lent's* first reflection, author Gary Zimak shares a personal story about one of the most troubling times of his life. His wife was pregnant with twin girls, but they were given only a ten percent chance of survival because they had a condition called twin-to-twin transfusion syndrome. After going for treatment at Our Lady of Lourdes Hospital in Camden, New Jersey, the couple would go to the chapel.

"When you're going through something like that," recalled Gary on *Christopher Closeup*, "you realize just how helpless you are and how much you need the Lord.

"Above the sanctuary were the words of Matthew 11:28: 'Come to Me, all who labor and are heavy laden, and I will give you rest.' I remember looking up at those words while my wife and I were kneeling...[and] saying, 'Lord, I need rest. I need You.' That's the message for each of us, especially those who are worried. He wants us to come to Him. That's the answer."

Thankfully, the Zimak girls are healthy and now 21 years old. But Gary can never forget about the lesson he learned during that experience.

I will give you rest. (Matthew 11:28)

Give me rest from my worries, Jesus.

Give Up Worry for Lent, Part Three

In Gary Zimak's book of daily reflections *Give Up Worry for Lent: 40 Days to Finding Peace in Christ*, he shares a wise quote from Blessed Fulton Sheen: "Nothing is more destined to create deep-seated anxieties in people than the false assumption that life should be free from anxieties."

Gary knows that quote is especially relevant in the modern age. During an interview with Tony Rossi of The Christophers, he said, "We are creating more anxiety because we buy into the false notion that the only way we can experience peace in life is to be problem-free. Jesus never said that.

"In John 16, He said, 'You will have problems, you will have tribulations, but be of good cheer. Why? Because I have overcome the world.' Jesus never promised a problem-free life. He didn't have one. His mother didn't have one. St. Joseph didn't have one...So when we look to eliminate all our problems, we're trying to control something we can't control. Peace is found in the Lord."

The peace of God, which surpasses all understanding, will guard your hearts and your minds in Christ Jesus. (Philippians 4:7)

Help me find my peace in You, Jesus.

A Spirit of Unity

Singer-songwriter PJ Anderson recently led a service pilgrimage for young people in association with Catholic Heart Work Camp. They traveled to Rome to volunteer in a soup kitchen called Casa Scalabrini, named after an Italian priest who was dedicated to caring for refugees and immigrants. Residents at the facility came from Africa, Tibet, and other countries.

PJ's group met with the refugees and found that they took great pride in their new home. The refugees also cooked foods from their homelands and served the retreat group because it made them feel good to be of service themselves.

Though some of the refugees didn't speak English, PJ called their time together "a community building event. A smile is a smile in whatever language." And he saw barriers between different peoples break down, creating an experience of unity.

PJ said, "We're living in a crazy world right now, with lots of hatred and violence...We need to unite our voices as one in love. Not in hate, not in being angry. But let that feeling of anger turn into love, so we can drive out hate with love."

Have unity of spirit, sympathy, love for one another, a tender heart, and a humble mind. (1 Peter 3:8)

Holy Spirit, help me drive out hate with love.

How McDonald's Went Meatless

The story of how McDonald's added the Filet-O-Fish sandwich to their menu is grounded in the Catholic tradition of meatless Fridays. *Reader's Digest* featured an article crediting the creation of the country's most famous (and widespread) fried fish sandwich to Lou Groen of Cincinnati, Ohio.

Groen had been in the restaurant business for a while when he purchased Cincinnati's first McDonald's franchise in 1959. He noticed that on Friday nights, typically one of the best for restaurant profits, his sales were plummeting.

Groen knew that the area's large Catholic population was looking for meatless options, so he sought out a fish sandwich with tartar sauce to add to the menu. McDonald's CEO Ray Kroc wasn't impressed, however. He wanted to try a meatless "Hula Burger" with a pineapple slice instead of beef.

The two made an agreement: both would be added to Groen's menus, and they would see which had higher sales. The rest is history, and since then Catholics (and all people) have enjoyed the Filet-O-Fish on Fridays—and any day of the week.

For he and all who were with him were amazed at the catch of fish that they had taken. (Luke 5:9)

Feed my soul this Lenten season, Jesus.

Lost and Found

Over six years ago, 17-year-old Rameil Pitamber had just lost his father, and was struggling to keep his grades up. "I was lost," he told *CBS News* correspondent Adriana Diaz. "I was a follower, and one poor decision led to the next."

Pitamber's string of bad decisions culminated in the worst decision of all: robbing a Little Caesars pizzeria at gunpoint with his friend who worked there. Pitamber was caught, convicted and sentenced to 11 years in prison. Brian Nugent, a deputy police officer in Avon, Indiana, was the person who arrested Pitamber.

Years later, Pitamber was released early for good behavior and started volunteering at a Goodwill store. There, he again encountered "Detective Brian," who remembered him. An impromptu lunch between the two led to a friendship that continues to this day. With Brian's help, Pitamber has found steady work, and is even attending school.

"[Detective Brian] treated me with compassion," Pitamber gratefully concluded. "To this day, he still builds my worth and self-esteem. With him in my corner, I can do anything."

Set the believers an example. (1 Timothy 4:12)

Christ, help us to be strong, positive mentors for our youth.

A B.O.L.D. Youth Ministry

During Lent 2019, young people from Memphis, Michigan, chose to fast for 30 hours and sleep outdoors to help those in need. As reported by the *Detroit Catholic*, B.O.L.D. Youth Ministry, which includes members from St. Augustine and Holy Family parishes, sponsored the event to raise money for the charity World Vision.

Youth minister Jennifer McClelland explained, "This is a program we did last year where the children give pledges and donations to raise money for countries with starvation and water shortages."

The students only consumed water and Gatorade the entire time. They also took part in challenges that helped them understand what poor people in other countries endure. For instance, they would carry two gallons of water a certain distance to recreate what villagers without nearby water do.

Tenth-grader Brennan McClelland said, "Doing a retreat like this makes you think hard about what God has given you, what you have to be thankful for, and it opens your eyes to the needs of others."

Is not this the fast that I choose...to share your bread with the hungry? (Isaiah 58:6-7)

Open my eyes to the needs of others, Jesus.

They Carried Him

When a storm brought quickly-accumulating snow to Edmonton, Canada, Shannon Ranger walked to pick up her six-year-old son, Matthew, from school. He has spina bifida and uses a wheelchair, so she knew the trip home would be a challenge.

Their struggles were noticed by those passing by. One man tried to shovel in front of them, but couldn't keep up. Another man soon joined in, and they decided the best way to make the over half-mile journey was to carry the boy in his chair. "It was amazing to see such kindness," Shannon told *CBS News*.

One of the men had his son with him, who immediately thought Matthew looked like a king being carried in his throne. That made Matthew laugh—and made the whole situation better. Shannon was so touched that she wrote a Facebook post that attracted media attention for how much the help of a few strangers meant to them.

Finding no way to bring him in because of the crowd, they went up on the roof and let him down...through the tiles...in front of Jesus. (Luke 5:19)

Jesus, where my strength is needed, may I always be willing to help.

"Do They Not Deserve the Best?"

Well-known for its Mardi Gras celebrations, New Orleans has another distinction as well: it is home to the only Catholic university in the U.S. that was founded by a saint. Born into a wealthy family in 1858, Katharine Drexel joined the Sisters of the Blessed Sacrament later in life and focused her attention on ministering to Native Americans and African Americans.

As reported by *Catholic News Agency*, she founded a secondary school for African Americans and "a preparatory school for teachers, one of the few career tracks available to Black Americans at the time." The latter school went on to become Xavier University of Louisiana in 1925.

University president C. Reynold Verret recalled a *New York Times* interview in which St. Katharine was asked, "Why are you using this expensive Indiana limestone for a school for black children?" Her response: "Do they not deserve the best?"

St. Katharine knew they did, and she spent her life promoting the inherent value of these young people who still suffered under segregation.

There is no longer slave or free...for all of you are one in Christ Jesus. (Galatians 3:28)

Free our hearts from prejudice, Creator of All.

A Doctor Who Revolutionized Transplants

Dr. Christoph Broelsch recently passed away in his native Germany at age 75. Throughout his career, he was a pioneering transplant surgeon, and one of the first to perform a successful living-donor liver transplant.

In the 1980s, Dr. Broelsch traveled to University of Chicago Hospital where he and other doctors, all experts in their field, theorized a way to take a section of a liver from a living donor and transplant it into a patient whose liver was failing. The first surgery was performed on a mother and daughter, where the child—only 21 months old—had advanced liver disease.

The surgery was a success, and was repeated at that hospital and at many others. Both the mother and daughter recovered fully, going on to lead normal lives. Thanks to Dr. Broelsch's work, pediatric patients (and some adults) no longer had to wait for a full organ from a deceased donor.

Dr. Broelsch and his team were public about the ethical issues at hand with living-donor transfers. They knew their work would save lives and add to quality of life, so they persevered.

There may come a time when recovery lies in the hands of physicians. (Sirach 38:13)

Thank You, Lord, for doctors and nurses that heal the sick.

A Message from Above

Baptist minister Jerome Jones of Monticello, Georgia, was working his day job as a lineman with the power company when a message literally came from above. It was a note tied to balloons that read: "God, help me go to college... Please help me get everything I need to leave Wednesday."

The writer of the note was Mykehia Curry, who was the first in her family to go to college. As reported by *CBS News,* she was worried about starting school and couldn't afford a few things she needed to set up her room. Jones, meanwhile, was struggling with his faith and considering leaving ministry. He had just $125 to his name, but the note touched his heart.

Rev. Jones got in touch with Curry. He purchased and dropped off a mini-fridge and a comforter to make her college start easier. What's more important is that both individuals were the answer to one another's prayers. Rev. Jones received the boost of faith he had been looking for, while Curry's balloon prayer happened to land with just the right person at just the right time.

At that very moment, the prayers of both of them were heard in the glorious presence of God. (Tobit 3:16)

Help me to be an answer to someone's prayer today, Lord.

How We Reflect God's Love

Gene Dodaro may be "deep in his senior years," as he puts it, but the memories of those who've loved him remain fresh in his mind. First, there was his grandmother, Frances Caputo, who died when he was only seven. "She was a little Italian lady, less than five feet tall," he recalled. "Whenever we would visit, she would cup my face in her hands and rain kisses all over it."

During those years, Gene also met his best friend, Ray Wiehn. Ray, who came from a devout Catholic family, was bigger and stronger than Gene, and served as his protector if anybody wanted to hurt him: "He was like my big brother: He would always direct me to do what was right, civilly and religiously. Surprisingly, I always listened! He's gone now also, and I miss his brotherly love."

Gene concludes, "When I hear of God's love for us, I think of the ways my grandmother and Ray loved me, and I understand: Our Father wants to cup our faces and shower us with kisses, and at the same time, protect and guide us to a lifetime of happiness and caring."

Faith, hope, and love abide...and the greatest of these is love. (1 Corinthians 13:13)

Help me to see Your love in those around me, Father.

A Country Singer Breaks New Ground

In April 2019, country superstar Brad Paisley broke ground for "The Store," a free supermarket in Nashville, Tennessee, to serve those in need.

The Paisley family was inspired to open The Store after volunteering at a similar establishment in Santa Barbara, California. They walked away from that experience realizing that most people didn't want handouts. "They want dignity and respect," Paisley said on The Store's website. "They want to be self-sufficient."

The Store will offer free groceries and be located at Paisley's alma mater, Belmont University. College students will volunteer their time serving others at The Store to help open their eyes about hunger in their area.

Paisley told *CBSNews.com,* "You can read statistics on hunger or you can read everything about this subject and never necessarily have it hit you in the heart like watching someone walk through this service, which is hopefully what's going to happen as a student is volunteering here."

Blessed are those who hunger...for they will be filled. (Matthew 5:6)

Open my eyes and heart to the needs around me, Giving Lord.

Grief, Then Hope

Larry Yeagley was a hospital chaplain in Fort Worth, Texas. He was ideally suited to this ministry because he knew first-hand the pain of grief. He himself lost a son in an accident.

He started Grief Recovery Seminars because he believed that "nobody should cry in their pillows all by themselves."

Yeagley said that it's important for us to allow grieving people to express their pain and tell us how they feel, deep down inside: "We have to let them drain off some of that pain, some of that agony, some of that doubt and frustration and anger before we can introduce them to hope."

If you want to help someone you know who is grieving, just be there. No one should have to grieve alone.

Be kind to one another, tenderhearted. (Ephesians 4:32)

Who needs my ear, my shoulder to cry on, my kindness and tenderheartedness today, Merciful Savior?

How Big is God?

On the website *Daily Devotion*, Jonathan Salomon shared a story about a young boy asking his father, "How big is God?"

The father responded, "It depends," then tried to explain what he meant. "Looking to the sky," wrote Salomon, "his father saw an airplane and asked his son what size did he think that airplane was? The child replied: 'Very small, I can barely see it!'

"Then the father took him to the airport and being close to a plane he asked: 'Now how big is the plane?'

"And the boy replied very amazed: 'Dad, it's huge. Wow! So, so big.'

"The father then said: 'This is how God is for you. His size will depend on the distance that you have from Him, and likewise that will affect your view of Him, your concept of Him and your experience with Him. The closer you are to God, the Bigger He will be in your life, and your concept of Him will be of a Great, Awesome, Loving and Powerful God that He is. If that is not how you see God right now, maybe you need to get a closer look.'"

Great is our Lord, and abundant in power; His understanding is beyond measure. (Psalm 147:5)

Help me move closer to You today, Father.

Smart Home Helps Military Family

Caleb Brewer, a retired Army Sergeant from Tucson, Arizona, was wounded in combat in Afghanistan on his 31st birthday in 2015. He lost both of his legs, sustained a traumatic brain injury, and was fortunate to have survived. However, thanks to a veteran's program, Sgt. Brewer, his wife, and their two daughters now have a new place to call home—a home specially designed and built to accommodate his needs.

As reported in the *Arizona Daily Star,* Brewer's story came to the attention of the RISE program and the Gary Sinise Foundation. RISE provides mortgage-free homes to severely wounded veterans. The home is a "smart house," designed with features that can be controlled by a phone or tablet to help in daily functions. It was also built to accommodate Brewer's wheelchair.

The family's gratitude reflects the love they've experienced though this good deed. "It's incredibly overwhelming in a good way," said Brewer. "It doesn't feel real. I never would've expected it in a million years."

Every house is built by someone, but the builder of all things is God. (Hebrews 3:4)

Strengthen families wounded by war, Prince of Peace.

Workers Find Success in Satisfaction

How do successful people describe the satisfaction they get from work? *Bits and Pieces* magazine reported an informal poll of men and women who admitted to both being good at what they do—and loving it.

One said: "I love to create something that wasn't there yesterday." Another said: "I like knowing I can do more than is expected of me—and I go ahead and do it." Still another admitted: "I get a thrill out of doing a job a little better than it was ever done before."

Everybody takes satisfaction in different ways. But each of us needs work that means more than a paycheck. Knowing that you give any task your best efforts brings a sense of accomplishment that no one can take away.

In the Lord your labor is not in vain.
(1 Corinthians 15:58)

Help me approach my work with humble pride, Lord, and guide me toward accomplishing Your will.

Project Embrace

After someone recovers from surgery or injury, what happens to all of their crutches, knee braces, etc.? More often than not, they end up getting discarded. 23-year-old University of Utah student Mohan Sudabattula thought of a much better use for these medical devices. Thus, Project Embrace was born.

"People get prescribed this stuff for a temporary amount of time to help them heal, and then what?" Sudabattula said to *KSL5 TV.* "It ends up sitting around and becoming clutter...so we decided to do something about it...I thought back to my entire family in India and the communities there. There are children and patients who...would do anything for these types of devices."

For now, Project Embrace is comprised of student volunteers. The used medical equipment they collect has been sent as far as India and Swaziland. The students hope to expand their outreach and are awaiting their pending nonprofit status.

"One thing that brings us all together as a team is a passion for this, and a passion to help," Sudabattula concludes.

Whoever is kind to the poor lends to the Lord. (Proverbs 19:17)

Savior, may we always seek to help those in need.

Teaching How to Save a Life

March 13, 2019, started out as a typical day for New Jersey science teacher Julianne Downes, when suddenly a student in her class started choking. Downes sprang into action and proceeded to do the Heimlich Maneuver. After 20 attempts, the food was finally dislodged from the student's throat.

After saving the student's life, a humbled Downes said that she is just one of many that could have helped, thanks to the Pascack Valley High School's mandatory policy of training each student and staff member to be CPR and AED certified. It was mandated back in 2015 after a student collapsed during track practice and a fellow teammate, who was an EMT, saved his life.

"It is impressive and powerful that we have all these people that can jump into action in any moment," Downes told *CBS2*.

Downes is heralded as being a hero by faculty and students, but she said, "As a mom, as an educator and as a human, it's our job to do the right thing."

For I will surely save you...because you have trusted in Me. (Jeremiah 39:18)

Loving Jesus, may we always seek to expand our knowledge of life-saving techniques.

As You Find Me

Meredith Bird would much rather listen to Taylor Swift than Christian worship music, but one Sunday in church, the song "As You Find Me" pierced her heart and soul. Originally recorded by Hillsong United, the lyrics include, "I know I don't deserve this kind of love/Somehow this kind of love is who You are/It's a grace I could never add up/To be somebody You still want/But somehow You love me as You find me."

Though Bird's adoptive family has been nothing but loving and welcoming to her all her life, she has struggled with feeling unwanted and unloved because her birth mother abandoned her at a hospital as a baby. That's why the song resonated.

On her blog, Bird writes, "When the little voice inside your head reminds you repeatedly of how disposable you are...you spend a lot of your time and energy trying to earn love and attention from people...But then there's Jesus, who loves us like nothing else compares. Who doesn't shy away from the messy, broken parts of us...I can't fathom why Jesus would want *me,* of all people. But, somehow, He loves me as He finds me."

See what love the Father has given us, that we should be called children of God. (1 John 3:1)

Help me to accept Your love, Jesus.

Minister to a World of Silence

If you were deaf and had to be rushed to the emergency room of a hospital alone, how would you give medical personnel vital information about yourself or your condition? This is a problem that faced millions of hearing-impaired people throughout the country.

Many years ago, Richard Russo, a deacon in the Catholic Church, led Cabrini Medical Center in New York City to take the lead in meeting the needs of the deaf. More than 40 employees completed a course to give them skills in communication such as sign language and finger spelling. In addition, Cabrini hired a deaf person for its staff.

"The deaf have traditionally stayed away from health settings," explained Deacon Russo at the time. "Experience has taught them that most people do not understand their special methods of communication...Their needs are not heard."

Deacon Russo passed away in 2017, but he is still remembered for the service and compassion he brought to an underserved community in our world.

Speak out for those who cannot speak. (Proverbs 31:8)

Guide me in serving others, Holy Spirit.

"What a Love Story!"

Sharon Gibbs-Brown was privileged to witness a once-in-a-lifetime love story firsthand when she got a job as caregiver to 88-year-old Frances DeLaigle and her 94-year-old husband Herbert.

As reported by Georgia's *WRDW News,* the DeLaigles celebrated their 71st anniversary in 2019. Six children, 16 grandchildren, and 25 great-grandchildren later, this couple was still going strong.

Brown's position with the DeLaigles sadly ended far too soon, when Herbert and Frances passed away within hours of each other. The impact of their love story, however, was beautifully recounted in Brown's Facebook post:

"They smiled, giggled and play[ed] like teenagers falling in love for the first time…They lived together, loved together, laughed together, and passed on the same day…Being in the presence of the DeLaigles was such a blessing, it even strengthen[ed] my marriage and the love my husband and I share. To God be the Glory for such an opportunity."

Set me as a seal upon your heart. (Song 8:6)

Abba, may we be inspired by the enduring bonds of love that surround us.

Mother and Child Reunion, Part One

Jim Ryan's parents had always been open about the fact that they had adopted him through Catholic Charities when he was nine days old, and that the first time they saw him, he was wearing a hand knit Irish sweater and a St. Christopher medal. But because Jim grew up in such a loving home, he never had any desire to find out about his biological parents.

At age 46, after his adoptive parents had passed away, Jim took a friend's advice to look into his origins. He contacted Catholic Charities and received a file from them that revealed his birth mother was an Irish immigrant named Ann.

In a speech, Jim explained, "She did not want to give me up for adoption, and cried every time it was brought up, but ultimately realized she couldn't afford to keep me...She knit during her pregnancy, which accounted for the sweater. I learned that she stayed in the hospital with me all nine days and fed me all my meals. And I learned that she left the hospital broken-hearted."

Jim knew he had to find his birth mother. That part of the story tomorrow...

You have received a spirit of adoption. (Romans 8:15)

Bless women who give up their children for adoption, Lord.

Mother and Child Reunion, Part Two

The day after reading the file about Ann, his biological mother, Jim Ryan received a call from Barb, an employee of Catholic Charities. Barb told him she'd been doing this kind of work for years, but never encountered a story as moving as this one. She promised to help him track down his mom.

Barb discovered that Ann had married a man named Jack, had four children with him, and lived in New Jersey 15 minutes away from where Jim grew up. Barb added, "[Ann] told me that she's prayed for you every day of your life, and that her only prayer was that someday you two would meet in heaven."

Jim called Ann, and they agreed to meet. He was in the process of moving from Virginia to Massachusetts to serve as the Dean of Harvard's Graduate School of Education. So with his wife and four kids in tow, Jim's happy reunion with his biological mother occurred at a rest stop on New Jersey's Garden State Parkway. Over time, he and his four half-siblings grew close as well. Jim said, "This is not a bridge I ever expected to cross, but it has enriched my life in so many ways."

Let her who bore you rejoice. (Proverbs 23:25)

May the loving and life-affirming bonds of family transcend any challenges from the past, Jesus.

Chores Lead to Happiness

Washing the dishes, vacuuming the floor, and dusting the furniture are all chores that need to be done in every family's home. But usually the adults finish these tasks because their kids whine and cry about doing them. A new study, however, shows that parents might want to make their children do chores anyway because they're good character builders and can also lead to greater happiness.

Using the Harvard Grant Study as research, *How to Raise an Adult* author Julie Lythcott-Haims said, "If kids aren't doing the dishes, it means someone else is doing that for them. And so they're absolved of not only the work, but of learning that work has to be done and that each one of us must contribute."

Lythcott-Haims elaborated to *Tech Insider*, explaining, "By making them do chores—taking out the garbage, doing their own laundry—they realize, 'I have to do the work of life in order to be part of life. It's not just about me and what I need in this moment, but that I'm part of an ecosystem. I'm part of a family. I'm part of a workplace.'"

Train children in the right way, and when old, they will not stray. (Proverbs 22:6)

May we build a good foundation for our children, Lord.

The Best Response to Reckless Hate

Following the murders of 49 worshipers at two mosques in Christchurch, New Zealand, blogger Larry Denninger recalled a line from the movie *The Two Towers,* based on Tolkien's *Lord of the Rings* trilogy: "So much death. What can men do against such reckless hate?"

"The best response to reckless hate," Denninger writes, "is reckless love. It sounds insensible and nonsensical to the world, and to be honest, it sounds that way to most Christians, too. But we know as Christians, by the example of Jesus' life and death, that is the only response."

"Evil's power lies in its ability to make us despair and feel hopeless. It endlessly batters against our hearts, minds, and souls, tempting us to believe all is lost...The truth? God doesn't expect you or me to solve all the problems. He expects us to love with a reckless love. That's what Christians are expected to do. Today, tomorrow, every day... May it never be said no one ever witnessed the love of God in us, because we failed to show the love we profess to possess. Let us be the ones to show what can be done against such reckless hate."

God is love. (1 John 4:8)

Where there is hatred, let me sow love, Lord.

Awesome Syndrome

Jeff and Sonia McGarrity of Colorado are the proud parents of eight children, four of whom are "typical" and four who have "Awesome syndrome." They're using a term created by author Mark Leach, who wishes that the doctor whom "Down syndrome" is named after had been named "Awesome" instead. Because that's how they see their kids with Down's: Awesome!

One of the McGarritys' sons was born with Down's, so the family adjusted and loved him unconditionally. Later, they adopted three daughters with Down's.

In countries such as Iceland, close to 100 percent of women whose unborn children test positive for Down syndrome abort their babies, purportedly to help spare the children suffering.

Jeff told Catholic Charities, "While families with children who have special needs—and all families, for that matter—certainly have their share of sleepless nights and frustrating days, we are glad to welcome the 'suffering' that has these four bright-eyed kiddos as a part of our lives."

As soon as I heard the sound of your greeting, the child in my womb leaped for joy. (Luke 1:44)

Jesus, may I see the awesome gift of life in all those around me!

Thousand Mile Taxi Ride

Many years ago, a New York cabbie drove 1,000 miles on an errand of mercy for a stranded Illinois family.

The driver had picked up a family at Kennedy Airport after an airline strike had stranded them in New York en route from the Virgin Islands to their home in Decatur, Illinois. When the family found that no accommodations to Illinois were available, the taxi man jokingly asked if they would like him to take them to Decatur for $300. The family agreed.

Driving straight through, the cab reached Decatur in 18 hours. After breakfast and a two hour nap at the home of his grateful passengers, the driver headed East again.

Commented the mother of the Decatur family, "He's a wonderful, helpful man. We'd probably still be stranded in New York if it weren't for him."

You and I may never be called on to display such a startling willingness to "go the extra mile." But in every life, God offers many opportunities for growth through service to others.

If anyone forces you to go one mile, go also the second mile. (Matthew 5:41)

Jesus, make us more aware that "it is in giving that we receive."

On God's Goodness

A little chapel in the foothills of the Appalachians bears this inscription on a beam above the pulpit: "God has always been as good to me as I would let Him be."

These words are from the last letter written by Sallie Howard, whose husband built the chapel in her memory.

This memorial, at the edge of DeSoto State Park in northern Alabama, was built around a large outcrop of rock, which forms its back wall. Visitors drawn by the unusual structure often linger to think about the meaning of the inscription.

Sallie Howard's words reflect her awareness of God's love. God delights in us and wants to guide and help us. He is waiting to give us peace and joy—if only we will let Him.

The compassion of the Lord is for every living thing. (Sirach 18:13)

How may I imitate Your compassion, Merciful Savior?

Fasting Like a 17th-Century Monk, Part One

Lent is a season of fasting, which can often feel unpleasant (it is supposed to be a sacrifice, after all). But modern fasting can't compare to the kind done by the Paulaner Monks of Southern Italy after they moved to Bavaria in the 17th century.

As reported by *Aleteia*, "The strict order required the brothers to refrain from all solid foods for the entire 40 days of Lent, which naturally brought about questions of how the order would maintain proper nutrition throughout the season. Turning to what they knew, they concluded that beer, or 'liquid bread' as they called it, could sustain them.

"The Paulaners brewed a special, unusually strong beer that would provide high levels of carbohydrates and nutrients to fight off malnutrition. This early doppelbock-style beer eventually became the original product of Paulaner brewery, founded in 1634, under the name 'Salvator.'"

Modern beer is much different, so this idea wouldn't work today. But one man did recreate a similar beer a few years ago and gave the fast a try. We'll share his story tomorrow...

I had eaten no rich food, no meat or wine had entered my mouth. (Daniel 10:3)

Give me the strength to make sacrifices for You, Lord.

Fasting Like a 17th-Century Monk, Part Two

J. Wilson had long known about the Paulaner monks and their "beer fast" in the 17th century, so he decided to recreate their type of beer with a professional brewer and adhere to the fast himself during Lent 2011. With permission from his boss at an Iowa newspaper, he drank "four beers a day during the workweek and five beers on the weekends."

Writing for *CNN*, Wilson said, "At the beginning of my fast, I felt hunger for the first two days. My body then switched gears, replaced hunger with focus, and I found myself operating in a tunnel of clarity unlike anything I'd ever experienced."

Wilson lost over 25 pounds and gained a sense of "self-discipline [that] can't be overstated in today's world of instant gratification." His experience, he concluded, "left me with the realization that the monks must have been keenly aware of their own humanity and imperfections. In order to refocus on God, they engaged this annual practice not only to endure sacrifice, but to stress and rediscover their own shortcomings in an effort to continually refine themselves."

I sat down and wept...fasting and praying before the God of heaven. (Nehemiah 1:4)

Help me renew and refine my spirit, Father.

Stars of Wonder

During the "in-between time of winter and spring," Elizabeth Scalia admired the night sky outside her Long Island, New York home, where stars are all too rarely seen. Writing for *Word on Fire*, she asked, "Does the fact that we can no longer see the stars have anything to do with our loss of wonder? These things over which we have no management—the stars, and all creation—they are more splendid, perfect, beautiful, and lasting than anything man can create."

She continued, "We have obliterated the stars with our artificial light, and in so doing have blinded ourselves. Without the wonder, the greatness of the galaxies in our sight, we've lost the ability to believe in, or expect, miracles.

"When you cannot see the glory of God's creation, how can you wish to glorify the Lord? No longer able to easily see and affirm anything greater than ourselves, we turn inward, we worship our own thoughts, our invention, our desires."

Today, choose to move beyond that narrow scope of vision and humble yourself before the greatness that surrounds you.

The heavens are telling the glory of God; and the firmament proclaims His handiwork. (Psalm 19:1)

Creator, open my eyes to the wonders of Your creation.

Has My Lent Been Enough?

"Has my Lent been enough? Have I prayed enough? Have I fasted sufficiently? Have I given alms with generosity and caring?" Those are the questions that author and blogger Lisa Hendey asked herself in 2018, during a particularly difficult year in which she found herself caring for her ailing mother.

She finally came to realize that nothing she does would ever be "enough" to make up for Jesus' sacrifice on the cross and His gifts of mercy and salvation. That was, after all, a free gift of His grace. But Hendey did learn something in the process.

She wrote, "Our family's situation has brought me into greater solidarity not only with the elderly who face this journey and their caregivers, but really with all of those in need. I see them everywhere: those who camp on the street half a mile from my home in LA. Those who labor at multiple low paying jobs to put food on their tables. Those who have been born with or developed disabilities, for whom basic daily tasks are a trial...This Lent has taught me that I can never do 'enough.'...I can only try to love."

I will boast...gladly of my weaknesses, so that the power of Christ may dwell in me. (2 Corinthians 12:9)

I offer my loving words and actions to You this Lent, Lord.

Getting Past Futility

Rogers Hornsby, Grover Cleveland Alexander, Bob Lemon, and Babe Ruth are all Hall of Fame baseball players. But all of them knew futility as well as success in the World Series.

Hornsby, one of the greatest hitters of all time, struck out eight times in 21 at-bats in the 1929 series and hit .238.

Pitchers Alexander and Lemon both allowed 11 runs in a four-game series. No pitcher ever allowed more.

Babe Ruth was the goat of the 1922 series, batting a feeble .118 in five games. Six years later, he compiled a .625 average in another World Series.

No one is protected from failure. A champion is an individual who can come back from a poor performance and maintain a standard of excellence.

Recognize that you'll have good days and bad days, and don't be discouraged when things go wrong. Learn from the past, but live in the present moment.

By your endurance you will gain your souls. (Luke 21:19)

Give me the needed endurance to face all of life's trials, Savior.

Have You Heard...?

Even scrupulously honest people can unwittingly spread false information. At some time or other, most of us have repeated a rumor that proved to be untrue. And even true stories easily become so distorted that they have little relation to fact.

Psychologists have identified common ways stories change as they pass from person to person: incidents may be exaggerated to make a more dramatic story; details may be forgotten; or what people hear may be influenced by their prejudices.

Rumors can damage businesses, ruin reputations, fan racial tensions, or at the very least cause needless anxiety.

When you hear a story, ask yourself: "What's the source of the story?" and "Is there any real evidence to support it?" Don't unthinkingly pass on rumors that could do harm. Take responsibility for your words.

A gentle tongue is a tree of life. (Proverbs 15:4)

Lord, make my speech charitable, honest, wise, and joy-filled.

Starting a New Life with Gratitude

"I was convinced I would become an adult when I turned 21. But now, I'm certain that turning 65 was the watershed moment that finally grew me up." So says Bruce Horovitz in *Kaiser Health News* about the age at which he found his life beginning—again.

The husband and father notes that hitting age 65 happily started a new and purposeful chapter in his life for which he created a playbook that others could follow.

He agrees with and quotes James Firman, CEO of the National Council on Aging: "There's really nothing to prepare us for the transition to this next phase of life."

Horovitz suggests reviewing such areas as health, finances, social relationships, and service to others. For example, he "re-established contact with a best buddy from college" and "bumped up my volunteer schedule."

Again quoting Firman, he concludes, "Life is a gift...Success in old age starts with an attitude of gratitude."

Do not lose heart. Even though our outer nature is wasting away, our inner nature is being renewed day by day. (2 Corinthians 4:16)

Guide us, Jesus, along the many paths life takes us.

A Little Boy's Empathy

Five-year-old Miguel Garcia didn't understand his father's sickness. But he did know that his father was losing strength and had to go to the hospital frequently for special treatments.

He also knew that his father was losing his hair due to the treatment, and that this made him feel sad. His father spoke of feeling strange and alone. Miguel's older brothers felt very bad and so did Miguel, who said he wanted to do something for his father.

One night, Miguel called his father into his bedroom. The five-year-old had cut off all his hair so his father wouldn't feel alone. He told his father, "I did it because I love you."

There are no words with more healing power than words of love. The more we express our love in words and deeds, the better we become as human beings.

See what love the Father has given us, that we should be called children of God; and that is what we are. (1 John 3:1)

Jesus, show us how to love each other as You love us.

Catholic Laughs

When Carl Kozlowski stayed home from school in the third grade, he didn't think it would be a career-defining moment. But after watching David Letterman's zany morning show at the time, it planted a seed that led Kozlowski to a career in stand-up comedy. Now, he has joined forces with another comic, Scott Vinci, to create a business called Catholic Laughs.

The duo, along with other well-known comedians, perform at parishes that are interested in doing fundraisers, so they work out a deal to split the profits from the show. And parishioners don't have to worry that they'll be inundated with swear words in the comedy routines. Kozlowski and Vinci's Catholic upbringings led them to keep things clean.

A profile in the *Detroit Catholic* noted Vinci as saying, "Contrary to popular belief, it is not necessarily more difficult for a comedian to keep his act 'clean' in the industry. Rather, clean shows cultivate a broader appeal, and usually result in more gigs." For more information, go to CatholicLaughs.com.

Our mouth was filled with laughter, and our tongue with shouts of joy. (Psalm 126:2)

When life gets too serious, send me something to laugh about, Holy Spirit.

Measuring the Value of Life

By what yardstick do you measure the value of life? British journalist Mary Craig offered an appealing standard in a book she wrote many years ago, titled *Blessings*. After a forthright description of her efforts to accept the disabilities of her second son, Paul, she explained her very real grief at his death:

"I owed him an incredible debt. If our value as human beings lies in what we do for each other, Paul had done a great deal: he had, at the very least, opened the eyes of his mother to the suffering that was in the world, and had brought her to understand something of the redemptive force it was capable of generating."

That is quite the accomplishment for a 10-year-old who was never able to speak, required constant attention, and lived what some would call a vegetative life.

Of suffering, Craig wrote: "The value of suffering does not lie in the pain of it, which is morally neutral—but in what the sufferer makes of it," which is the essence of Christ's acceptance of the cross.

Father...not as I will but as You will. (Matthew 26:39)

Jesus, help me bear my crosses.

Abandoned Church Finds New Life

Greg Thomas sat on the steps outside the abandoned wooden church in Montgomery, Minnesota, and prayed. He had received a diagnosis of stage four neck and head cancer, and required a feeding tube in his stomach along with intense chemo and radiation. He told the *Star Tribune* he was "terrified."

Thomas returned to those steps every day. Finally, an idea struck him. Maybe he could give the church a new coat of paint and fix it up. It was called St. John's Catholic Church, and had been built by Czech settlers, many of whom were buried in the cemetery on its grounds. But it had been closed for 70 years.

Thomas got the church keys from a nearby farmer and discovered the statues and pictures inside remained untouched. He painted, put up shingles, and soon attracted help from the community. He also started feeling better, noting, "It was like as I was rebuilding the church, God was rebuilding me."

Thomas's cancer went into remission, and St. John's now welcomes worshipers who, like Thomas, are in need of a house of prayer.

Like living stones, let yourselves be built into a spiritual house. (1 Peter 2:5)

Holy Spirit, guide me in building Your spiritual house.

A Ride of Compassion

An Illinois man started a new job at FedEx and has a police officer to thank for his second chance.

In April 2018, Ka'Shawn Baldwin, 22, was pulled over by Police Officer Roger Gemoules for driving with an expired license plate and an invalid driver's license. Baldwin told the officer that he knew his license was expired, but that he had borrowed the car from a friend so that he could get to his job interview that day.

Gemoules told *NBC* affiliate *KSDK*, "He was polite when I pulled him over and he seemed like a good young man, so I wanted to give him a chance."

Instead of towing his car and giving him a ticket, the officer showed Baldwin compassion and drove the young man to his interview, where he landed a job at FedEx as a package carrier.

Gemoules' actions have been commended by Cahokia Mayor Curtis McCall Jr. as being "a great example of how community-oriented policing actually works."

Saul said, "May you be blessed by the Lord for showing me compassion!" (1 Samuel 23:21)

Loving Creator, teach me how to walk through life in Your footsteps and show compassion toward others.

A Payless Donation

When a Payless shoe store in Hays, Kansas, was going out of business in early 2019, one woman was inspired to buy out nearly 200 pairs of shoes—not for herself, but for flood victims in Nebraska.

Fort Hays State University graduate Addy Tritt heard that her alma mater was taking part in the Nebraska flood relief effort, so she decided to help. "I have been so blessed," she told the *Hays Post*. "So many people have helped me when I was down. I want to help if I can."

When she heard that her local Payless was going out of business, Tritt walked in to buy out the remaining shoes in the store. After some negotiation, she bought 204 pairs of shoes for $100 out of her own pocket. The retail value was $6,000.

Tritt hopes that her donation inspires others to volunteer and help however they can. "I think everything is a part of God's plan," she said. "If you can do something for someone else, you need to find a way, even if it is a pair of shoes."

The Lord sits enthroned over the flood. (Psalm 29:10)

Merciful God, help me be a lifeline to others.

Finding God in the Darkness, Part One

At age 35, Kate Bowler's life seemed blessed. She had a loving husband and newborn son, she'd written a successful book exploring the prosperity gospel, and she worked as a professor at Duke Divinity School. Then, she was diagnosed with incurable stage four colon cancer.

Kate was understandably shaken to her core. She had been raised around Mennonites and Catholics, so she didn't officially subscribe to the prosperity gospel, an American religious movement which believes that if your Christian faith is true and deep, God will make you healthy and even wealthy. But after her diagnosis, she saw that she had absorbed the belief that she could control her life through sheer determination and faith.

Kate confronted her new reality and wrote about it in her Christopher Award-winning memoir *Everything Happens for a Reason and Other Lies I've Loved*. Instead of feeling like a failure for not healing herself, she came to find God in the midst of brokenness and suffering, especially during the season of Lent.

More of Kate's story tomorrow…

The Lord is near to the brokenhearted. (Psalm 34:18)

Bring Your peace to those with fatal illnesses, Savior.

Finding God in the Darkness, Part Two

Though Kate Bowler isn't Catholic herself, she has found solace in certain aspects of the faith following her diagnosis with incurable stage four colon cancer.

During a *Christopher Closeup* interview, Kate said, "I've learned from the Catholic tradition, especially in Lent, that there are times of deep and important lament, when Catholics are good at saying and performing what it feels like to come undone...A Catholic cross has a suffering Jesus to remind us that we're in our bodies, Jesus was in His body, and that our suffering is not an affront to God."

Kate has also come to a new understanding of Easter. She used to view life as something where "you love all the right people, do the right things, and, in a way, you don't really need the Kingdom Come...That's why Good Friday [and] Easter [are] so important. First, the world has come apart and only God can put it together. And then in Easter, we're hungry for the fact that God's going to come back and there will be a new kingdom and new earth. Before, I didn't need a new kingdom. Now, I do."

I am the resurrection and the life. Those who believe in Me, even though they die, will live. (John 11:25)

May Lent bring me closer to You, Jesus.

Finding God in the Darkness, Part Three

The hospital in which Kate Bowler had surgery and received treatment was right next to the Methodist Seminary where she worked at Duke Divinity School. That experience gave her a new appreciation of community.

Kate explained that Americans in particular often subscribe to a hyper-individualism ("I can do it on my own!") that she also bought into because she's a high achiever. But once she got sick, her work colleagues rallied around her out of love and demonstrated "that we have to belong to one another."

"The more helpless and reliant I became," Kate observed, "the more I realized how important it is to have that web of obligation in which we don't feel embarrassed by our neediness. We just know, 'I can't do this on my own. Also, could you bring some food tomorrow?' My lovely, sweet local Methodist church fed me for a year. I mean, they just took turns bringing food over when we couldn't take care of ourselves. So I've been absolutely held up by the people who've chosen to love me."

More of Kate's story tomorrow...

If they fall, one will lift up the other. (Ecclesiastes 4:10)

It's difficult for me to admit my neediness, Lord. Give me the wisdom and strength to ask for and accept help.

Finding God in the Darkness, Part Four

Though doctors initially predicted Kate Bowler would die quickly from her cancer, she remains alive several years later because of an experimental treatment with immunotherapy drugs. She's not cured, but remains stable for the time being.

The extra time has deepened Kate's gratitude for life's simple moments, such as holding her son's hand while walking him to his first day of kindergarten because she never thought she'd get to see that day.

Her experiences also broadened her feelings of connection to others. During a *Christopher Closeup* interview, Kate noted that being in pain led her to a deeper understanding of the struggles that all people go through, because no one's life is problem-free.

Kate's perception of God has also evolved. She concluded, "I wanted to be an earner: someone who earned God's love and approval...I found that I shifted some of the way that I think of God from a contractual one, into one in which I mostly think of God as overwhelming love, as one where even in the midst of the worst moments, I felt the sweetness of God's love."

God is love. (1 John 4:8)

Help me experience the sweetness of Your love, Jesus.

Time to Examine Our Motives

Jesus' last words before dying included a prayer of forgiveness for those who executed Him: "Father, forgive them; for they do not know what they are doing." (Luke 23:34)

This outstanding gesture of pardon reveals the compassion of Jesus. It also illustrates how easy it is for men to perform unworthy deeds in the name of the highest causes.

Among those who executed Jesus, at least some were acting in the name of "defense of religion" or "the interests of public peace." Similar explanations have been given throughout history to justify persecutions, wars of aggression, or restrictions on the rights of individuals and groups.

During the celebration of Christ's death and resurrection, it is well to take stock of our motives. Are we purifying them in the light of the Gospel's message of love? Or are we using high-sounding excuses to rationalize courses of action that have little or nothing to do with the message of Jesus?

Father, into Your hands I commend My spirit. (Luke 23:46)

Holy Spirit, help me to be open and honest in analyzing my intentions.

Your Debt is Forgiven

As Easter approaches every year, many churches advertise their holiday masses or services. But in 2018, Pathway Church in Wichita, Kansas, tried something different. They spent the money they would have ordinarily used for ads to pay off the medical debt of 1,600 families in the state.

As reported by *Relevant* magazine, Pastor Todd Carter coupled the church's promotion funds with money already allocated to help needy families, totaling $22,000. These families then received a note stating, "We're Pathway Church. We may never meet you, but as an act of kindness in the name of Jesus Christ, your debt has been forgiven."

Addressing his congregants, Carter said, "I want you to imagine for a moment what those 1,600 people felt like last week when they got that letter in the mail...and all of a sudden they realize that their debt, this debt that has been hanging over their head, has been forgiven...That's exactly what God, in the person of Jesus Christ, wants you to feel each and every day: that your debt has been forgiven."

Forgive us our debts, as we also have forgiven our debtors. (Matthew 6:12)

Help me to accept and practice forgiveness, Savior.

Look for God in Ordinary Places

Two of Jesus' followers were traveling to Emmaus on the first Easter, when the risen Lord approached them and joined them in their journey. Unrecognized, He discussed the events of the last few days with them, explaining why it was necessary for the Christ to die and so "enter into His glory."

When they reached the village, the two invited Jesus to stay with them, which He did. St. Luke explains how the Master broke bread and gave it to them—and how they suddenly recognized who their companion actually was.

Like the two disciples, we all tend to look for the Lord to act in grand and dramatic ways. Yet, the events of everyday life are filled with His presence, had we but the eyes to see. A meal, a job to be done, a chance meeting on the street—all can be occasions for encountering God in our neighbor.

Their eyes were opened, and they recognized Him; and He vanished from their sight. They said to each other, "Were not our hearts burning within us while He was talking to us on the road, while He was opening the Scriptures to us?" (Luke 24:31-32)

Father, help us to realize that it is in each other that we find You.

After the Storm

Writer Leticia Ochoa Adams followed some dark paths in her life as a result of being sexually abused as a child. She began moving toward self-respect and healing as an adult after finding a welcoming priest and church in her Texas community.

Adams now shares her story with others in the hopes that they, too, can overcome the emotional wounds of their pasts. On her Facebook page, she shared the following observations:

"After a storm, the sun comes out and all the plants begin to lean towards the warmth of its rays. The rain from the storm and the rays from the sun help that plant grow and bloom. Without both, the plant will die.

"So life comes with both storms and sun also. Suffering and mistakes are the storm and God is the sun. When you know Him, you can't help but be like a plant and lean towards Him for some sunshine to help you grow and heal.

"Here's to healing and to a God who never abandons us, even when we have abandoned ourselves. And here's to getting out of His way to finally bloom."

Incline your ear to My sayings...They are life to those who find them. (Proverbs 4:20,22)

Help me to grow and to heal, Divine Messiah.

A Teacher's Helping Hand

"I'm not coming back to school," said 13-year-old Damien to his math teacher, Finn Lanning, at AXL Academy in Aurora, Colorado. When Damien explained why, Lanning was shocked.

Damien lived in foster care and suffered from kidney disease. Since no foster family was willing to take him in, he would have to live in the hospital. On top of that, Damien's chances of qualifying for a kidney transplant were low because he didn't have a stable home.

As reported by Steve Hartman of *CBS News,* Lanning said, "It hit me like a ton of bricks. I mean, you just can't sit across from somebody that you care about and hear them say something like that and know that you have room to help." And help he did.

The teacher, who believed he was perfectly happy being single and childless, took Damien in and became his foster parent. Lanning was at Damien's side through dialysis and eventually, the kidney transplant he needed. He is now looking into adoption, proving that selflessness can lead to a level of happiness we never expected.

Give justice to the weak and the orphan. (Psalm 82:3)

Lead adults to open their hearts and homes to children in need of families, Father.

Friendship and Fortitude

In 2011, Micah Herndon returned home from four years of active duty in Iraq and Afghanistan. He took up running to cope with post-traumatic stress and survivor's guilt.

In 2019, he entered the Boston Marathon. Written on small plates affixed to his shoelaces were the names of three of his fallen comrades: Juarez, Ballard, and Hamer.

At mile 20, Herndon's legs began to lock up. "That last 4.2 miles I ran is the hardest, longest 4.2 miles I ever ran in my life," he said on *NBC's Today Show*. It became so difficult for him to move that he dropped to the ground and began crawling.

He low-crawled until his legs loosened up enough to allow him to crawl on all fours. He made it across the finish line to honor the fallen and send a message.

Herndon said, "I just hope that what everyone gets out of this whole message is to bring awareness to PTSD and all the other issues that come from war, and not to be ashamed of it if you're a veteran."

My flesh and my heart may fail, but God is the strength of my heart and my portion forever. (Psalm 73:26)

Lord, sustain me through the trials of life.

Changing the World One Suit at a Time

While working at New York City's Department of Motor Vehicles, PK Kersey noticed many young men arriving for job interviews dressed inappropriately. Kersey felt motivated to help.

He assumed the applicants either didn't own a suit or didn't realize the importance of getting dressed up to make a good impression. At first, he and his brother simply gave away their extra suits. But much more was needed.

Kersey started a nonprofit called "That Suits You," which has grown to include job-skills training, workshops, and partnerships with various schools and organizations.

Participants learn how to get jobs and succeed in them. Kersey told *AM NY*, "It's about the relationships they're building from us teaching them, the mentorship, and how they're learning to communicate and express themselves."

When Kersey sees the impact that his work is having on people's lives, he knows it's all worth the effort.

Do not neglect to do good and to share what you have, for such sacrifices are pleasing to God. (Hebrews 13:16)

Help us, Lord, to notice what needs to be done and to pitch in.

Helping Is All That I Know

"People appreciate my dad for what he did as a right fielder for the Pittsburgh Pirates, sure, but they also remember him as someone who always wanted to help," Roberto Clemente, Jr. told Michael Anft for *AARP: The Magazine.* "That's how we lost him. His plane went down over the Atlantic in 1972 as he was traveling to Nicaragua to deliver aid to earthquake victims."

Clemente Jr., who was a boy when his father died, carries on the generous spirit of both his parents. "Helping is all that I know," he said. While playing Little League, he saw kids and adults asking players for food and wanted to do something.

Today, Clemente Jr. is a sports broadcaster and also serves as global ambassador for Food for the Hungry and its Striking Out Poverty enterprise. He not only wants to get people food and clean water, he wants to teach them how to help themselves.

Come, you that are blessed by My Father, inherit the kingdom prepared for you from the foundation of the world; for I was hungry and you gave Me food, I was thirsty and you gave Me something to drink. (Matthew 25:34)

Instead of focusing on the negative, give us the strength, Jesus, to maintain hope in the face of challenges.

Volunteer in a Wheelchair

Many years ago, Mrs. John Nichols completed more than 1,000 hours of voluntary hospital work. And she did it all as a paraplegic, confined to a wheelchair.

Propelling herself around the corridors of New Jersey's Englewood Hospital, Mrs. Nichols headed the volunteer services committee, the visitors' aid service, and was a member of the hospital's executive board.

Attracted to hospital work at age 18, she began as a clinic aide in New York Presbyterian. With a few years interruption for a long series of operations, she kept at it afterwards.

"She makes all the visitors feel relaxed and comfortable with her big smiles," commented an associate. "Then you're startled when she leaves her desk on an errand and goes zipping around in that wheelchair."

Succumb to self-pity and you'll accomplish little or nothing. But "go with what you've got," whatever your limitations, and you can be an effective instrument of God's love.

**Do not neglect the gift that is in you.
(1 Timothy 4:14)**

Father, may we stress our assets and minimize our liabilities in our efforts to serve others.

A Prayer to Open Hearts and Spirits

Some of the prayers of the Rev. Dr. Martin Luther King Jr. have been collected in Lewis V. Baldwin's book *Thou, Dear God: Prayers That Open Hearts and Spirits*. Here is one that addresses human beings falling short of our Christian ideals:

"O Thou Eternal God, out of whose absolute power and infinite intelligence the whole universe has come into being, we humbly confess that we have not loved Thee with our hearts, souls and minds, and we have not loved our neighbors as Christ loved us. We have all too often lived by our own selfish impulses rather than by the life of sacrificial love as revealed by Christ. We often give in order to receive. We love our friends and hate our enemies. We go the first mile but dare not travel the second..."

"O God, have mercy upon us. Forgive us for what we could have been but failed to be. Give us the intelligence to know Your will. Give us the courage to do Your will. Give us the devotion to love Thy will. In the name and spirit of Jesus, we pray. Amen."

Do not be conformed to this world, but be transformed by the renewing of your minds, so that you may discern what is the will of God. (Romans 12:2)

Conform my will to Your will, Father.

Young at Heart

100-year-old John Cook recently wed 102-year-old Phyllis. These twice-widowed centenarians have certainly proven that you're never too old to be young at heart!

John and Phyllis met in Kingston Residence, an assisted living facility in Sylvania, Ohio. They had been dating for about a year before they made the decision to tie the knot. "We were just compatible in a whole lot of ways, found ourselves enjoying each other's company," World War II veteran Cook told *WNWO-TV*.

"To tell you the truth, we fell in love with each other," Phyllis added. "I know you think that may be a little far-fetched for somebody our age, but we fell in love with each other."

The key to the Cooks' successful union, according to the new bride? Valuing the other's privacy. "We keep both our apartments," the new Mrs. Cook concluded. "He's upstairs and I'm down." The newlyweds always share meals together, and their favorite pastime is sitting outside, enjoying each other's company in the sunshine.

The Lord God said, "It is not good that the man should be alone. I shall make him a...partner." (Genesis 2:18)

Abba, foster love and fidelity between married couples.

Dream Small to Win Big

Though Jack and Judy Jurries' second son, Joey, was born with Down syndrome, they were determined to raise him to reach his full potential. When Joey showed an interest in swimming, his small dream inspired not only his family, but the world to realize he could achieve great things.

"My every dream was that my kid would be accepted and have peers and a social situation to interact with," Judy shared with the *Catholic Herald*.

In 2018, Joey's swim times qualified him to participate in the Down Syndrome World Championships held in Truro, Nova Scotia. The Jurries took a "leap of faith," and after overcoming multiple training, financial and health challenges, Joey and his mom traveled with the U.S. team for the world-level meet. Joey medaled in three events and broke a national record.

Proud of her son, Judy said he is an inspiration to others with disabilities: "God gave him a gift, there's no question about that, but they can all strive for whatever their gift might be."

Jesus said to him, "Stand up, take your mat and walk." (John 5:8)

Lord, may our disability not define us, but make us stronger.

One Man Changed Our Language

Can one person really make a difference? An obscure young school teacher in Somers, New York, thought so. In 1783, he compiled a book that eventually sold 100 million copies.

Noah Webster thought that political independence from England wasn't enough. He said he had "too much pride to stand indebted to England for books to teach our children." His "Spelling Book" was an important step in the liberation of American literature. He deleted the "u" from such words as "honour" and shortened words like "programme" and "musick."

History and science, as well as rules for proper behavior, were contained in his famous "blue-backed speller," which was a prelude to his landmark dictionary, published in 1828. Later came a grammar book and reader. Not wanting his books pirated, Webster was influential in getting copyright law passed in Congress in 1831.

Noah Webster had a sense of mission. He pursued his goal day and night, though he never made much money on his writing. Let us pursue our goals with the same passion.

Our steps are made firm by the Lord. (Psalm 37:23)

Father, when we need it, remind us of where we came from, why we are here, and where we are going.

Realistic Optimism

A crippling disease gave a new direction to the life of Jacqueline du Pré. She was a successful cellist who traveled extensively on concert tours with her pianist husband.

In 1971, du Pré felt her hands going numb. She discovered that she had multiple sclerosis. She could no longer play the cello, or, eventually, even walk or dress herself. She had to learn to handle her frustrations and to reorganize her life.

From her wheelchair, du Pré began teaching music to a dozen students. She also led a research project on multiple sclerosis to which musicians donated their fees from four concerts a year. With performers like Arthur Rubenstein and Isaac Stern, the project raised money for the work.

Jacqueline du Pré passed away in 1987, but her mantra remains a good one: "I believe in realistic optimism, but not in wishful thinking."

You, too, may be suffering from a disability. Don't give up on life. Explore your potential, believe in yourself, and trust in God to help you find and reach new goals.

As You share in our sufferings, so also You share in our consolation. (2 Corinthians 1:8)

Lord, even in life's worst struggles, may I find a renewed sense of purpose.

From Orphan to "Bon Pasteur"

Saint Mary Euphrasia Pelletier was born at the end of the French Revolution into a family living in exile on an island off the coast of France. Her father died when she was 10 years old, at which point her mother sent her to a boarding school in Tours, France. Her mother died three years later, so she remained at the school as an orphan.

Near her school in Tours was a convent for the Order of Our Lady of Charity of the Refuge, founded in 1641 to help poor and homeless girls at risk of exploitation. Inspired by their mission, she joined the order while still a teenager, eventually becoming Mother Superior.

As Larry Peterson reported on *Aleteia,* Mary Euphrasia felt it was her calling "to help the orphaned, abandoned, and vulnerable young girls that seemed to be everywhere." In Angers, France, she established a home for them called "Bon Pasteur" ("Good Shepherd"), and continued founding these shelters for young women throughout the country.

Give justice to the weak and the orphan; maintain the right of the lowly and the destitute. (Psalm 82:3)

Lord, guide me to find my purpose in service to others.

Gallup to the Truth

The late pollster George Gallup was a man of faith: faith in his work and faith in God. In part, he came to God through his work with statistics.

He once said he could prove the existence of God statistically. As an example, he used the human body.

"The chance that all the harmonious functions of a human body would just happen is a statistical monstrosity," he said. The existence of human beings, in other words, defies all the laws of probability and implies the existence of God.

We all have different ways of coming to God. But give God a chance. Take time each day to search for Him in your way.

Ever since the creation of the world His eternal power and divine nature, invisible though they are, have been understood and seen through the things He has made. (Romans 1:20)

Guide me to You, Almighty Lord.

A Not Quite Solo Flight

The first time Mrs. Editha Merrill ever sat behind the controls of a plane, she had to fly the plane in an emergency. The 78-year-old woman was in the co-pilot's seat when the pilot suffered a severe heart attack at 7,500 feet. They were a hundred miles from the nearest airport.

Also on the plane was a woman who had been instructed on what to do in an emergency. But the two could not change seats in the cramped cockpit so it was up to Mrs. Merrill to do the flying. Somehow, the two succeeded in landing the plane.

Later, a spokesman for the airport said that they had made a good team, bringing in the plane without damage to it or themselves.

Two people working together can often accomplish miracles. When there's a difficult job to be done in your life, why not ask a friend to share your burden?

If they fall, one will lift up the other; but woe to one who is alone and falls and does not have another to help. (Ecclesiastes 4:10)

Grant me the ability to act with grace under pressure, Jesus, and the willingness to help someone in need.

What Makes You Smile? Part One

Christopher James Bohinski moved to New York City to pursue an acting career, but noticed that many of the talented people he encountered suffered from a negative attitude. Having experienced the pain of losing his father to cancer, he knew that he wanted to do something to add positivity to the world.

As he recalled in *Guideposts*, Bohinski created a blog called *NYC Smile 4 Me*, and started posting videos of himself asking strangers, "What makes you smile?" It became a hit and even attracted celebrities ranging from Helen Mirren to Kristin Chenoweth. Bohinski observed, "God smiled on my efforts."

Then, he got the news that his mother in Pennsylvania had been diagnosed with lung cancer. He made the three hour trips back and forth for a while to be with her when she received chemotherapy, but came to see she needed him there full-time as a caretaker. Bohinski uploaded a video explaining his move, thinking that was the end of his smile ministry. But God wasn't quite through with his efforts just yet. More tomorrow...

A glad heart makes a cheerful countenance. (Proverbs 15:13)

Help me to recall the things that make me smile, Father.

What Makes You Smile? Part Two

Christopher James Bohinski grew accustomed to his role as caretaker for his cancer-stricken mom in her hometown of Wilkes-Barre, Pennsylvania. He did the laundry, took her to doctor's appointments, served her meals, and more. But he also felt a sense of dissatisfaction at having left behind his smile ministry. His mother finally told him, "People need smiles everywhere. There's a lot you can do for others right here."

After suggesting a fall festival (or Smile Festival) to the mayor, Bohinski got the go-ahead to put it together. When word spread, everybody got involved. Bohinski wrote in *Guideposts,* "A dentist donated prizes. A college fraternity offered to oversee the ring toss...The police department offered a meet and greet with its K-9 unit." Even his mother started helping, as it gave her a happy distraction from chemo.

The Smile Festival became "the most attended town event in recent history." Bohinski concluded, "In that moment, I realized the power of a smile. And I knew I was exactly where I was supposed to be. My own dreams weren't delayed; they were just coming true in a different way than I had ever envisioned."

God...fulfills His purpose for me. (Psalm 57:2)

Teach me to trust in Your vision for my life, Divine Healer.

A Foster Care Success Story

Justin Nieves of Oviedo, Florida, has known hardship and struggle in his young life. His mother was addicted to drugs and his father died when he was in middle school.

Justin went to live with his aunt and uncle when he was in high school, but continued conflicts led to him being placed in foster care at age 16. That was a crucial point when Justin could have chosen to drop out of school. However, he decided to commit to his education, if for no other reason than to buck the low expectations of foster care kids.

Once he saw his academic success, that initial reaction turned into hope for a better future. Justin told the *Orlando Sentinel,* "I started meeting case workers, going to church, and decided I was going to do good for myself...As I started going through college, I thought...that other kids could do the same."

Today, at 21, Justin has mended his relationship with his aunt and uncle, and mentors other foster care children on how to have a successful future. He was recently recognized for his community work.

Cast all your anxiety on Him, because He cares for you. (1 Peter 5:7)

Help me to show my gratitude by sharing Your gifts, Lord.

God's Inspiration in Hollywood

Visual set designer Philip Metschan has a unique job in the movies: he designs sets for animated films, such as Pixar's *The Incredibles 2*.

In a recent interview with *Catholic World Report*, Metschan explained his love of nature and how he takes inspiration from the divine when creating the highly-detailed world of a Pixar film: "In a sense, I feel like whenever I'm using [real-world environments] as inspiration, I'm using God as inspiration."

Metschan is a Catholic and brings his faith into his work, in a way that expresses his artistic talents. He also wants his work to reflect the beauty of the world and of the human experience, a vision that is not too readily found in the matinee features of today.

He concluded, "As an artist, you feel like you've been given some kind of special skill, or a special view of how to execute these new things, and you also feel a responsibility that these things you create will be positive and enlightening."

The heavens are telling the glory of God; and the firmament proclaims His handiwork. (Psalm 19:1)

May my work today reflect Your beauty and glory, Lord!

Redefining Romance

For a long time, Jenny Albers perceived romance as defined by fairy tales: a big diamond engagement ring, bouquets of flowers sent to the office, surprise exotic getaways. However, it wasn't until she experienced marriage and parenthood that Albers realized what true romance means.

As a Colorado mother raising two children (with two other children already in heaven), Albers sees that her relationship with her husband is better than any fairy tale. In a blog post for the *Today Show,* she writes, "It's not the expressions of love based in fantasy that matter, it's the expressions of love shaped by reality."

Albers says that love and romance shouldn't be measured by big luxurious gifts, but instead by the "rather ordinary": helping with the dishes, changing a baby's diaper, and being a source of comfort when things get tough and messy. Romance, she concludes, is the "million little acts of service that are done simply out of love."

I will recount the gracious deeds of the Lord... according to...His steadfast love. (Isaiah 63:7)

Lord, thank You for Your million little acts of love.

One Day, It Will Be You

Twice in one week, Adele noticed elderly people struggling through a task without anyone offering to help them. The first instance happened in a supermarket where an older man searched and searched for a particular product. Adele stopped to help him.

Next, she was in a cafe when she saw a senior citizen, with a gash on his leg from falling down, struggling to walk to his car. No one offered to help, so Adele accompanied him herself.

On her Facebook page, Adele said, "When you see an elderly person walking down the street, searching in the supermarket or struggling to their car, take a minute…and ask them if they need a hand. Think about your grandparents and your parents and how upset you would be if someone didn't stop to help them. But more, think of them as you."

"Once upon a time they were you. They were busy, they had work, they had children, and they were able. Today, they are just in an older body that is not going as fast as it used to and this busy life is confusing. They deserve our utmost respect and consideration. One day it will be you."

Do not cast me off in the time of old age; do not forsake me when my strength is spent. (Psalm 71:9)

May I be a help to someone who is elderly, Father.

"Come On, Kid, Fight Back"

In May 2019, in the Hermosa neighborhood of Chicago, a mother and daughter were walking along the street when they heard screams emanating from a canvas shopping bag left on top of a garbage can. Inside was a newborn baby boy. As reported by the *Chicago Tribune,* "His naked body was covered by a towel and the umbilical cord was still attached."

The mother and daughter immediately took the child to a nearby firehouse where firefighters discovered he was no longer moving and "cold as concrete." An ambulance arrived and they all started working on the baby together, trying to warm him and will him back to life.

In the ER, doctors inserted an IV and breathing tube in the baby. Larry Langford, a spokesman for the Chicago Fire Department, noted that many people gathered around the child, some making the sign of the cross and praying, others cheering him on, saying, "Come on, kid, fight back."

Suddenly, the baby's vital signs improved. He became more stable over the next few days, gaining a second chance at life thanks to the hard work and prayers of everyone involved.

I will restore health to you. (Jeremiah 30:17)

Bring love and life to all babies, Creator of All.

When God Calls the Heart

Brian Bird is the creator and executive producer of the family-friendly, faith-affirming, Christopher Award-winning *Hallmark Channel* series *When Calls the Heart*. The show is so popular with Christian fans that Bird co-authored a devotional book series with Michelle Cox, titled *When God Calls the Heart*. It uses plotlines as jumping off points for prayerful reflections.

Here is one of their prayers for times when you're facing a challenge and don't know what to do: "Father, why do I always try to fix my own problems? Why do I make a mess of things when I should just turn to You first? Please help me to trust You more in situations where I feel as if I'm trapped in a corner with no idea how to escape.

"Help me to get out of Your way so that You can take charge. Teach me what You want me to learn from each situation, and provide the strength I need. Help me to also be vulnerable enough to ask my friends and loved ones for help. And, in turn, help me to be available when life has them in a bind. Thank You for never failing me."

In all your ways acknowledge Him, and He will make straight your paths. (Proverbs 3:6)

Remind me to turn to You in good times and bad, Jesus.

A Leadership Lesson from Caterpillars

Processionary caterpillars are strange creatures. They travel in long, undulating lines, one behind the other. French naturalist Jean-Henri Fabre once led a group of them out onto the rim of a large flowerpot, so that the leader found himself nose-to-tail with the last caterpillar in the procession.

Through sheer force of instinct, the ring of insects circled the rim for seven days and nights until all died from exhaustion and starvation. This was in spite of a clearly visible source of food nearby. The caterpillars ignored the food because it lay outside the beaten path.

Going around in circles can be unhealthy for people too, especially for those charged with any degree of responsibility for leadership. Take a look around you and see if there might be some opportunities for good that you never noticed before.

Sow for yourselves righteousness, reap steadfast love. (Hosea 10:12)

Holy Spirit, give me the vision to see where I can exercise the leadership today's world needs.

A Graduation to Remember

Aldo Amenta was never supposed to walk again after breaking his neck in a 2015 diving accident, which left him a quadriplegic. As reported by *CBS News*, the Florida International University student considered dropping out of school, but changed his mind after receiving support from loved ones and a scholarship to continue his education.

In 2018, Amenta earned a degree in electrical engineering, but also accomplished an even greater feat: he walked.

Rehabilitation and physical therapy had helped him make progress in regaining minor use of his limbs—and an exoskeleton did the rest. The device, which contains motors and levers, was attached to the lower half of Amenta's body, allowing him to take slow but steady steps across the stage to accept his diploma at his graduation ceremony.

He said, "You have to keep hope, faith, have perseverance and a lot of patience towards that particular situation. Even if you find yourself in a really dark place, there's always a little light that will shine your way through to succeed."

The crowd was amazed when they saw...the lame walking. (Matthew 15:31)

Bring hope to those with medical problems, Lord.

A Hollywood Legend's Conversion, Part One

Actor Gary Cooper was beloved by his family and friends, as well as by fans who admired the heroic characters he played in films such as *High Noon, Pride of the Yankees,* and *Sergeant York.* But he also had flaws, the biggest of which was having affairs with other women despite being married to his wife, Veronica Balfe.

An affair with actress Patricia Neal led Cooper to separate from his wife and their daughter Maria. But guilt from the whole situation made him physically ill and, eventually, repentant, leading to him moving back in with his family.

As reported by Mary Claire Kendall for *Forbes.com,* Balfe's Catholicism was a regular part of hers and Maria's life—and it came to have an influence on Cooper, too. He started attending Sunday Mass with them, and befriended their parish priest, Father Harold Ford. Though the actor and clergyman initially bonded over a shared love of hunting and fishing, their conversations also turned to God and left Cooper contemplating some of life's bigger questions. More of the story tomorrow...

The Lord...is patient with you, not wanting any to perish, but all to come to repentance. (2 Peter 3:9)

Lead sinners, including me, to repentance, Jesus.

A Hollywood Legend's Conversion, Part Two

Gary Cooper joined the Catholic Church in 1959, explaining his conversion in this way: "This past winter, I began to dwell a little more on what's been in my mind for a long time (and thought), 'Coop, old boy, you owe somebody something for all your good fortune.' I guess that's what started me thinking seriously about my religion. I'll never be anything like a saint...I just haven't got that kind of fortitude. The only thing I can say for me is that I'm trying to be a little better. Maybe I'll succeed."

Cooper's newfound faith brought him comfort and confidence in 1960 when he was diagnosed with cancer. Author Mary Claire Kendall, writing at *Forbes.com,* quotes Cooper's wife Veronica saying, "He'd been perfectly wonderful throughout the entire illness. What helped him most was his religion." In addition, he found spiritual strength in the sacraments and books like Fulton Sheen's *Peace of Soul.*

As he lay dying, Cooper placed himself in God's hands and told others, "I am not afraid of the future." He passed away in May 1961.

I love those who love Me, and those who seek Me diligently find Me. (Proverbs 8:17)

Help me to trust in Your love and forgiveness, Father.

Serving Cups of Kindness

If you're looking for one of the nicest places in America, *Reader's Digest* suggests you visit Bothell, Washington, where a cup of coffee is served with something extra special: kindness.

Will Tinkham, who was born with developmental disabilities, works at the coffee stand, Beca's Brew, and greets guests with a smile and a warm "hello" every day. His kindness inspired the coffee stand's owner, Beca Nistrian, to start Kindness Day on May 10th, which is Tinkham's birthday.

"[Will] finds the smallest things to be happy about...He finds joy in everything," Nistrian told *KOMO News.*

To spread kindness on this day, Nistrian delivered free cookies and coffee to police officers, firefighters and all "who serve other people, but not for the money." Others quickly joined in these acts of generosity, and the town of Bothell established May 10th as "Cup of Kindness Day."

Will Tinkham proved that kindness can be spread all year long and have a lasting impact. It all just starts with a smile.

Whoever pursues righteousness and kindness will find life and honor. (Proverbs 21:21)

Lord, may I choose to spread kindness today and always.

One Mother's Greatest Mission

Stella Spanakos feared for her son Nicholas's future. Nicholas was living with autism, and Stella worried there weren't many opportunities for him as he was heading into adulthood. This fear led to action, and Stella founded the Nicholas Center.

The Nicholas Center offers services to teach social and vocational skills to people living with autism, and provides them with employment and essential job training skills through three businesses that Spanakos cofounded. She told *Forbes* her "son and his classmates inspired our team to create opportunities that wouldn't have normally existed." Her business model has helped pave the way for other industries to employ people with autism.

Stella Spanakos is a beacon of light to families struggling with autism, and her purpose is to ensure that her son, and those like him, have a future and are taken care of. She's a mother whose "greatest mission in life is making sure my son is safe and can live a life that is fruitful and productive."

Keep forever such purposes...and direct their hearts toward You. (1 Chronicles 29:18)

Jesus, help me find my mission in life and go after it with all my heart.

The Greatest Victory

In 2018, Jockey Mike Smith rode Justify to a Triple Crown victory, winning the Kentucky Derby, the Preakness Stakes, and the Belmont Stakes. He was 52-years-old, making him the oldest jockey to ever win the Triple Crown.

"I don't want to give it up, not yet anyway," Smith said of his love for racing in a *Catholic News Service* article in which he also talked about his faith in God. "My faith means everything to me," Smith said. "I would not have anything if I didn't have it."

Smith recalled how his parents and grandparents first taught him about the Catholic faith and said it was his grandmother, Rosita Vallejos, who instilled in him a life of prayer.

Now, Smith prays throughout his day, but he doesn't pray to win. He prays for safety and for the grace to be a good person. "We are put here to do the great things the Lord wants us to do," he said, "to help others if we can, be there for people, love people, to be humble, gracious, kind, considerate, caring."

I can do all things through Him who strengthens me. (Psalm 119:20)

Lord, help me to build a life of character.

Mark Wahlberg is Grounded in Prayer

Actor Mark Wahlberg is at the top of most Hollywood producer's lists when the role calls for an action hero. The 47-year-old maintains a strict eating and exercise schedule to stay in shape. But his spiritual health is also important. One thing that he begins each day with, without fail, is 30 minutes of prayer.

The prayer time was noticed when he posted his daily schedule on social media. As reported in *The Christian Post*, Wahlberg's day seems more monastic than movie-star. He wakes up at 2:30 a.m. for a half hour of prayer. That's followed by exercise, eating specific small meals, and more exercise. He does this so that when his wife and young children get up after 7:00 a.m., he can spend time with them.

Family and faith are central to Wahlberg, grounding him in a Hollywood world that's built on illusion. "My Catholic faith is the anchor that supports everything I do in life," he said. "In my daily prayers, I ask for guidance, strength in my vocation as a husband and as a father."

He said, "Cornelius, your prayer has been heard and your alms have been remembered before God." (Acts 10:31)

May my prayers to You, God, set the tone for my day.

Youthful Offender Finds a Home

Many years ago, a volunteer librarian in a prison changed one teenage convict's life by adopting him. The 16-year-old boy, sentenced to a year in the Maryland Correctional Institution for nine burglaries, met the woman when he was assigned to clean the library. Discovering his love for books, the 47-year-old mother of three gradually won the embittered boy's confidence.

Learning of his grim past—a patchwork of foster homes and institutions—the librarian decided to give him his first real home through legal adoption.

The boy then went on to become a high school graduate, and even collaborated with his new mother in writing a book titled *Thirteen to One*, after the 13 different institutions, jails, and homes he was in.

When even one person cares enough, wonders can happen. God has given us the power of love to be an instrument for changing the world. But He leaves to us the decision of when and how to show meaningful concern in a world wracked by discord.

Beloved, since God loved us so much, we also ought to love one another. (1 John 4:11)

Holy Spirit, increase in us a love that spills over into every facet of our lives.

The Little Library that Could

With a desire to share his love of books and reading, retired Italian school teacher Antonio La Cava transformed his three-wheeled van into a mobile library called the Bibliomotocarro to transport books to children who otherwise would not have access. "Without a book, so often the child is alone," La Cava told the *BBC*.

Worried about "growing old in a country of non-readers," La Cava drives throughout Italy, bringing books to children in remote villages to help promote literacy to those with little access to reading material. He even takes time to travel to San Paolo Albanese, which only has two children of primary school age, because everyone deserves the chance to read.

La Cava strongly believes in spreading the joy of literature to as many children as possible and hopes his Bibliomotocarro brings the message that culture is made by and for everyone. He said, "Carrying out such action has a value, not only social, not only cultural, but has a great ethical meaning."

Reading...will enable you to perceive my understanding of the mystery of Christ. (Ephesians 3:4)

God, help me share the Good News with those who long to read and hear Your words.

Waving Granny Says Goodbye

For the past 12 years, 88-year-old Tinney Davidson has been quite a fixture in her town of Comox, British Columbia. In 2007, she and her husband moved into a house that was located very close to the Highland Secondary School.

It was then that Tinney got into the habit of waving cheerfully from her living room window to the students walking to and from school. Even after her husband passed away, she continued these daily greetings, leading these youngsters to give her the affectionate nickname, "Waving Granny."

After a dozen years of waving, however, Tinney moved into an assisted living home. In gratitude for her warm salutations, the pupils from Highland decided to give her a proper personal send-off.

In a touching video posted by *CBS News,* approximately 400 students were shown walking by Tinney's house, carrying flowers and colorful signs thanking their "Waving Granny" for her kindness. Tinney watched through tear-filled eyes as all of the youngsters waved and blew her one last kiss goodbye.

Gray hair is a crown of glory; it is gained in a righteous life. (Proverbs 16:31)

Lord, may we always respect and learn from our elders.

The Father of the Tin Can

A man whose name is virtually unknown started the canning industry in America. Here is his story.

In September 1847, Harrison Woodhull Crosby performed the first experiments in canning stewed tomatoes. Using six tin pails, he soldered tin lids on them, leaving a square hole in the center. Packing each pail with freshly stewed tomatoes, he sealed over the openings and stored them for several months. When opened, the tomatoes were fresh and delicious.

Later, at New Jersey's Lafayette College, he tried selling 1,000 tin cans of tomatoes, but failed. Doggedly, he sent shipments of canned tomatoes to newspapers, senators, Queen Victoria, and President James Polk. Glowing newspaper accounts followed, and canning was on its way to becoming a common practice.

It's easy to think that people will snap up a good idea, but it isn't always so. Trust in God and perseverance to provide a more certain formula for promoting sound projects on the job, in the home, or wherever others need services you can offer.

We want each one of you to show the same diligence so as to realize the full assurance of hope to the very end. (Hebrews 6:11)

Holy Spirit, guide my creative ideas toward success.

Above and Beyond

As a teacher in Chicago, LaShonda Carter is used to going the extra mile for her students. But a recent example of how she offered to help garnered some attention from national media, as well as a surprise for the student she was assisting.

Former student Larresha Plummer had recently been accepted to a college program and was looking for work. She had an infant daughter, and couldn't find anybody to babysit so that she could attend a job fair.

That's when she reached out to Carter, who not only agreed to stay with the child, but also to give Plummer a ride to the job fair. A Facebook Live video from the car by Carter is what made the story spread.

That small act of kindness inspired others, and even sparked some surprise job offers for Plummer, who hopes to repay her former teacher's good deed someday. For Carter, it's all in her approach to her students. "I'm no more special than any other teacher. Teachers do things like this every day. We don't need recognition," she told *Good Morning America*.

Everyone who is fully qualified will be like the teacher. (Luke 6:40)

Rabbi, bless and strengthen all teachers who go above and beyond the call of duty.

Talk to Each Other

The Curry Pizza Company has many locations, one of which is in Fresno, California. One of the co-owners, Varinder Malhi, runs a special promotion offering a free pizza pie to any group of four or more. There is one catch, however—the individuals in the group must relinquish their smart phones to the wait staff, who then secure them in the employee lockers.

Malhi first got the idea for the "Talk to Each Other Discount" when he saw the benefits of turning off his phone during family meals at home. If patrons can make it through their pizza without asking to check their phones, they are entitled to one free pizza. Alternatively, if the group is not in the mood for a pizza that day, they can instead opt to donate their pie to the homeless through a nonprofit called Khalsa Aid.

"We make 40-to-50 pizzas [for the homeless] every other week from each [of our] locations," Malhi told *Your Central Valley* writer Dennis Valera. "Khalsa Aid volunteers to serve it, we volunteer to make it." What a wonderful way to promote both generosity and real-life "face time" in our day-to-day life!

Pleasant words are...sweetness to the soul. (Proverbs 16:24)

God, may we always value the power of communication.

Stargazer Finds a Comet

Would you like to have a comet named after you? Don Machholz had that wish. The stargazer eventually succeeded, but it took him 1,700 hours of comet hunting before his perseverance paid off. "I was so excited when I found it," said the California man in 1978, "because I was familiar with that part of the sky, and I knew it shouldn't have been there."

Machholz became interested in astronomy at age 13 and began his pursuit of a new comet in earnest in 1974. Comets are the only celestial bodies named after the discoverer. "At first," said Machholz, "my goal was to find a comet and have it named after me. But later it was thrilling just to study the sky, and I no longer felt disappointment when I didn't see anything new."

The true amateur—the word means "lover"—takes joy in the action itself, and not in the reward. Each of us can be an amateur, finding delight in loving service to the people that God has called us to serve.

The glory of the stars is the beauty of heaven, a glittering array in the heights of the Lord. (Sirach 43:9)

Inspire us, Jesus, to find happiness in what we do for others.

Grateful American, Part One

Actor Gary Sinise grew up in Chicago and, during his teenage years, made some bad choices having to do with getting high, partying, and even stealing cars. He credits his high school theater program with pointing him "toward redemption."

In 1994, Sinise's life changed when he portrayed Lt. Dan Taylor in the Tom Hanks hit *Forrest Gump*. In the movie, Lt. Dan inadvertently leads his platoon in Vietnam into an ambush in which some of them are killed. And Lt. Dan loses his legs in battle.

After the war, observed Sinise on *Christopher Closeup*, Lt. Dan tries "to drown himself in alcohol because he's dealing with terrible guilt and post-traumatic stress. But at the end of that story, he's standing up again on prosthetic legs. He's successful in business and moving on with his life. He's able to make peace.

"[For] so many troubled, injured, or wounded veterans that I met in hospitals—that's the story they want. They want that story of being able to move forward, put their war experiences behind them, and be successful...It was a hopeful story, and I found that our veterans related to it and wanted to talk about it."

You are the God of the lowly...savior of those without hope. (Judith 9:11)

Bring hope to veterans with PTSD, Messiah.

Grateful American, Part Two

The role of Lt. Dan in *Forrest Gump* led Gary Sinise to get more involved in veterans causes. At the same time, he was facing his own battles on the home front. His wife, Moira, was struggling with alcoholism and was unwilling to admit her problem. Faced with the loss of her family, she finally pursued the help she needed and moved toward recovery.

While attending an AA meeting at St. Michael's Church on the North Side of Chicago, a woman walked up to Moira one day and told her, "My dear, you need to become a Catholic." Moira's mother had been Catholic, but they didn't practice the religion when she was growing up. As Moira explored the Catholic faith, she decided this was a step she wanted to take.

Moira converted, and she and Gary began sending their kids to Catholic school and attending Mass together as a family. Gary himself had not yet joined the Church, but he had become more open to God and the spiritual part of life due to various experiences in recent years. Then came 9/11.

More of the story tomorrow...

Call on Me in the day of trouble; I will deliver you. (Psalm 50:15)

Lead spiritual seekers toward faith in You, Jesus.

Grateful American, Part Three

As involved as he was with veterans causes, Gary Sinise felt devastated at the loss of life that occurred on 9/11. He and his family went to their local church in California for a memorial Mass that Friday.

During a *Christopher Closeup* interview about his memoir *Grateful American*, Sinise said, "I remember crying through the Mass and feeling with [my] broken heart that service to others was a great healer."

Sinise began using his spare time and musical talents to entertain members of the military being sent to Afghanistan and, later, Iraq. "I started going to war zones, hospitals, entertaining on military bases across the country and around the world.

"I started raising money for multiple military charities, all as a volunteer...I found that the more I gave, the more relief I received...because I could see that I was doing some good. Was it God calling me to service? It very well could be...This is a life mission."

More of the story tomorrow...

The greatest among you will be your servant. (Matthew 23:11)

Lead me to take advantage of the healing gift of service, Jesus.

Grateful American, Part Four

During a 2003 flight to Iraq for the USO, Gary Sinise found himself seated next to a man he didn't recognize. The man didn't know who Gary was either, so the two started talking. The stranger introduced himself as retired fireman John Vigiano Sr. His two sons, Joe and John Jr.—one with the NYPD, one with the FDNY—were killed on 9/11 in the Twin Towers' collapse.

Vigiano Sr. went down to Ground Zero to dig through the rubble, looking for his sons. On *Christopher Closeup*, Gary recalled, "[John told me that] he looked around and saw people from all over the world who came to Ground Zero to help pass out food and water and help in any way they can...He saw all these people lined up for days, and the spirit of America coming together to help everybody at Ground Zero. He said to me, 'You know, I think more good came out of that terrible day than evil.'"

Gary credits his friendship with Vigiano (who passed away in 2018 at age 79), along with many of the firefighters he met, with helping him decide to become Catholic himself in 2010.

The conclusion of the story tomorrow...

Do not be overcome by evil, but overcome evil with good. (Romans 12:21)

Teach me to bring good out of evil, Holy Spirit.

Grateful American, Part Five

After attending Mass with his wife and children for many years, Gary Sinise finally took the next step and converted to the Catholic faith himself. During a *Christopher Closeup* interview, he said, "[Our] little church became such a positive force in our lives...I secretly went through a Confirmation process and surprised my family by taking them to church on Christmas Eve. Our priests brought me into the Church, confirmed me into the Church. And that was a big surprise to my family."

Gary continues to live his faith and mission of service through the Gary Sinise Foundation, which includes outreach efforts, such as the building of specially-adapted houses for disabled veterans. And his hope for people who read his memoir *Grateful American* is this:

"If the book can inspire others to look at what they're grateful for and to think about our country not as a place where people are divided all the time...But look at the blessings that we've had because of the freedoms we have in this great country. If I can inspire people to go out there and serve others, the book is going to be worth the year it took to put it all down."

Kindness is like a garden of blessings. (Sirach 40:17)

I promise to count my blessings today, Father.

Remembering Those Who Serve

For Memorial Day 2019, the community of Locust Valley, New York, mourned the loss of Sgt. Robert Hendricks, age 25. A local resident, he was killed by a roadside bomb in Afghanistan just a few weeks earlier.

As noted in *Newsday*, he was the "first fallen service member from the quiet town since Army Sgt. James Harrington, Jr. was killed in the Vietnam War."

The town spent Memorial Day as many do: watching parades with school bands, laying wreaths, gathering for cookouts, and remembering the war dead. But this year, the reality of what service and sacrifice mean hit close to home in a poignant way.

"People generally think that it's our grandfathers and great grandfathers who we honor on this day for their service," said one resident, "but it's also for young soldiers."

This is My commandment, that you love one another as I have loved you. No one has greater love than this, to lay down one's life for one's friends. (John 15:12-13)

God, may we never forget our unsung soldiers and their families who sacrifice so much.

Ear for the Lonely

During the 1970s, when workers in a door-to-door survey in Iowa reported that loneliness and boredom were a major problem for older persons, one county set out to do something about their need.

"Dial-a-Listener" was set up to provide volunteers, who would staff phones between 1:00 p.m. and 9:00 p.m., to talk with anyone who cared to call. A positive attitude and a pleasant voice were among the traits looked for in the "listeners." Many recruits were themselves retired and expressed a deep satisfaction in taking part in an activity that helped so many people. Response to the program was extremely positive.

Given enough motivation, any community could undertake a similar service for the aged or infirm. Even more basically, any individual can try to be a sympathetic listener when the opportunity arises. With God's help, resolve never to turn a deaf ear to another's cry of loneliness.

If you will not listen, my soul will weep in secret. (Jeremiah 13:17)

Father, You always hear us. Help us to learn to listen to one another in love and patience.

A Kid's Best Friend

When a child is sick or injured, what he/she needs may not necessarily be another prescription, but the kindly wag of a tail.

Wrangler is a Labrador and the first full-time facility dog at Providence St. Vincent Medical Center in Southwest Portland, Oregon. His important job is to help comfort patients in the children's emergency room, where they can be in a lot of pain, feel out of control, and fearful of the environment and situation.

Facility dogs, such as Wrangler, receive extensive specialized training from an accredited organization and learn specific skills that make them like part of the medical staff.

"Kids tend to be animal lovers, and they will be petting Wrangler and, without realizing it, they are being soothed," Kasie Walker-Counts, a pediatric nurse, said to *Catholic News Service*. "He's adorable, but he also adds so much in an often terrible situation."

Wrangler knows more than 90 commands and can snuggle on command. In a stressful situation, he is just what the doctor ordered.

And God said, "Let the earth bring forth living creatures of every kind...And it was so." (Genesis 1:24)

Creator, let me be gentle and kind to all of Your creatures.

The Pressure to Be the Best

When singer-songwriter PJ Anderson performs at retreats and Catholic Heart Work Camps, his hope-filled songs find a receptive audience in youth who fear failure while enduring tremendous pressure to succeed.

During a *Christopher Closeup* interview, PJ said, "At a lot of these youth events...the thing I hear most about from high school kids is the pressure that they feel to be the best at everything. When I was in high school, you went to summer school if you needed a little extra help. But now, you go to summer school so you can get extra credit...so you can go to college early so you can graduate early so you can go to a job that you end up not even liking that much. It's all this pressure to be the best in academics, the best in sports. I hear that a lot.

"But not everybody can be the best," continued PJ. "So with that comes feelings of failure from high school kids and younger. [They need to hear] that we are enough with Jesus, with our Creator, with God. We need to do our best to be close to Him. But He doesn't call us to be busy and the best. He calls us to be holy and to keep Him close."

Draw near to God. (James 4:8)

Guide me in dealing with the pressures of life, Messiah.

God's Plan All Along

Jackie and Travis Allor of Warren, Michigan, had been thinking about expanding their family through foster care and adoption. Once they began praying about it, "the signs were all around us," they told the *Detroit Catholic*.

The Allors soon found a child who needed a placement, Elicia. After a few weeks, the Allors got a call from a social worker saying that Elicia's mother was about to lose her rights to all her children, and would they consider adopting Elicia's three brothers as well? "I joke I was praying for four years for kids, and God gave us four kids at once," Jackie said.

Life in foster care had been difficult for the children, adjusting to new homes and having a life marked by constant change. But the family soon settled in, and worked through the challenges that came with fostering and adoption. The one thing they all agreed on was that this was their family, and this was the way God planned to bring them all together in love.

He destined us for adoption as His children through Jesus Christ, according to the good pleasure of His will. (Ephesians 1:5)

Jesus, let me always trust and be open to Your plan for my life.

A Garden Blooms in the Bronx

In 1989, Daniel Chervoni couldn't take it anymore. The Bronx, New York native noted how ugly his neighborhood's Brook Park looked with its overgrown weeds and bushes, garbage, and general lack of care.

Chervoni told *NY1 News'* Pat Kiernan, "I went to sleep one day, woke up, and it was like, you know something needs to be done with this space. Next thing I know, I become a gardener, a farmer, a bee keeper, a chicken man! And I enjoy it, I love it."

After taking some gardening classes, Chervoni took it upon himself to clean up the park and turn it into a community garden where neighbors gather to socialize and help out. And all these years later, Brook Park is till thriving.

Kiernan notes, "Garden boxes line the space and garlic grows in the greenhouse. Chickens lay fresh eggs for local residents to enjoy. And during warmer months, Chervoni tends to the beehive. Local school kids are invited to help out, too."

Chervoni concludes, "I get enjoyment out of seeing people smile...and getting to help other people less fortunate than me."

I made myself gardens and parks, and planted in them all kinds of fruit trees.
(Ecclesiastes 2:5)

May we nurture the gardens around us, Lord.

Holy Spirit Guides Boston Dad

Daryl Silva, also known as "The Boston Dad" on Facebook and Youtube, told a story online about a road rage incident that he feels was defused by the Holy Spirit.

As Silva was pulling out of a parking lot, a pickup truck taking up two lanes zoomed towards him, with the driver honking his horn and screaming obscenities. Instead of responding the same way, Silva says he felt the Holy Spirit inspire him to lean out his window and say to the angry driver, "Would you like me to buy you a coffee? It seems like you've had a bad day."

Though taken aback, the driver followed Silva into a nearby Dunkin' Donuts parking lot, still wondering if this offer was for real. Silva bought him coffee and started praying with the man, who broke down in tears and started sharing all the troubles in his life.

Silva concluded his video by saying, "If somebody is acting cruel to you, mean to you, they need that heart of yours. They need God more than anyone. So don't react to their anger. Answer with love."

A soft answer turns away wrath, but a harsh word stirs up anger. (Proverbs 15:1)

Whenever possible, help me to defuse anger with kindness and love, Prince of Peace.

Paula Faris' Journey of Faith, Part One

ABC News' Paula Faris seemingly had it all. A great husband, wonderful kids, and high-profile jobs as co-anchor of *Good Morning America's* weekend edition and co-host of the *The View.* But Paula also felt overextended, as if God was telling her that she needed to step back from some of her professional commitments. She discussed the idea with a network executive, who told her, "You'd be crazy to do that."

During a *Christopher Closeup* interview, Paula said, "I allowed fear to paralyze me from doing what I knew was right." Then, her eight month "season of hell" began.

Paula suffered a miscarriage that required emergency surgery; she endured a severe concussion when someone threw an apple at her head while she was reporting a story; she sustained injuries in a car crash; and she got pneumonia.

During that period, Paula felt like God was asking her to trust His will about changing her work schedule. She also realized that she had invested "too much of my identity in what I did and not who I was as a child of God." And so, she listened and trusted. More tomorrow...

Pay attention to what you hear. (Mark 4:24)

May I hear You and trust Your will, Jesus.

Paula Faris' Journey of Faith, Part Two

After enduring what she calls her "season of hell," Paula Faris told her bosses at *ABC News* that she couldn't maintain her current schedule anymore, and asked if she could work on news stories Monday to Friday instead.

She also pitched them the idea of starting a podcast in which she would interview newsmakers about their spiritual beliefs. *ABC News* obliged Paula's requests, and she has since launched her podcast, "Journeys of Faith."

"The genesis [of the podcast]," said Paula, "is my own personal faith. It's been my rock, my glue, my foundation. It has kept my marriage together. It has pulled me through the most difficult and trying times."

"Secondly" she continued, "as a journalist, I recognize that if you mention Jesus or God or Allah, we cut that from the interview. I don't want that to happen. That's why we created this. It's to give people a space to talk about something that's deeply personal to them and something that they're very passionate about." More tomorrow...

Do not be ashamed, then, of the testimony about our Lord. (2 Timothy 1:8)

Help me to share my faith humbly yet honestly, Jesus.

Paula Faris' Journey of Faith, Part Three

Though Paula Faris is a lifelong Christian, her aim with her "Journeys of Faith" podcast isn't to proselytize or even talk only with people who think and believe exactly as she does.

During a *Christopher Closeup* interview, she explained: "Jesus was out there talking with people that didn't see eye to eye with Him. He was with the worst of sinners, and yet having conversations—even some tough conversations...This is me sitting down with and listening to or respecting somebody else's faith...and also showing them, hopefully, the love of Christ in me. We can agree to disagree, and we can do so respectfully.

"I think that as a society, we've lost the ability to do that...We tend to just sit down with people that think exactly like us...[Through] these conversations with people that I don't see eye to eye with, I'm growing...And I think you will earn people's respect if you sit down and engage in a conversation with them and show them the love of Christ. Really, that's the calling, isn't it? To love God and love people. We overcomplicate it. That's what I'm trying to accomplish here."

Conduct yourselves wisely toward outsiders... Let your speech always be gracious. (Colossians 4:5-6)

Allow me to show someone the love of Christ, Father.

Paula Faris' Journey of Faith, Part Four

Though Paula Faris is a successful anchor and correspondent with *ABC News* now, she almost didn't pursue that career path. She had felt God calling her to be a broadcaster early in life, but she let fear paralyze her.

Paula studied TV production in college, staying behind the scenes despite her professors telling her she would be perfect for on-air work. After graduation, she took a job in radio sales, until 9/11 caused her to follow God's promptings and pursue a career in news. "If God calls you, God's going to equip you," reflected Paula. "We can't trust ourselves. We have to trust God."

Paula also acknowledged that living a life of faith isn't all sunshine and roses. She concluded, "[Jesus said], 'In this world you will have trouble, but take heart because I have overcome the world.' You're going to have issues as Christians. In fact, you may have more problems...But we can have peace because Christ has overcome it all. That's the end game. If we're getting too comfortable here, then we need to really question our priorities. We were never called to be comfortable."

Let Your steadfast love become my comfort. (Psalm 119:76)

Equip me to do Your will despite my fears, Jesus.

Nurses in Normandy

American sisters Ellan and Dorothy Levitsky became inseparable at a young age. When they got older, they even attended nursing school together and volunteered to join the Army as World War II continued in Europe. A need arose for nurses in France, so Ellan offered to go if Dorothy joined her. Ellan told the *Los Angeles Times,* "The war was on, they needed nurses badly, and I just felt I had to do something."

In August 1944, the sisters arrived in Normandy to work at a "makeshift hospital," where they tended to the physical, emotional, and spiritual wounds of the injured. Their kindness and commitment made them so beloved by the locals that in 2012, they were awarded France's highest honor: the Legion d'Honneur.

Dorothy passed away in 2015, but Ellan, age 99, made the trip to Normandy for the 75th anniversary of D-Day on June 6, 2019. Wearing her Legion d'Honneur pin, she was constantly approached by people wanting to thank her for her service. We join with them in applauding her service—and the service of all who sacrificed during wartime.

May the Lord bless His people with peace! (Psalm 29:11)

Bless all nurses who bring comfort to the sick, Divine Physician.

A D-Day Remembrance

On June 6, 1944, Allied forces fighting Hitler's occupation of Europe made the bold move to liberate the continent by storming the beaches of Normandy, France. More than 4,000 Allied troops were killed during the attack. Irving Locker, though, was a survivor. He recalled his experiences for *NBC News* for the 75th anniversary of D-Day in 2019.

The 94-year-old from New Jersey was a part of the 116th AAA Gun Battalion. He recalled, "It's terrifying and believe me when I tell you, when we were in the Higgins boat coming in, the long life that we thought we were gonna have could be shortened very, very fast because of the bullets that were coming at us."

Locker, who is Jewish, is willing to talk about his time in the Army, but admits that thinking about the Holocaust still keeps him awake some nights. Regarding his service, he said, "We did what we had to do. Freedom is not free. There were a lot of people that gave their lives, millions of people gave their lives so that they— the children today—could be free."

Precious in the sight of the Lord is the death of His faithful ones. (Psalm 116:15)

May we remember those who fought and died for our freedoms, Prince of Peace.

The Light of the Trinity

On his blog, Deacon Greg Kandra noted that the concept of the Holy Trinity can be understood through the concept of light. The first words God speaks in Scripture are, "Let there be light." He later gave us His Son, "the Light of the World," as our Savior. And on Pentecost, said the deacon, "the Holy Spirit, arrived in...tongues of flame settling over the apostles to ignite their hearts and light the way."

The deacon then cited John Wesley's description of the Trinity: "In this room, there are three candles—and only one light."

Deacon Kandra continued in his own words: "The world will do all it can to extinguish the light. With violence. With bigotry. With persecution. With cruelty and hate."

"If you want to know how to make the mystery of the Trinity alive in the world...I would suggest this simple advice: Remember God's love for the human race, His love for every one of us—a love so vast, it stretches across eternity and gave us His son, the Light of the World and then gave us the Spirit, the light that never goes out. Let that light shine...Let us be that light."

Let your light shine. (Matthew 5:16)

May I reflect Your light to all I meet, Holy Trinity.

A Love That Defied the Odds

"He opened up my world," said Kris Scharoun-DeForge about her husband, Paul, on their 25th wedding anniversary. But at the time they got married, the world wasn't exactly supportive of their relationship. You see, both Kris and Paul have Down syndrome, and many people didn't believe they had the intelligence and maturity to make a marriage work.

As reported by *Reader's Digest,* the couple has faced obstacles in their lives, but they've always risen to the occasion. Paul spent years successfully working in the vocational department of the Arc, an organization that helps the developmentally disabled. And Kris became a skilled cook and goes to work every day in an office mail room.

Unfortunately, the couple couldn't defeat their final challenge. Paul developed dementia and died in 2019 at age 56. Throughout his illness, Kris was at his side whenever possible, even when Paul was moved to a medical facility. Susan Scharoun, Kris's sister, said, "They have an unconditional love."

Set me as a seal upon your heart...for love is strong as death. (Song of Solomon 8:6)

Strengthen couples through all the challenges of marriage and help them deepen their love, Jesus.

"It's Time You Come Work For Me"

In June 2019, Russ Martin was recognized with a special honor. The Director of Broadcast Operations at *KLUX 89.5 HD* radio in Corpus Christi, Texas, received an award for 25 years of service.

As reported by *South Texas Catholic*, KLUX General Manager Marty Wind congratulated Martin "for his unceasing dedication to Catholic broadcasting for the past 25 years...We couldn't have done it without you. And we appreciate you."

Before joining *KLUX*, which is run by the Diocese of Corpus Christi, Martin worked in secular media in California, Florida, North Carolina, and Texas. He said, "I still get up in the morning and look forward to going to work. For 25 years I worked in commercial radio and the Lord said, 'Okay, you have some talent so it's time you come to work for Me."

Not all of us can leave our jobs and go work for God full-time. But each of us, in our own ways, can serve Him in some way every day. Take a look at your life and see where God is calling you to be a messenger of His hope and love.

Your ears shall hear a word behind you, saying, "This is the way; walk in it." (Isaiah 30:21)

Lord, make me aware of Your voice in my life.

A Squirrely Visitor

It was a gorgeous summer day when Catholic Charities of Rockville Centre, New York, held an orientation meeting for new employees in its Hicksville office. Part of the day involved a fire drill, which prompted everyone to go outside and enjoy the sun's invigorating warmth. When the employees re-entered the office, however, they discovered a visitor had come in with them. There was a squirrel on the table in the boardroom.

As recounted on the Catholic Charities blog, the employees tried shooing him towards the front door and enticing him with peanut butter. Neither approach worked. Finally, someone removed the screens from the windows and opened them wide, so the squirrel could "feel the breeze on his whiskers." That approach worked, and he scurried out!

The writer concludes, "That day, [God] revealed the merciful spirit of our employees and their determination and perseverance in resolving unusual problems. If they go that extra mile for a squirrel, imagine how much more they're prepared to do to serve their neighbors in need!"

Ask the animals, and they will teach you. (Job 12:7)

Help me to see Your presence, Lord, in all creatures, great and small.

The Gift Wrap & the Jewel

At age 92, Wanda Goines read her poem about aging, "The Gift Wrap & the Jewel," in a video that went viral. Here is the poem: "I looked in the mirror and what did I see/but a little old lady peering back at me/With bags and sags and wrinkles and wispy white hair,/And I asked my reflection, 'How did you get there?/You once were straight and vigorous and now you're stooped and weak/when I tried so hard to keep you from becoming an antique.'

"My reflection's eyes twinkled as she solemnly replied,/'You're looking at the gift wrap and not the jewel inside./A living gem and precious, of unimagined worth/Unique and true, the real you, the only you on earth.

"The years that spoil your gift-wrap with other things more cruel,/should purify and strengthen, and polish up that jewel./So focus your attention on the inside, not the out/on being kinder, wiser, more content and more devout./Then, when your gift-wrap's stripped away, your jewel will be set free/to radiate God's glory throughout eternity."

Let your adornment be the inner self with the lasting beauty of a gentle and quiet spirit. (1 Peter 3:4)

Father, may I always polish my inner jewels of kindness, faith and wisdom.

The Happiest Bus Driver in London

After almost 50 years, Londoner Patrick Lawson reached a profound turning point in his life. "My whole teenage years, if I wasn't on the street, I was in jail," he confessed to *CBS News* reporter Caitlin O'Kane. "My mind was just focused on drugs and violence."

"I saw the big issue," Patrick continued. "I thought of my young teenage children and I thought, 'If I make it through this, I've got to turn my life around.'"

True to his word, after his epiphany, Lawson wasted no time in getting help for his drug addiction. Through the SHP (Single Homeless Project), he was able to find a job driving buses. In becoming a bus driver, Lawson found the new beginning he needed, and the purpose in life he always wanted.

His unfailingly cheerful demeanor soon earned Lawson the title of "the happiest bus driver in London." After nearly a year of employment, he even became the proud recipient of the Hello London Award for Outstanding Customer Service at Transport. "I love what I do," Lawson concluded.

There is nothing better than that all should enjoy their work. (Ecclesiastes 2:24)

Father, may we find passion and purpose in our vocations.

Persistence in Prayer

Have you ever felt the need to pray, but didn't know how to go about it? Here are two suggestions that might help.

One, set aside some time *each* day. It doesn't have to be long. Three minutes at the start of the day—or just before going to bed—would be fine. If you give three minutes to reflection each day, you will be surprised at the spiritual progress you will make in a few months.

Second, start *simply*. Say the Our Father slowly, thinking about each phrase; or read a line of Scripture and think about what it means to you. Even a poem or a passage from a favorite book can help focus your thoughts.

God did not intend prayer to be a burden, but a time to draw closer to Him   to recognize His presence and enjoy it.

When you call upon Me and come and pray to Me, I will hear you. (Jeremiah 29:12)

May we set aside time each day to rejoice in Your presence, Lord.

Good Neighbors Cut Crime Rate

During the 1970s, a tidal wave of burglaries swept over the Whispering Oaks section of Austin, Texas, until policeman George Vanderhule did something about it.

The community was being hit by 35 major offenses a month: burglaries, vandalism, sexual assaults on adults and children. Officer Vanderhule found that the residents were strangers to each other: "Nobody knew anybody else."

Added to that, there were too many bushy trees, high privacy fences, and places to hide. In five meetings with concerned residents, Vanderhule showed them how to use light and noise to make it harder for criminals to break in.

"If your neighborhood criminal can't enter your home in four minutes," said the officer, "he'll give up the attempt." Crime dropped in Whispering Oaks by nearly 70 percent over a two-month period.

Knowing your neighbors is good for more than crime prevention. It's a chance to make friends—and to be a friend.

Better is a neighbor who is nearby than kindred who are far away. (Proverbs 27:10)

Keep us from being narrow in our concerns, Father, so we will have friends in times of need.

Michaels Desserts

Thirteen-year-old Washington native Michael Platt has always enjoyed baking. As a youngster, he was also greatly inspired by Dr. Martin Luther King, Jr.'s famous "I Have a Dream" speech. Michael recently found a way to use his affinity for creating pastries to make a positive difference in the world.

Three years ago, Michael received a pair of shoes from "TOMS: One for One," a nonprofit that gives a free pair of shoes to a child in need for every new pair of shoes it sells.

The youngster decided to do the same with baked goods and created a company called Michaels Desserts. The absence of an apostrophe in his charity's name is deliberate, "as a reminder that he is baking for others, not himself."

Even more impressive is the fact that Michael is accomplishing all this while dealing with epilepsy. Due to his frequent seizures in class, his mother made the decision to homeschool him.

"I always wanted to have a purpose for what I do," Michael told *Washington Post* reporter Hannah Nathanson. "It's all about helping people."

A gift opens doors. (Proverbs 18:16)

Abba, help us utilize our talents for the greater good.

The Strange Case of Dr. Couney

If you were a woman who gave birth to an extremely premature baby during the early 1900s, your best odds of saving your child's life came from going to a sideshow in Coney Island or Atlantic City and looking for the exhibit run by Dr. Martin Couney. Dawn Raffel tells his story in her Christopher Award-winning biography *The Strange Case of Dr. Couney.*

Couney's exhibit featured premature infants in incubators. It might sound exploitative, but the care these babies received from his staff was the best—and Couney genuinely wanted to save them. He said he was doing "propaganda for preemies!"

Why did preemies need propaganda? Because the eugenics movement was gaining in popularity at the time, and its proponents believed that the weakest members of society should be allowed to die (or even actively killed) to keep society strong. It was a worldview later adopted by the Nazis.

In her research, Raffel met with several of the babies, now senior citizens, for whom Couney cared. They all appreciated learning more about the mysterious doctor who saved them.

Before I formed you in the womb I knew you. (Jeremiah 1:5)

May our society treasure all human life, Creator.

The Beauty in a Blade of Grass

At the age of 34, Mrs. Vita Buckley of Dix Hills, New York, became almost totally blind. She could see colors, but not details. The mother of three developed keratoconus, a disease that attacks the cornea, the transparent tissue that covers the iris and transmits light to the optic nerve.

But Buckley was lucky. Within a week, she was able to receive a corneal transplant in one eye. A year later, the other eye received the same treatment.

What was it like to regain her sight? "I was sitting in my kitchen one day," she said in an interview, "when I noticed I could see the veins in the leaves, make out the bark on trees and the individual blades of grass. I was suddenly aware of details that I'd forgotten."

Do we appreciate the gift of sight? Do we ever thank God that we can behold a leaf, a tree, a blade of grass, a loved one's face? Don't take this precious gift for granted.

Thank the Lord for His steadfast love, for His wonderful works. (Psalm 107:15)

Help us to slow down, Lord, and begin to take in the beauties of the universe You let us share.

A Non-Traditional Wedding Banquet

When Ana Paula Meriguete and Victor Ribeiro got married in Brazil, instead of having a wedding dinner, they chose something a bit less traditional but much more generous: a banquet to feed the hungry.

Following the couple's wedding ceremony in church in 2019, the real banquet was being prepared in Guarapari, in the Brazilian state of Espírito Santo, where 160 hungry children and their families were waiting, grateful for food in their stomachs.

"We decided to feed those who really need it, because our family members have what they need," Ribeiro told the newspaper *Estadão*.

The bride and groom were ready to finance the celebration on their own, but monetary donations from friends and family started pouring in, including from a professional catering company who generously donated food for the banquet.

It was a beautiful way to commemorate the union of this special couple whose love extended beyond themselves to help so many in need.

When you give a banquet, invite the poor, the crippled...And you will be blessed. (Luke 14:13-14)

My Lord, help guide my generous spirit to feed others.

Building a Dream Job

Carlyn McClelland was a stay-at-home mom until she realized her passion for carpentry and fought through stereotypes and financial challenges to make her dream a reality.

It started when McClelland wanted renovations done to her house in Middlebury, Indiana, but was overwhelmed by the type of work involved. Then, in 2015, she took that first step to learn to do them herself.

"I was about two weeks into my [associates degree] program when I realized that I should have done construction my whole entire life," she told *Good Morning America*.

Afraid of getting further into debt with this life-changing decision, McClelland applied for a scholarship through *Dirty Jobs* host Mike Rowe's foundation, mikeroweWORKS. It aims to close the skills gap and challenge the stigmas and stereotypes that discourage people from pursuing a trade job.

Carlyn was granted the scholarship and finished her degree. She is now proud to be doing the work she is passionate about, while also building her dream home.

Go now, and work (Exodus 5:18)

Lord, thank You for all my special talents.

Adoption Changes Lives

With all but one of their children grown and out of the house, Lisa and Gary Fulbright decided to welcome two new children into their family through adoption.

Then, in 2017, they became foster parents to three more children: Jaxon, Journey, and Jace, brothers from a family of seven children, all in the custody of the state.

The Fulbrights would often invite the boys' other siblings—Emerson, Autumn, Piper, and Sawyer—over to visit on holidays. Then one day, St. Francis Ministries, an organization that provides care for children in state custody, asked the Fulbrights if they would be willing to adopt all of the siblings in order to keep them together. The Fulbright's immediate response was, "Yes."

The children were ecstatic, and the Fulbrights got everyone matching football jerseys to wear on the day of the adoption. Lisa told *Good Morning America,* "They had been through so much, they didn't need to lose each other...It's kind of chaos, but it's a fun type of chaos because we just love them."

Blessed are you because you had compassion. (Tobit 8:17)

Lord, help my heart grow in love and compassion.

A Father's Quiet Sacrifices

On the day that former *NBC News* correspondent and Christopher Award-winning author Bob Dotson graduated college many years ago, he discovered that his father, Bill, had never made it past the fifth grade. The reason, his dad explained, was that his own father abandoned the family, leaving his mother to raise three kids by herself. Money was so tight that his mother turned Bill over to a farmer to work as an indentured servant.

He was eventually rescued by his aunt, and started working as a janitor at age 11. When Bill got a job in an optical store, his boss encouraged him to go to night school to make up for his missed education. And so he did—for 23 years.

As Bob recalled on his Facebook page, "By the time I turned two, my father had earned an honorary Master's Degree in Ophthalmics for his study of the eye...He opened Dotson Optical Company. His partner stole most of the profit that first year and disappeared...Undaunted, dad saved and struggled until he could open a new business that eventually bankrolled the first Dotson to graduate from college—me."

Let each of you look not to your own interests, but to the interests of others. (Philippians 2:4)

Bless fathers who make sacrifices for their families, Lord.

Denzel Washington's Inspiration

Actor Denzel Washington was raised in a hard-working family in New York. He didn't have a lot of material things, but he did have excellent mentors, one of whom was Billy Thomas from the local Boys Club.

Billy would hang up college pennants of the schools where Boys Club's graduates went on to study. Dozens of pennants, from schools all over the country, made a young Denzel feel like anything was possible. Though he stayed close to home, going to Fordham University in the Bronx, he continued to have good mentors. As an adult, Denzel reflected on his life and saw just how much their influence mattered.

In his autobiography he wrote, "I had tremendous help along the way. That was a huge blessing from God. Behind every great success there's someone and often more than one person. A parent, teacher, coach, role model. It starts somewhere. As the Bible says, 'Train up a child in the way he should go, and when he is old he will not depart from it.' There's no reason it can't start with you."

Whoever becomes humble like this child is the greatest in the kingdom of heaven. (Matthew 18:4)

Jesus, I am humble and grateful for those who have led me to where I am today.

Teamwork: Their Lives Depend on It

What's it like to do your job perched nearly 300 feet in the air? The men who painted New York's original Tappan Zee Bridge in the mid-20th century answered that question for a newsman.

"You have to be crazy," said one. "I've been crazy about this job for five years. House painting is dull. This is more challenging and I love it." A 62-year-old crew member, on the job for 45 years, added, "It keeps me young. It seems like 45 days."

The supervisor explained, "We practice the idea that each man is his brother's keeper. We must have teamwork or we're in trouble."

On the ground, this adage is no less true. In a world beset by divisions, one of our primary tasks is to work together as a "human team." Whether you are a bridge painter, a student, or anything else, there is a positive contribution that only you can make. God's help is assured. Our cooperation is needed.

To this day I have had help from God, and so I stand here, testifying to both small and great. (Acts 26:22)

Father, make us energetic in putting into practice Your command to love our neighbor as ourselves.

A Deacon (and Cows) Come to the Rescue

During a recent interview on *Christopher Closeup*, Deacon Don Grossnickle recalled becoming good friends with a Ugandan seminarian who was studying at his Chicago parish, St. Mary of the Lake. When that seminarian was ready to be ordained back in Uganda, he invited Deacon Don to concelebrate his first Mass.

The trip was eye-opening for the deacon, who visited orphanages, water projects, and St. Luke Clinic, run by a nurse named Teophista. There, he saw six mothers and babies slowly dying from malaria fever, hooked up to IV.

Malaria is preventable and treatable, but the people of Uganda had no money to afford those resources in many cases.

Deacon Don came home and said, "God, help me do something to help those people who are too poor to afford medicine." Deacon Don started a microfinancing program, which allows people in the U.S. to donate money to Ugandan families to get a cow, sell its milk for profit, then donate ten percent of the profits to the clinic for buying medicine. The program has been successful. Says Deacon Don, "Through the Lord's gifts here, we're expanding."

**He does not let their cattle decrease.
(Psalm 107:38)**

Creator, allow me to help the poor today.

An Unexpected Airport Encounter

Singer-songwriter Sarah Hart felt frustrated that her flight would be delayed by two hours. She sat at the airport, grumbling to herself, until an elderly woman approached her saying, "Honey, I know you don't know me from Adam, but I'm 88 and can you please take me to the bathroom? I have macular degeneration and I can't see where I'm going."

Hart happily obliged, and learned the stranger's name was Donna. Afterwards, the two women began chatting. Hart wrote on her Facebook page, "[Donna] was on her way to visit her daughter, a theater actress in New York City who is dying of ovarian cancer. Hospice had called and asked her to come right away. After that, I was not about to leave this sweet woman alone. I spent the last two hours with her...So many tears, but a little laughter sprinkled in, too."

Hart helped Donna board her plane, gave her a big hug, and promised she'd write. Hart concluded, "I was so truly reminded...no matter how bad you have it, someone else has it so much worse. And angels are everywhere, to keep you centered in reality and in what truly matters."

Comfort My people, says your God. (Isaiah 40:1)

May I be a comfort to the lonely, Messiah.

A Garden of Love

When Toshiyuki Kuroki's wife, Yasuko, went blind after complications with diabetes, he transformed their Japanese dairy farm into a garden to help remind her of the joys of living.

Yasuko lost her sight 25 years ago. *Goodnewsnetwork.org* reported that "she began to withdraw from life, no longer talking to people and locking herself away inside their house." One day, Toshiyuki noticed a shibazakura—a bright, fuchsia colored flower—and although his wife couldn't see it, the strong fragrance ignited an idea that blossomed in his mind.

Toshiyuki planted flowers near and around their house until their entire farm was transformed into a giant flower garden. It was so beautiful that it even caught the attention of tourists who came to see the pink-blanketed grounds. And the fragrance led Yasuko to venture outside, walk through the gardens, interact with visitors, and rediscover the beauty in living again.

Today, the flowers are still blooming, and the couple is able to enjoy life together in their "garden built by love."

And the Lord God planted a garden in Eden. (Genesis 2:8)

Creator, even in darkness please show me the light.

Climb the Highest Mountain

Sir Edmund Hillary, the first man to climb Mount Everest, once told an interviewer that the greatest explorers were frequently motivated not by confidence, but by fear. "They can often perform better as a consequence," he said. "If you're absolutely sure you'll be successful, why bother starting? Maybe you're doing something that's a bit too easy for you."

To reinforce his point, Sir Edmund expressed the opinion that his own talents are rather modest. "But," he added, "having a certain amount of stubbornness and a vigorous strength, I was able to get by on many of these projects."

Besides climbing Everest, Sir Edmund also made a dogsled trip across the Antarctic and a 1,500-mile journey up the Ganges River in India.

There are limits to what stubborn determination can achieve, but few of us reach them. We sometimes fail because we give up too soon. So set high goals. Sprinkle stubbornness with common sense. Pray to God for guidance. And then climb your mountain.

Look! On the mountains the feet of one who brings good tidings. (Nahum 1:15)

Instill in us a spirit of adventure for high achievement, Lord.

From Prison Cell to Broadway Stage

For actor Charles Dutton, one decision made all the difference in his troubled life.

Dutton grew up on the streets, was in and out of reform schools, and landed in prison after fatally stabbing a man in a fight. Even there, his temper continued to get him into trouble.

While he was in solitary confinement, he read an anthology of plays and became interested in drama. He decided his life was going to change. While he was still in prison, he got his high school equivalency and two-year college diplomas.

After his release, Dutton studied at Yale Drama School and went on to become a successful actor. He won a Tony award for his role in a Broadway hit and became the star of a TV sitcom.

Dutton's story demonstrates that in many ways, large and small, our decisions can change our lives—and we can change ourselves. If there's an aspect of your life that needs transformation, exercise your free will to change it for the better.

As servants of God, live as free people, yet do not use your freedom as a pretext for evil. (1 Peter 2:16)

Free us, Jesus, from whatever enslaves our hearts, minds, souls, or bodies.

A Grand Opening a Day Late

The grand opening of Billy's Donut Shop turned out to be not so grand. The Missouri City, Texas store's first day in business didn't draw any customers.

The owner's son, Billy By Jr., tweeted out a picture of his father looking disappointed inside his empty shop, writing, "My dad is sad cause no one is coming to his new donut shop." He hoped people would see the tweet and come down to support this new mom-and-pop business. And that's exactly what happened.

Billy's tweet got shared 300,000 times, leading customers to come to the donut shop in droves. The next day, Billy tweeted, "Just wanted to update y'all! We completely sold out of donuts and kolaches! You are all amazing. I can't thank everyone enough for coming out and supporting local businesses. This means so much to my family."

Billy also tweeted out a new picture in contrast with the old one. This one showed father and son, side by side, smiling and feeling happy that their new venture would be a success after all.

The father of the righteous will greatly rejoice; he who begets a wise son will be glad in him. (Proverbs 23:24)

Father, may we support our parents' hopes and dreams as ardently as they support ours.

A Dancer's Praise

If we're making the most of the talents God gave us, we are praising Him in our own unique way. That truth was highlighted in a *Humans of New York* Internet post about Silas Farley, a member of the New York City Ballet.

He said, "I was first exposed to ballet at the age of seven when a traveling company came to my church in North Carolina. By the time I was eleven I was practicing six days a week. It became my all-consuming monastic devotion.

"I eventually made it to the New York City Ballet. I've always seen ballet as my way of serving God. I think it's what God has called me to do. You can call it frivolous, or superficial. But you can stretch that argument to infinity. Why do we have painting? Why do we have architecture? I think it's all a form of worship. In a secular age, the theater becomes the cathedral.

"There can be such a lack of empathy and collaboration in this world. But in the theater, we see beauty and order and harmony modeled for us—two hours at a time. And it took a lot of sacrifice to make that possible."

We have gifts that differ according to the grace given to us. (Romans 12:6)

May I praise You through my words and actions, Father.

A Question Can Change a Life

Rusty Schimmel was a high school senior in Evansville, Indiana, working his summer job as a lifeguard at an Easter Seals swimming pool. Then, a single question changed his life.

Like many teenagers, Rusty was trying to figure out what he wanted to do with his life. He was a mediocre student who never really applied himself in school. He did, however, enjoy his job working with disabled kids and giving them swimming lessons. One day, a therapist told him that he had a great way with the kids, and asked if he'd ever consider being a therapist.

The question threw Rusty for a loop. His first thought was that he never saw himself doing anything so life-changing. But the fact that somebody else believed he could do it made Rusty believe it for himself for the first time. He soon buckled down at school and got his grades up, went into a competitive college program, and became a therapist.

Now, over 20 years later, Rusty has built an impressive career helping others and is still working for Easter Seals, currently as the vice president for adaptive technologies.

So if anyone is in Christ, there is a new creation! (2 Corinthians 5:17)

May my words encourage others and extend Your grace, Lord.

How Al Smith Faced Prejudice, Part One

Al Smith may be best known today for the annual Catholic Charities fundraising dinner named in his honor, but in the early 1900s, he made history by becoming the first Catholic on the ballot for the U.S. presidency.

Smith grew up on Manhattan's Lower East Side, which included Irish, Italian, Jewish, and Chinese immigrants. His family was working class, though many around him were poor. When Al's father died, his mother had to take a job to support the family, and Al himself dropped out of his Catholic grammar school to find work.

Through political connections he made with the Irish Catholics who ran Manhattan's Democratic Party, he was elected to the State Assembly in 1903 and became a self-educated politician who got things done on issues that affected working men, women, and children, like the ones he grew up with.

Later, Smith became one of New York's greatest governors. But when his attention turned to running for national office, he had to deal with the anti-Catholic prejudices still held by many at that time. More of the story tomorrow...

When the righteous are in authority, the people rejoice. (Proverbs 29:2)

Help us choose good and honest public servants, Lord.

How Al Smith Faced Prejudice, Part Two

Despite making inroads into the halls of power in New York, Catholics like Al Smith weren't always embraced on a national level. During a *Christopher Closeup* interview about his biography *Frank and Al,* Terry Golway explained, "The overt discrimination against Catholics, particularly the Irish, dates back to the 1840s when the first wave of Irish Catholic immigrants came over to the United States during the potato famine.

"By 1873, which is when Smith was born, there's still a lot of contempt for Catholics based on religion, but also based on the fact that many of them were poor and didn't speak English, like the Italians...And there was a great sense that Catholics were threatening the Protestant identity of the United States."

The main person who helped Smith overcome that bias was Franklin Delano Roosevelt, whom Smith dubbed "Frank." Their alliance was unusual, however, because of their differences. Smith grew up in New York's working class; Roosevelt came from money and prestige. And when FDR was first elected to the New York Assembly in 1911, he was seen as a snob. So how did they come together? More tomorrow...

Do not judge by appearances. (John 7:24)

Creator, help us overcome our prejudices.

How Al Smith Faced Prejudice, Part Three

Al Smith and Franklin Roosevelt didn't like each other initially, but polio humbled Roosevelt. He came to appreciate all the traits that made Smith a beloved and successful politician, so the two became friends. And without Roosevelt's support, Smith might not have been able to convince the Democratic Party's Protestants to make him their candidate in 1928.

The anti-Catholic prejudice was so bad among some Democrats that Alabama Senator Tom Heflin and his supporters in the KKK suggested that Catholics in the United States should be deported because they can never be good citizens due to their allegiance to Rome. Thankfully, the Klan lost that argument.

Author Terry Golway hopes that people who read his biography *Frank and Al* are left with this message: "I hope they're reminded what a great man Al Smith was. He suffered through the most bigoted campaign in American history in 1928. He was deplored around the country because of his Catholic beliefs. I think that many Catholics may have forgotten that part of history...I hope this reminds them of what it was like to be a Catholic in the United States 100 years ago. It wasn't easy."

God shows no partiality. (Acts 10:34)

Help me see Your presence in everyone, Father.

"On Sundays, He Serves the Lord"

Eighteen years ago, the *Today Show's* Al Roker and his wife, Deborah Roberts, noticed that their baby son, Nick, wasn't developing the way he was supposed to. At age three, Roker writes in *Guideposts,* "he hardly talked and could barely walk."

Doctors diagnosed Nick as being on the autism spectrum. But the young man didn't let that limit his life. Al says, "[Nick] started working with speech, behavioral and occupational therapists, developing strength, conversational skills and mobility. We enrolled him in a program at a school to suit his needs, watched him make friends, signed him up for Tae Kwon Do—at his insistence—and took him to Sunday school."

Today, Nick is a black belt in Tae Kwon Do and an acolyte at St. James Episcopal Church. Roker says, "Ever since he's become an acolyte, Nick has the clearest focus, Sunday after Sunday... lighting the candles, carrying a torch, holding up the Bible for the lesson to be read and marching down the center aisle with the cross, concentrating on that altar. On Sundays, he serves the Lord."

God chose what is weak in the world to shame the strong. (1 Corinthians 1:27)

Lead special needs children to fulfill their potential, Lord.

Amen to the Rescue

Heather Brown and Tyler Smith headed to the beach for a day of fun with their friends. The high school seniors at Christ Church Academy in Jacksonville, Florida, jumped into the water and started swimming, hoping to reach a nearby island. But as *ABC News* reported, the pair "were quickly caught up in a current that continued to pull them out deeper into the ocean."

Panic set in, and Smith started experiencing cramping. "While I was laying on my back, the best I could, floating, I just called out, 'God, please don't let this be the end. I still want to see my family...Send someone to save us,'" Smith said.

After an hour and a half, Brown and Smith finally saw a boat coming toward them. Its name? "Amen." Captain Eric Wagner picked up the teens, saving their lives. He said, "We were the only boat there, too. It was a day that only the fishing boats were going out, and they go straight out to the Gulf Stream. They don't go up and down the coast, so I don't think any boats would have found them. I don't want to call it dumb luck, it wasn't. It was the hand of God."

He reached down from on high...He drew me out of mighty waters. (Psalm 18:16)

Send help to those in distress, Holy Spirit.

A Close Shave and a Fresh Start

In July 2018, Phil wanted to apply for a job at McDonald's and was told he could get an interview if he groomed himself and shaved his beard. Phil was determined, but there was one problem. He was homeless, living on the streets of Tallahassee, Florida, and lacked a proper razor.

While attempting to shave in a gas station parking lot, Phil was approached by police officer Tony Carlson. Carlson noticed Phil was using a defective razor, so he decided to help him. He tightened the razor's screw and proceeded to shave Phil's beard himself.

"I like to think of us more as peace officers first, law enforcement officers second," Carlson told the *Today Show.* "[Phil] was excited that there was a chance he was going to get the chance to get a job if he just did this single thing."

Phil's interview with McDonald's went great, and they hired him shortly thereafter. His life is being changed for the better, thanks to one police officer's random act of kindness.

During a severe ordeal of affliction, their abundant joy and their extreme poverty have overflowed in a wealth of generosity on their part. (2 Corinthians 8:2)

Loving Father, lead me to someone in need of assistance.

A Cry of Hope

Expectant parents Mindy and Christopher Koehler received devastating news during their baby Arabella's ultrasound: she had a rare birth defect called congenital diaphragmatic hernia, or CDH, which hinders normal lung growth. Half of the children with CDH nationally don't live past six months.

Doctors advised the couple to terminate the pregnancy. "I felt so lost and confused," Mindy recalled to *ABC Action News.*

Heartbroken, the Koehlers were referred to Johns Hopkins All Children's Hospital in St. Petersburg, Florida, where they met Dr. David Kays, who gave them hope. He told them that there was enough lung for their daughter to survive and an 85 percent survival rate. Dr. Kays performed repair surgery after Arabella was born, and today she continues to thrive.

This hospital is sparking a surge of patients around the world with its survival rate of CDH at 95 percent, believed to be the highest in the world. And now, whenever the Koehlers listen to the sound of Arabella crying, they feel joy that she has the lung capacity to do so.

Protect me, O God, for in You I take refuge. (Psalm 16:1)

Lord, please protect and give strength to the healers.

Chaplain to the Team

Father Jerry Herda of the Archdiocese of Milwaukee may be one of the biggest Brewers fans in the priesthood—and he has good reason to be. For the past 12 years, he has served as the team chaplain, offering Masses and building the Catholic community among the people who work for the team.

Speaking to *Catholic News Service,* Father Herda explained that he was appointed to the Major League Baseball team in 2006 when the Brewers signed Jeff Suppan, a player who was a devout Catholic. Suppan had asked if there could be Mass on the weekends in the ballpark for the people who worked there.

Since then, Father Herda has offered Mass in the press room of the stadium, where a mix of players, grounds crew, concessions staff, security guards, and others join in. In addition to Masses, he has heard confessions, done baptisms, and even a funeral Mass. "It gives me some joy in the sense there is a connection to something I love," Father Herda said. "I love being a priest and I love sports, so it is nice to connect them together."

Athletes exercise self-control in all things; they do it to receive a perishable wreath, but we an imperishable one. (1 Corinthians 9:25)

May I not be afraid to bring my faith into my work, Lord.

Love Conquers Orphan's Fear

Adopting a four-year-old Korean boy was a heartwarming adventure for the late baseball pitcher Jim Bouton. But it started out with nothing but heartbreak.

During the 1960s, Jim and Louise Bouton decided to adopt a Korean orphan when their own children were three and five. Homesick and unaccustomed to American ways, the little fellow cried almost continuously for days.

Finally, a combination of patience, love, and medical care transformed the thin, frightened boy into a happy, healthy child. He became "just one of the Bouton family" and settled contentedly into his new life.

"What the world needs now is love," was how one popular song put it. And love can only come from people like you and me. There are ways by which all of us can become instruments of God's love in a world divided by hate. Ask God to help you find them.

There is no fear in love, but perfect love casts out fear. (1 John 4:18)

Spirit of Love, make us more willing to take the risk of reaching out to those in need.

Heart to Heart Parables

As a child, Sister Ave Clark, O.P., always loved the parables of Jesus and hoped that she could write some herself one day. As an adult, she fulfilled that goal with the publication of her book *Heart to Heart Parables.* The stories include "The Lonely Star," "An Ant Named Charity," and "Bird with Two Broken Wings." The point of them all is to help readers "see in the ordinary the wonderful gift of God's love."

Sister Ave ends each parable with a series of questions the reader can ask himself or herself, along with a prayer, such as, "Creator of Love, grant us the greatness of heart to walk Calvary without a pretense of our humanity; to ask for help, reassurance, and companionship; to share one another's burden; and to be Christ incarnate for each other."

During an interview with The Christophers, Sister Ave said she hopes her book motivates readers to reach out to others and make a positive difference in their lives. She concluded, "I think all of our life is like a parable that's unfolding."

He began to teach them many things in parables. (Mark 4:2)

Holy Spirit, bless me with the wisdom to understand Your lessons in the parables of life.

The Challenge of Depression

"The world knows me as a 28-time medalist, but for me, sometimes my greatest accomplishment is getting out of bed." That was the message shared on Twitter by Olympic swimmer Michael Phelps, who has opened up about his struggles with depression.

During an interview with *CBS This Morning*, Phelps recalled, "I spent three or four days in my room in 2014 not wanting to be alive. Since the Olympics, I've gone through one major depression spell, maybe two."

So how does he deal with those moments when they come? "I was really good at compartmentalizing things...and not bringing them up and letting them just build, build, build. Then I explode. So the biggest thing for me is opening up and communicating."

Phelps acknowledges that depression can strike different people in different ways. The key, though, is to ask for help when you need it by talking to a therapist and/or loved ones.

When the righteous cry for help, the Lord hears, and rescues them from all their troubles. (Psalm 34:17)

In times of depression, open me to asking for help and remind me that I am loved by You, Creator.

A Simple Memory Booster

Are you reading today's *Three Minutes a Day* entry silently right now? Well, it might benefit you more to read it out loud.

As reported by *Reader's Digest*, "Researchers from the University of Waterloo in Canada have uncovered what may be the easiest way to improve your memory ever. Their research, recently published in the journal *Memory*, suggests that reading out loud yourself can increase your recall skills by up to 15 percent."

Psychologist Colin MacLeod, the study's co-author, explained, "Say the information that you want to remember out loud and you'll have a higher likelihood of remembering it. Yes, it's that simple!"

Reader's Digest adds, "The combined effect of speaking and hearing oneself talk is the key to giving your memory a boost, scientists say. Called 'the production effect,' reading out loud allows our brains to save that information in our long-term memories."

His memory will not disappear, and his name will live through all generations. (Sirach 39:9)

Lord, help me to remember the important things in life.

The World is Awake

During her 12 years as a correspondent for *ABC News,* Linsey Davis has covered stories ranging from the Miracle on the Hudson to the Boston Marathon bombing. But after giving birth to her son Ayden five years ago and reading books to him every day, she started thinking about using her storytelling skills in a different way: namely, writing children's literature.

Linsey wasn't sure what form that story would take until Ayden, then age two, asked her one day, "Mommy, does God open up the flowers?" Linsey said, "I was so pleasantly surprised by his curiosity and his ability to make that connection between God, nature, and the world around him. That was when I had the 'a-ha' moment that that's what I'm going to write about."

That book became a Christopher Award winner: *The World is Awake.* It tells the story of a brother and sister enjoying the great outdoors and a trip to the zoo. Along the way, they come to appreciate the wonders of God's creation. The theme can be summed up in the lines, "The world is awake/it's a wonderful place/alive with God's power/and glad with His grace."

The heavens are telling the glory of God; and the firmament proclaims His handiwork. (Psalm 19:1)

Thank You for the beauty of creation, Father.

Making Water Out of Air

You can't create money out of thin air, but how about water? It's a challenge that Beth Koigi took on after a drought hit her Kenyan community in 2016.

While taking part in a U.S. program in Silicon Valley, Koigi met environmental scientist Anastasia Kaschenko and economist Clare Sewell. *The Guardian* reports that they joined forces "to create Majik Water, which captures water from the air and converts it into drinking water using solar technology."

Kaschenko explained, "There's six times more water in the air than in all the rivers in the world. With every one degree Fahrenheit increase in temperature, water begins to evaporate on the ground but increases by about 4% in the atmosphere, and that's water that's not being tapped."

The term "Majik" originates "from the Swahili *maji* for water and 'k' for *kuna* (harvest)." Though costs remain high, the team is working to lower them so they can bring this life-saving creation to people who lack a basic water supply.

You visit the earth and water it, you greatly enrich it; the river of God is full of water. (Psalm 65:9)

Fill my body and soul with life-giving waters, Creator.

Putting Christ at the Center of Marriage

Marriage is a beautiful vocation, but one that has been presented a bit misleadingly in our culture, says author Laci Swann. Writing on *Lightworkers'* website, Swann observes that a foundation for a lifelong marriage has to be built on Christ.

Modern views, often gleaned through popular media, show marriage as the blissful end to finding one's soulmate—the two needing nothing more than each other. The image of one spouse completing the other can easily turn marriage itself into an idol, and one that will disappoint if expectations are set too high or unrealistically.

Swann offers a way forward: each spouse should put their love of Christ first so they can help one another along the Christian journey. She writes, "If you want to gift your partner a love that will surpass all understanding, make God's presence the center of your home. Ask God to help you affirm, encourage and love your spouse; ask Him to help you cherish and delight in your partner." Good advice for any lifelong commitment!

Let marriage be held in honor by all. (Hebrews 13:4)

Savior, please bless and sustain the marriages in my family, and be at the center of their lives.

Something For Me to Do

"In a world where there is so much to be done," Dorothea Dix once said, "I felt strongly impressed that there must be something for me to do."

Dix was born in Hampden, Maine, in 1802. At the age of 12, she went to live in Boston with her wealthy grandmother, who intended to introduce her to high society. But Dix was more interested in the plight of the poor and used her grandmother's barn as a makeshift school for neglected children.

Dix learned of the reform movement for the care of people with mental illness and began to investigate the conditions of poor and indigent people with mental illness, eventually delivering a series of scathing reports to the state legislature to bring about reform.

Her crusade continued for another 40 years as she helped found 32 hospitals, 15 schools, and a number of training facilities for nurses. During the Civil War, she led nurses to provide care for soldiers on both sides. On her deathbed she was quoted as saying, "I think even lying on my bed I can still do something."

Brothers and Sisters, do not be weary in doing what is right. (2 Thessalonians 3:13)

Lord, help me to be a tireless advocate for good.

Stabbing Leads to Youth Program

After his son was stabbed in New York's Central Park many years ago, Sidney Augstein decided to offer an alternative to young boys whose anger and idleness might touch off violence.

Soon after his company bought a firm that makes airplane training equipment, he started a program to offer high school students a chance behind the controls of two flight simulators.

"I felt it would be a good thing to do if we took kids who never had an opportunity to fly and let them learn something about it from the ground up, since flying is held in awe by most people and particularly by young people," explained Augstein. "It promotes an attitude of confidence in one's self."

Outrage and anger are normal reactions to individual or group violence. But rooting out the causes of violence is another worthwhile goal, as we try to find the right balance between justice and redemption.

Put away violence and oppression, and do what is just and right. (Ezekiel 45:9)

Father, help us to create a more peaceful society.

A Great Untapped Resource

During an interview with *Columbia Magazine,* Linda Fried said, "I see older people as a great untapped resource." The dean of Columbia University's Mailman School of Public Health, she added, "Psychological research has shown that older people have a strong desire to make a difference in the world."

Many elders "are eager to remain involved in work or in volunteer activities. So why not connect these large numbers of wise and experienced older Americans with important social initiatives that could use their help?"

For various reasons, not everyone can remain active, and some still face age discrimination. But, because finding meaningful pursuits supports healthy aging, let's do all we can to open up opportunities for the benefit of our elders and ultimately ourselves.

So even to old age and gray hairs, O God, do not forsake me, until I proclaim Your might to all the generations to come. (Psalm 71:18)

Holy Spirit, inspire us to work with older people, encouraging them and learning from them.

Dreams Into Reality

Most likely, men, women and children dreamed about going to the moon long before America made it a reality in 1969 with the Apollo 11 voyage. For many of those alive when astronauts first landed on the moon, it was unforgettable. *AARP: The Magazine* quotes a few of them.

"To me it was the most magnificent moment in human history," said William Shatner. Actress Ali McGraw understood 1969 was in many ways a violent and divisive year. Yet she saw people come together to watch the event on a TV someone brought onto the street for the occasion: "The energy was so hopeful."

The politician Bob Kerrey was recovering from wounds received in the Vietnam War. But he was hopeful too: "Anything that takes your mind out of despair is a good thing."

When I look at Your heavens, the work of Your fingers, the moon and the stars that You have established; what are human beings that You are mindful of them, mortals that You care for them? (Psalm 8:3-4)

Inspire us, Holy Spirit, to dream even seemingly impossible dreams.

A Marvel of God

Though she stars in movies on the Hallmark Channel, where happy endings are guaranteed, actress Nikki DeLoach has faced struggles in real life with far more uncertain outcomes. In the fifth month of being pregnant with her son Bennett, Nikki and her husband learned the child had multiple heart defects. They didn't know if Bennett would live.

As related in *People* magazine, Bennett was born and taken to Children's Hospital Los Angeles where a cardiothoracic surgeon "did the impossible by successfully completing procedures that most kids do not survive." The baby's chest was left open for a few days, so Nikki actually saw her son's heart beating outside his chest.

Thankfully, Bennett recovered. Nikki credits her faith in God, and the compassionate support of family, friends, and medical staff with getting her through the ordeal. She said, "This experience, while certainly the most difficult and terrifying of my life, has been the most transformative and inspirational. I gave birth to the strongest, most mighty human I've ever known. He is a superhero. He is a marvel of God."

The physician heals and takes away pain. (Sirach 38:7)

Bring healing to suffering children, Divine Physician.

Share Your Story

Her son's heart issues are not the only challenges actress Nikki DeLoach has faced recently. Sadly, her father was diagnosed with Pick's disease, an aggressive form of dementia. She told the Alzheimer's Association that her dad used to be the most "kind, loving, honest, patient" man she knew. He has now largely lost those personality traits due to the nature of this debilitating illness.

Nikki went public with her father's condition because she thought it could help everyone involved. She explained, "When it came to Dad's diagnosis, I said to my family: 'People want to help us. People want to reach out. There are other people going through this, and we will never know how sharing our story may help another family.'

"When I know someone else is going through what I am going though, it helps me as much as it helps them. It helps us all feel less alone. I want people to be able to speak more openly about the help they need, because I have been there, and I know how important it is."

More tomorrow…

Whenever we have an opportunity, let us work for the good of all. (Galatians 6:10)

Allow my challenges to be a help to someone else, Father.

Turning Pain Into Purpose

Actress Nikki DeLoach's father may suffer from dementia, but as his primary caregiver, her mother endures substantial stress, too. "We have to be super mindful of the spouses of people with [dementia]," Nikki told the Alzheimer's Association. "They often experience a decline in health as well."

Nikki calls her mother's response to the situation "nothing short of heroic. However, heroes also need a team of people that lift them up and support them. This is why I encouraged her to reach out to her local chapter of the Alzheimer's Association. The people who have been supporting her there are angels. They are helping her learn how to cope with what is happening to her and how to help my father."

The Association even helped Nikki's mom create a support group at her local church: "She is bringing in speakers and people involved with the Association who can help anyone and everyone who needs it. I am beyond proud of my mother for doing this. She has turned her pain into purpose, which is so courageous. I hope the group will grow as more people see how important it is to talk about what they are going through."

**Love one another as I have loved you.
(John 15:12)**

Give caregivers divine strength and patience, Father.

An Orthodox Christian First

Novak Djokovic is one of the biggest names in sports, racking up wins on tennis courts all over the globe. For a period of time, he was the number one player in the world, with 68 titles including 12 Grand Slam tournaments. However, he stays grounded in all of his success by leaning on his Orthodox Christian faith.

In a recent story on *Aleteia,* Djokovic recalled being named to the Order of St. Sava, the highest distinction in the Serbian Orthodox Church. "This is the most important title of my life, because before being an athlete, I am an Orthodox Christian," he said of receiving this honor in his native Serbia.

In addition, Djokovic supports charities and organizations that help the poor and children. He has opened a restaurant in Serbia that feeds the homeless and the poor, and established a foundation to help provide young people in his native country with access to good schools. He has been lauded for his generosity, but still roots his success (and his giving spirit) in regular prayer and Bible reading.

In the case of an athlete, no one is crowned without competing according to the rules. (2 Timothy 2:5)

Lord, may I realize that Your word is the true path to eternal life.

Outcast Becomes a Christ-Bearer

St. Christopher's reputation has taken a hit, but that shouldn't be the case, says Brother Silas Henderson, SDS, on *Aleteia*. Brother Silas relates the story of "Reprobus" (translated as "Outcast"), who was a fierce figure.

The story goes that Reprobus was looking for the most powerful king to serve and eventually came to Christianity. A hermit who was instructing Reprobus told him to carry travelers across a river. One day, while carrying a small child, the weight became heavier and heavier, nearly crushing Reprobus.

Only on the other side of the river did the child reveal himself to be Jesus, who told Reprobus that he felt the weight of the world. It was then that Reprobus's name was changed to Christopher ("Christ-bearer").

After Vatican II, there was a story that the Church had revoked Christopher's sainthood because he was a "legend," but that simply isn't true. First noted in written works going back to the 13th century, St. Christopher remains a recognized saint. He is an inspiration for all of us to be "Christ-bearers" in the world.

I try to please everyone in everything I do...so that they may be saved. (1 Corinthians 10:23)

My prayer today is to bear someone's burden to Christ.

Creating a Universe

In her book, *Just Kids from the Bronx*, Arlene Alda shares the oral histories of consequential people whose early years shaped not only them but the wider world. A few of these Bronxites include Carl Reiner, Mary Higgins Clark, General Colin Powell, A.M. Rosenthal, and Dava Sobel.

Some said that growing up in the Bronx offered them access to good educations, exposure to the arts, freedom to explore, or the opportunity to mingle with people from various cultures.

Obviously it isn't just those who become prominent whose early lives are significant. Each child, influenced by their environment, is important. As Chazz Palminteri put it, "I always tell people when you create a child … (you create) a universe because that child will grow up and affect a lot of people, like ripples in water."

[Children] are indeed a heritage from the Lord, the fruit of the womb a reward. (Psalm 127:3)

Father, may we always remember the preciousness, potential, and inherent dignity of all children.

A Cold One and a Shoulder to Cry On

It was a typical Wednesday in St. Paul, Minnesota. *Breakthru Beverage* beer deliverymen Jason Gabel and Kwame Anderson were driving along the Interstate 94 Overpass, when to their horror, they saw a man dangling off a fence. Gabel and Anderson immediately called 911, knowing this man intended to jump to his death.

Andreson, a big fan of Denzel Washington, quickly decided to channel the latter's character in the movie *Inside Man,* determined to keep the man occupied because, as he surmised to *WCNC,* "If I wait for police, this thing may be over."

To that end, Anderson thought that offering the man a beer might be a good icebreaker—and he was right. After nearly an hour, Anderson and Gabel convinced the man to come back to the safety of the overpass.

Both deliverymen were hailed as heroes, but Anderson gave the Almighty all the glory. "We have a route that we do every Wednesday," he told *WCNC* reporter Jenni Fink, "and that wasn't the way I would normally go...It was God's plan."

I know the plans I have for you...to give you a future with hope. (Jeremiah 29:11)

Lord, may we always treasure life as our greatest gift.

A Grandparent is a Blessing

Over nine years, Elizabeth Broadbent and her husband only had two "date nights" because they had no family nearby and couldn't find a reliable babysitter for their three sons with ADHD. That finally changed when Broadbent's mom moved to town. Suddenly, the couple could spend time alone together, trusting that their kids were in safe and loving hands.

In addition, having their grandmother in their lives is a blessing for her sons. On the website *ScaryMommy*, Broadbent writes, "A grandparent who shows up is present. They hug your kids. They ask about their day. They love them. Your kids get one more person in their lives who care about them, and that's worth more than anything else."

Broadbent also makes sure that she is there for her mom when she needs help. She concludes, "When she was sick, I brought her dinner in the middle of a storm. You show up for sickness. You show up to nail on roof tiles. You show up to hang pictures and decorate trees and run errands. You don't do it because you have to. You do it because you love them."

Grandchildren are the crown of the aged. (Proverbs 17:6)

Bring generations of families together, Jesus.

The Comic and the SEAL

The relationship between comedian Pete Davidson and Texas Congressman Dan Crenshaw didn't start too promisingly. After all, during an episode of *Saturday Night Live,* Davidson mocked Crenshaw, who lost his right eye during an IED attack in Afghanistan where he served as a Navy SEAL.

A few weeks later, Davidson apologized publicly and even welcomed Crenshaw to *SNL* to poke fun at him. In an era of anger and pettiness, this display of maturity stood out.

The following month, Davidson, who has struggled with mental health issues, posted a message on social media that suggested he might be suicidal. One of the people who personally called him was Crenshaw.

The congressman told *CNN,* "We don't go back very far. We're not good friends. But, I think he appreciated hearing from me. I told him everyone had a purpose in this world. God put you here for a reason. It's your job to find that purpose. And you should live that way."

Once again, this was a display of compassion between political opposites that the world needs more of.

Pray for those who persecute you. (Matthew 5:44)

Make me more understanding toward others, Lord.

One Teacher Who Won't Be Forgotten

If you're lucky, you have at least one teacher who stands out in your memory as somebody who made a real difference in your life.

For many young people of the Tarrytown school district in New York, Ronald Tucci was such an outstanding teacher. He was widely respected for his interest in his students, for always making time to talk and make others feel comfortable.

When Tucci died of cancer at age 53, one student said, "When I called him at the hospital to see how he was doing, all he wanted to know was how I was doing."

Sometimes it's only after we've lost someone that we appreciate just how much they've meant to us. Don't wait to let the folks who matter to you know you're grateful. Tell them today.

I did not listen to the voice of my teachers. (Proverbs 5:13)

May it never be said of us, Master, that we did not listen to our Teacher.

TechBridge

According to a recent AARP poll, 83 percent of Americans, ages 50 to 64, own smartphones. A far lower percentage of these Americans, however, actually know how to work them. Enter Girl Scout Troop #60013.

This Virginia-based troop created a "smartphone clinic" of sorts, the aptly named TechBridge. It's a program in which the girls show older people how to properly use their cell phones. The troop hopes this project will qualify them for the highly coveted Girl Scout Silver Award.

"It has to be something that helps your community," 13-year-old Cadette Tara Udani explained to *CNN* reporter Julia M. Chan. "And so for us, that was teaching the elderly in our community how to use their technology better."

"Those girls were just marvelous," 90-year-old Nancy Taylor exclaimed. "They…had a very mature attitude about answering our questions." And 14-year-old Sarah Middleton concluded, "I think this is really important to do, to help everybody stay safe and well-educated."

Serve one another with whatever gift each of you has received. (1 Peter 4:10)

Paraclete, foster love and respect between generations.

Commitment Leads to a Better You

Commitment. Some say it's still popular. Others say it's non-existent today. But most agree that any life commitment, especially marriage, is important.

Glen Argan, writing in a Canadian newspaper, noted that a lifetime commitment means that "one is no longer free to go wherever one wills. Life, to some extent, becomes limited and channeled."

But, he continues, "One cannot fully be oneself without giving of oneself...We become more human by seeing our own faults through the disappointment of another person, who loves us without reservation.

"When one has the option of walking out... one isn't challenged in the same way to change oneself, be patient, and enter into reconciliation."

Commitment, in other words, is a vehicle for growth, for becoming a better person. It is a pledge worth taking.

Commit your way to the Lord; trust in Him, and He will act. (Psalm 37:5)

Help me to become more fully myself by giving of myself, Jesus.

New Hope for a Mysterious Disease

Brandon Noblitt of St. Louis, Missouri, was a normal six-year-old, playing sports and going to school, until what seemed like a run-of-the-mill virus left him paralyzed.

Brandon's condition, known as acute flaccid myelitis, or AFM, strikes about one in a million and has polio-like symptoms, such as sudden weakness and an inability to use arms or legs. Doctors don't know what causes the condition, but a spike in cases in 2017 led to more media attention of the rare disorder which primarily affects children.

Brandon's family told *CBS News* that they turned to Dr. Amy Moore of Washington University in St. Louis, a pediatric surgeon with a new approach. Brandon had a first-of-its-kind surgery for children with AFM: a nerve transfer. Today, he can walk again.

"It's been amazing," Brandon said. "Thanks to Miss Doctor Moore, I can go outside, play with my brothers, play football." He added that he now wants to be a surgeon like Dr. Moore.

For [physicians] too pray to the Lord that He grant them success in diagnosis and in healing, for the sake of preserving life. (Sirach 38:14)

Jesus, bless the healers who reflect Your divine healing.

About My Mother, Part One

Peggy Rowe isn't the most famous member of her family. That distinction goes to her son Mike Rowe, host of *Dirty Jobs* and Facebook's Christopher Award-winning series *Returning the Favor*. But Peggy has become a celebrity in her own right, thanks to her warmth and writing talent.

During a *Christopher Closeup* interview about her humorous memoir *About My Mother*, Peggy recalled that her mom, Thelma Knobel, was a refined, sophisticated woman who enjoyed ballet and opera. Then, in 1954, an unknown side of Thelma arose when the Orioles started playing in her hometown of Baltimore. "My mother," recalled Peggy, "[became] a baseball fan who shouted obscenities at umpires and threw underwear at the television set."

And it wasn't just a phase. At age 90, Thelma fell and broke her hip when she was at Peggy's house. Despite being in excruciating pain, Thelma insisted that Peggy call the neighbors so they could carry her to the sofa to watch the Orioles game until the ambulance arrived. Peggy still smiles at the memory and eccentricity of her mom's behavior.

God has brought laughter for me. (Genesis 21:6)

Help me find humor in everyday life, Holy Spirit.

About My Mother, Part Two

Peggy Rowe treasures the gift of faith that her mother, Thelma Knobel, passed on to her. During a *Christopher Closeup* interview, Peggy said, "We lived just one block from the little gray shingled church, Kenwood Presbyterian. My father was the Sunday school superintendent. My mother was the president of the women of the church, and they were involved in every phase of the life and work of the church."

One of the ways that Thelma lived out her faith was in her devotion to her husband Carl. Peggy recalled, "I've never seen a love story quite like that of my parents. Both of them grew up poor and married during the Depression...She was always at his side, right up until the time they passed away in 2005 and 2003.

"Her one wish in her senior years was that she would outlive my father so that she could continue taking care of him. She outlived him by two years. He was an invalid for the last 11 years of his life. He had glaucoma and had lost his eyesight, and he had a stroke earlier on which left him very weak on one side. So she took care of him."

Do not hesitate to visit the sick, because for such deeds you will be loved. (Sirach 7:35)

Give spouses the strength to care for each other, Lord.

About My Mother, Part Three

Peggy Rowe is grateful for the example of marriage she saw modeled by her parents. She is also appreciative of her own husband of 58 years, John, whom she often calls "Prince Charming" on her Facebook page.

Peggy noted, "My husband is the best gift that I [ever gave] to my parents. He was there for them throughout their senior years...When Dad could no longer drive because of glaucoma and John had retired, every morning John would take Dad back to McDonald's so that he could meet his retired friends. They had a wonderful relationship."

John's willingness to help others is one of the qualities Peggy admires most about him. She said, "It's been good for me through the years to see his giving nature. If it's Tuesday, [he's doing] Meals on Wheels. If it's Wednesday, he's volunteering at the oncology unit at our local hospital...It's such a priority, and people are so appreciative."

Each of you, however, should love his wife as himself, and a wife should respect her husband. (Ephesians 5:33)

Guide married couples to be loving towards their in-laws and each other as they build a family life together, Jesus.

Teamwork Made the Dream Work

There's an old truism that nobody succeeds alone. This certainly applies to sports, even individual athletes. For all that is written about grit, determination, and practice, without coaching and teamwork, even the most gifted athlete can fall short.

Gertrude Ederle is a perfect example. Author Brenda Byrne Greene wrote about Ederle's road to becoming the first woman to swim the English Channel. Encouraged by her father and sister, Ederle hired a coach and made an attempt in 1925, but her swim was cut short when her coaches observed her faltering in the water and pulled her into the boat. She was livid and decided to fire them all.

Ederle hired a new coach, a man who had completed the swim himself, and he was 100 percent in her corner. He taught her a new swim stroke, and they trained hard. Ederle's sister and coach were her chief motivators. When Ederle made the attempt again in 1926, she completed the swim in record time: 14 hours and 39 minutes. Having the right team made all the difference.

If they fall, one will lift up the other; but woe to one who is alone and falls and does not have another to help. (Ecclesiastes 4:10)

Lord, may I be a friend and teammate to those in my life.

Living With Those in Need

To deeply understand something, it is sometimes necessary to experience it personally. Father James Harvey took to the streets of New York City to become more aware of the plight of the homeless.

He donned sneakers, sweatpants, and a ragged sweatshirt to conceal his identity. Then he went out to feel the effects of deprivation that the young street people with whom he worked dealt every day. Some of the homeless people were able to communicate well and even looked out for one another. Others had lost their grip on reality.

Father Harvey experienced the overwhelming sense of isolation and alienation experienced by the men, women and youngsters who had no place to call home. His time on the streets convinced the priest that a solution will come only with the cooperation of government, business, and private individuals. He grew determined to do his part to make things better.

Open your mouth, judge righteously, maintain the rights of the poor and needy. (Proverbs 31:9)

May we do all we can to help those who are not as fortunate as we are, Father.

A Mother's Unexpected Gift

Many 13-year-old boys save their money to buy clothes or video games, but not William Preston. He went to work to buy a car for his mom.

Krystal Preston is a financially-struggling single mother of three in Fernley, Nevada. She needed (but couldn't afford) a car to travel to work, as well as take her kids to school and other appointments. William decided to solve her problem. He found a used car listed online—a 1999 Chevy Metro—and worked out a deal with the owner to do odd jobs for her in exchange for the vehicle.

One day, William walked into the family's home and told Krystal, "Mom, I got you a car." She didn't believe it, but he led her outside where the car's original owner waited. The lady drove them to her home where the Chevy was waiting for Krystal. "I lost it, I bawled," Krystal told *KOLO-TV*. "And then she gave me the keys and the paperwork." And regarding William, Krystal said, "He has so much life and spirit in him. He's just an amazing kid."

Let her who bore you rejoice. (Proverbs 23:25)

Instill children with a selfless love for their parents, Holy Spirit.

Unity of Greater New Orleans

Following Hurricane Katrina in 2005, more than 11,000 people in New Orleans were left homeless. But thanks to the efforts of the nonprofit Unity of Greater New Orleans, which aims to end homelessness, that number has decreased 90 percent.

Martha Kegel, the charity's executive director, told *WBUR* that their approach was threefold. First, they assembled an outreach team that "was willing to go anywhere and do anything to rescue and rehouse a homeless person." Next, they successfully lobbied Congress to support a rent assistance fund.

Finally, they followed a "Housing First" model, which accepts people as they are (sober or not), provides them a home, then "wraps all the services around them that they need to stay stable and live the highest quality life that they can live."

Kegel notes this approach is more cost-effective than people realize because homeless people often wind up in the hospital or prison, which costs taxpayers a lot of money. The amount of rent assistance necessary to keep them housed is far less, and has better long-term results.

Open your hand to the poor and needy neighbor in your land. (Deuteronomy 15:11)

Guide us to sensible solutions for homelessness, Messiah.

A Friendly Shark Tank

Keira, Christian, and Kaley Young are siblings—ranging in age from 15 to 25—who have faced tremendous loss. Their mother Beth died of cancer in 2012. And in 2018, their father, New York City Firefighter Keith Young, died of cancer that was caused by working at the World Trade Center following 9/11.

Determined to keep their father's memory alive, the Young siblings devoted themselves to expanding his business selling a food cutting board that he designed, called the Cup Board Pro.

They took their pitch to the TV series *Shark Tank*, hoping to get one of its hosts to invest $100,000 in exchange for 10 percent of their business. Instead, they got a deal with all five sharks, including Mark Cuban and Lori Grenier, for 20 percent of the business, with a promise that all the sharks' profits would go to a 9/11-related charity.

Christian told *Newsday*, "I'm seeing comments and messages from people who really appreciate us sharing our story, and saying it inspires them to continue whatever they're going through, whatever life throws at them."

Rejoice in hope, be patient in suffering, persevere in prayer. (Romans 12:12)

Help me bring good out of tragedy, Father.

The Motto of a Minister

Many years ago, The Christophers received a letter from a retired Episcopal priest in Maryland. He wanted to let us know that we had been helpful to him over the years, and he wanted to share the story of his vocation.

He remembers having a vision in his youth of the vast amount of work to be done in the world, but he also experienced a feeling of unworthiness. "What could I do to ease the burdens of worry and care in so many people?" he asked himself.

And then one day it came to him: he could become an Episcopal priest and simply offer his friendship, a smile, and comfort to those needing it. The idea captured him. He entered the ministry and adopted these words as his motto: "I'll do what I can."

You know, that's not a bad motto for anyone because it's simple and realistic. Why not decide to make it yours? Do what you can, and pray for what you cannot yet do!

Let each of you lead the life that the Lord has assigned, to which God called you.
(1 Corinthians 7:17)

God, support us in our efforts to make the world a better place.

Couple Adopts 16 Disabled Children

During the 1950s, New Jersey couple Kurt and Julie Lerke read a newspaper account of a veteran's return to Korea to aid children of American GIs. They felt inspired to help, so into their own family of two children, they adopted 16 more over the years.

"They are all races and have every physical disability imaginable," said Mrs. Lerke, "brain damage, cerebral palsy, hemophilia, asthma, and meningitis."

The youngsters, ages two to 20, were all formerly rejected in other homes, but they found happiness with the Lerkes. They help take care of the family's two-acre farm. Mrs. Lerke said, "If someone had told me years ago [that I'd have]... 18 children...I wouldn't have believed them. It seems very natural, normal now."

All God's children deserve a chance for a reasonably happy life. Maybe you can't be an adoptive parent. Or maybe you can. Consider all the ways in which you might help make a child's life better.

Whoever welcomes one such child in My name welcomes Me. (Mark 9:37)

Jesus, may every child be given the chance for a loving, fulfilling life.

A Life-Saving Catch

You should always keep your eyes and ears open because you never know what opportunity life will place in your path. This was the case for 17-year-old Algerian Fawzi Zaabat, who wound up saving a child's life.

"I was just walking [in the Fatih district of Istanbul] when I saw the little girl at the window," Zaabat told *AFP* (Agence France Presse). "She fell and thanks to God, I caught her before she hit the ground."

The toddler in question, two-year-old Syrian Doha Muhammed, had wandered away from her mother, who was cooking in the kitchen, and accidentally slipped right out the open window of the second-story apartment. Thankfully, Zaabat, who happened to see Muhammed from the street below, had already positioned himself to catch the youngster.

Amazingly, thanks to Zaabat's quick thinking (and catching), Muhammed escaped her fall unscathed. Though the girl's family gave Zaabat a reward, the teen was just grateful to God that he could help.

God, the Lord, is my strength. (Habakkuk 3:19)

Savior, may we always keep our eyes and ears open to Your call.

A Eulogy for an Unlikely Friend

When Katie Brocker moved to Detroit, she made an unlikely friend on her way to work: a homeless man named Gordy King. But when Brocker heard King passed away, she couldn't rest until she found out if he had the burial he deserved.

In August 2018, Brocker eventually tracked King's body to the Wayne County Morgue, where she learned that they had failed to find his next of kin. Brocker believed it her Catholic duty to give her friend a proper memorial and burial.

She held fundraisers to raise money for his tombstone, and the local funeral parlor donated the casket. Friends and the community came together to pay their respects.

As reported by the *Detroit News,* Brocker said during her eulogy, "I don't know Gordy's favorite color or favorite childhood memory. What I do know is that he was a child of God, and we were meant to meet."

Brocker believes every act of kindness makes a difference, and she hopes this inspires her children and others to make a difference in someone's life.

Whoever does not love does not know God, for God is love. (John 4:8)

Help me, Lord, make a difference in someone's life today.

A Deacon's High-Flying Ministry

Deacon Daniel Michaud of the Archdiocese of Baltimore has a servant's heart wherever he goes. Whether ministering in the Church or working as a flight attendant for Southwest Airlines, he's found a way to be himself.

When Deacon Michaud and his wife got married, they designed their own wedding bands with symbols of their Christian faith: a cross, a fish, and a grapevine. "People see it," he said. "It's just one way that you start conversation."

He compares his flight attendant job to being a bartender because he encounters so many people interested in opening up to him: "I'm able to go to work and still be Deacon Dan in a sense... I can still treat people with respect; I can still see the good in people."

In a story for the archdiocese about life after ordination, Deacon Michaud said, "It's been more about the power of the spirit working through things. It's nothing different about me as far as gifts or talents, but the spirit that was...instilled upon me during ordination has made a difference."

Go into all the world and proclaim the good news to the whole creation. (Mark 16:15)

Holy Spirit, help me to share my faith with all people.

Not Giving Up on the Race

While Andrew Silverman was training for his first half-marathon in 2015, he started experiencing symptoms that made him unsteady on his feet. After seeking help, the 27-year-old Staten Island native learned the disheartening truth: he was diagnosed with multiple sclerosis (MS).

While others were crossing the finish line, Silverman was walking around his block with a walker, still weak from a flare-up and devastated by the diagnosis. But he was determined to not give up on his goal.

Four years later, Silverman feels stronger than ever. He has crossed six half-marathon finish lines and is prepared to start training for a full marathon. Even though it can be difficult at times living with MS, Silverman says that running continues to be his form of meditation. He now hopes his story will help inspire others facing similar health issues.

"I know what it's like to go through something life-altering, that changes your world," Silverman told *NY1*. "But you move along and you just readjust how you envision your life."

**"Come what may," he said, "I will run."
(Samuel 18:23)**

Dear God, no matter how hard life gets, give me strength to never give up on the race.

The Best Medicine

A 30-year-old lawyer with a flair for theatrics used to run one of New York's most successful "off Broadway" shows—for patients in the city's hospitals. Called Hospital Tours, his production enlisted performers of all ages and professions who were willing to spend one night a month entertaining patients. The lawyer-producer conceived the idea in Paris in 1965.

"I knew a lot of musicians, and I thought I might make use of their talent," he explained. "It was such a smash in France that I decided to try it here when I came home. Our first performance was in Bellevue Psychiatric Ward in December 1965. It has since become very much part of my life."

A hospital recreation director called Hospital Tours "the best medicine since penicillin."

Maybe you and I can't go "on the road" for the ill and infirm. But wherever we are, if we look hard enough, each of us can do something to lighten the burden of suffering humanity. God will surely be with us in our efforts to do so.

Do not hesitate to visit the sick, because for such deeds you will be loved. (Sirach 7:35)

Jesus, increase the number of those who are willing to imitate Your compassionate service of the sick.

Credits Parents for World Record

Tom Dempsey, former placekicker for the New Orleans Saints, didn't let the fact that he had only half a kicking foot and no right hand prevent him from becoming a standout football player. In fact, Dempsey broke the world record for field goal kicking in 1970, sending the ball 63 yards.

What enabled Dempsey to win a place in the record books? He said: "I'll always be grateful for my parents' attitude towards me when I was a small boy. They simply refused to let me feel sorry for myself because I was different than other people. They taught me to get out and compete. My father, especially, made me try everything."

Each child has a spark of potential which can remain largely buried without the right kind of support. You and I can play a key role in God's design by encouraging children to go as far as they can in developing their talents. Remember, young people need backers to guide them down the right path.

In the case of an athlete, no one is crowned without competing according to the rules. (2 Timothy 2:5)

Father, may we encourage people, not impose unnecessary restrictions on them.

Contemplating Prayer

Trappist monk Father Thomas Keating was known by many as one of the pioneers of the modern Centering Prayer movement. It's a form of silent prayer whereby a person aims to be in the presence of God in a special way.

When Father Keating died at age 95, Katharine Q. Seelye wrote his obituary for *The New York Times*. The article noted how he'd been born into wealth and privilege, attending exclusive private schools and, for a time, Yale University before the course of his life changed.

Seelye wrote, "As he studied Christianity, he was drawn to the mystics and came to believe that the Scriptures call people to a personal relationship with God."

Eventually, Father Keating helped found Contemplative Outreach, with chapters in 39 countries and thousands of people following its precepts.

Be still, and know that I am God! I am exalted among the nations, I am exalted in the earth. (Psalm 46:10)

Teach me how to pray, Lord.

A Doctor's Call

Several times in his life, Dr. Scott Ross of Manassas, Virginia, had to practice patience in waiting for something good to happen. The first was when he was a boy and wanted to be an altar server. He needed to reach the minimum age, and his parish priest kept telling him he had to wait, no matter how enthusiastic he was about the possibilities.

The second time was when Dr. Ross applied to become a deacon. His home diocese had opened up the permanent diaconate program for new applicants. He talked with his wife about it, applied, but was turned down. That was not something he was used to, but he trusted God's plan.

More than four years later, he felt the call to apply again and this time he was accepted. The timing was also right for him to work at a free health clinic set up by Catholic Charities. "The diaconate allows me to help people with spiritual issues," Dr. Ross told *The Arlington Catholic Herald*. "My medical profession helps me to help people with their physical needs and issues... They're really brought together in service."

I know the plans I have for you, says the Lord, plans for your welfare and not for harm. (Jeremiah 29:11)

God, help me to trust in Your plan always!

The Power of Hope and Literacy

John Bunn of Brooklyn, New York, spent 17 years in jail on a wrongful conviction of murder. At age 14, he was arrested for killing a corrections officer. The detective in charge of the investigation was later revealed to be corrupt. But despite Bunn maintaining his innocence, he was convicted and sentenced to nine years to life.

Once in prison, Bunn's isolation was made worse by the fact that he was illiterate. He grew determined to learn to read and write so he could send letters to his mother. Reading opened new doors for Bunn. "I felt trapped without a voice for so long, but the power of reading could take my imagination, and take me to anywhere in this universe," he told *CNN*.

Bunn was released from prison in 2006, and in 2018 he was exonerated, citing evidence and the arresting detective's string of wrongful arrests. Bunn didn't get embittered, though. Instead, he uses his story and his literacy work to help disadvantaged kids focus on the positive in life.

He will not break a bruised reed or quench a smoldering wick until He brings justice to victory. (Matthew 12:20)

May my struggles be used for Your greater glory, Jesus.

MicroShifts, Part One

Author Gary Jansen titled his latest book *MicroShifts: Transforming Your Life One Step at a Time* because he knows that "making small changes in the way that you live, pray, communicate with people, and communicate with God can, over time, have big, powerful results."

During a *Christopher Closeup* interview, Gary recalled a particular example: "For a long time, I thought I was going through a very bad depression. I was struggling through work, struggling through life, struggling through my relationships. I got so tired one day that I actually fell asleep and got eight hours of sleep. Before that I was getting four and a half, five maybe."

Gary woke up the next morning feeling like a new man. He was more energetic and hopeful than he had been in a long time. His body's weariness, he realized, had affected his mind, his soul, and his relationship with God. From that point on, Gary made sleep a priority and discovered that his physical, mental, and spiritual health all benefited greatly.

More about MicroShifts tomorrow…

I will both lie down and sleep in peace; for You alone, O Lord, make me lie down in safety. (Psalm 3:5)

Grant me restful sleep, Prince of Peace.

MicroShifts, Part Two

"The power of one percent." That's one of the ideas that author Gary Jansen addresses in his book *MicroShifts: Transforming Your Life One Step at a Time*.

During a *Christopher Closeup* interview, he explained, "Each of us has 24 hours a day: 1,440 minutes...What if you just took one percent of your day: that's 14 minutes and 24 seconds? Can you set aside 15 minutes of dedicated time to pray to God in a new way, [or spend time] with your spouse, or exercise?"

Another major player in Gary's approach to MicroShifts is St. Ignatius Loyola and his spirituality that searches for God in all things. Gary said, "If there was garbage on the street, St. Ignatius would say, 'Where's God in the garbage?' We can find God in sunsets, in flowers, in times when we feel in love with people and the work that we're doing. But what about those times we're going through the garbage of life? How do we find God in that? Once I started...trying to find God in all the good stuff, and all the bad stuff too, that was transformative."

More on MicroShifts tomorrow...

If you seek Me with all your heart, I will let you find Me, says the Lord. (Jeremiah 29:13-14)

Help me to seek and find You, Jesus.

MicroShifts, Part Three

Dealing with difficult people is a challenge for everyone, so Gary Jansen tries to remind himself that each of us is a unique individual in "this great mosaic of God's creation." As an example, he recalled an encounter he once had with a homeless man, known as "the town drunk" in his community. The man, who often gets aggressive with people, approached Gary for money, but Gary didn't have any so he began to move away.

Suddenly, said Gary, "I had this vision of him as a little boy. I don't know what happened to him since then, but at some point, his mom held him or a nurse held him and showed him love." Gary wondered, "What if that was me?"

He concluded, "Everybody out there...was at one point a child, and there was a lot of hope there. At some point, something changed. I think God calls us to compassion...I'm not asking you to be a doormat to people. But at the same time, there's an opportunity to take a step back and live with compassion. One of the ways to do that is to imagine this person was a child at some point, and to uplift that and value that."

Unless you change and become like children, you will never enter the kingdom of heaven. (Matthew 18:3)

Help me to see others as You see them, Father.

English Couple Pedaled Cross Country

Back in 1978, Bert and Queenie Barnes of Norfolk, England, celebrated their retirement by bicycling 4,000 miles across the United States in 85 days. They averaged 45 miles a day, and traveled from West to East to have prevailing winds at their backs. And the couple did it all on nine dollars a day.

Both had cycled all their lives. They prepared for the journey by cycling all around England and Norway. Why did they do it? "I saw so much of people retiring and fading away," said Bert.

He added, "Coming through the little townships, we thought, 'This is the real America.'" People took them in and proudly showed them the local sights. "We never met a bad American," said Queenie, smiling. "There must be some, but we didn't meet any."

Some people retire from life at an early age. Others stay active to the end. Much of the difference lies in attitude. You don't have to ride a bike to be active. What is required is a desire to reach out, to touch another's life in some positive way.

Do good to friends before you die.
(Sirach 14:13)

Help us, Lord, to look up, not down, in all we say and do.

Perseverance Pays Off

During the 1970s, Mary Stevens was a public school teacher in Harlem who felt discouraged. For years, under trying conditions, she had been teaching problem children. Her dedication did not seem to produce any results.

As Stevens' seriously considered a change in career, she also made an effort to try a little harder. Finally, her efforts paid off. Half the children who came to her were illiterate. She strove to make them believe they were not losers, encouraging them to overcome their oppressive environment and teaching them the value of education.

The children responded, and in two years time, they were transformed. They could read at their grade level and had acquired a new outlook on life.

Giving up is the easy way out of problems. But through constant effort, a situation that seems hopeless can be changed for the better. If you're considering quitting on a goal, give it a second thought.

The one who endures to the end will be saved. (Matthew 10:22)

Lord Jesus, who persevered to the point of death, give us the courage to keep going in spite of our daily troubles.

Shelter from the Storm

Heavy rains drenched the spectators paying their respects to murdered Alabama police Sergeant Wytasha Carter as her funeral procession made its way through Birmingham's streets. On hand was Sheriff's Deputy Tiffany Dial, standing in silent salute without an umbrella.

Shawn Allen, a civilian who worked in the area, noticed Deputy Dial's silent homage, so he walked up behind her and held his umbrella over her for 30 minutes. People noticed and started taking pictures, which then went viral online.

Allen told Dial, "The procession was just about one of the most powerful kind of emotional displays that I hope I never see again, and I was just really impressed that you were out there paying your respects to Sgt. Carter."

Deputy Dial told *WABC*, "It meant a lot, in ways you can't even put into words...People do care about us, and that's very uplifting. It can be very easy to get jaded in this job, so it's nice to see the good in people and to be reminded of that, too."

You have been a refuge to the poor, a refuge to the needy in their distress, a shelter from the rainstorm. (Isaiah 25:4)

Inspire me to perform simple acts of kindness, Lord.

Redemption in Veterans Court

Since 2015, millions of people have viewed the viral video of Rebecca Mills, age 42, getting into a brawl with another woman in a Beech Grove, Indiana Walmart. Mills had served "nine honorable years" in the Navy, noted the *Indianapolis Star*, but had hit a low point in her life due to a battle with depression, migraine headaches, and a painful divorce. She became dependent on pills, which led her to an even lower point: breaking into a stranger's home and stealing some items.

However, that was also a turning point. Mills said, "I look at getting arrested as a blessing in disguise. I was a sick person who needed and wanted to get well."

Mills was assigned to the Indianapolis Veterans Court, which "helps veterans and current service members grapple with...substance abuse and mental health problems." Counseling and support helped her give up drugs, find a job, rebuild loving relationships, and even start going to church. She said, "[Veterans Court] met me where I was and accepted me with all my flaws. They believed in me when I didn't believe in myself."

Put away your former way of life...Be renewed in the spirit of your minds. (Ephesians 4:22-23)

Lead troubled souls to second chances, Jesus.

"Miracles do Happen Here"

"Miracles do happen here." That's the motto of Chris Miracle's family's towing and recovery truck company in Baker County, Florida. One fateful Thursday evening, Chris had the chance to experience this inspirational tagline become a reality.

As he was driving along County Road 125, he saw a distant flickering of lights. Chris immediately followed his gut, turning his truck around to follow the source of the light, which led him to a clearing near the local Manntown Church.

There, he saw a sedan plunged "nose down" into a creek. As it turned out, a 77-year-old woman, who wishes to remain anonymous, had veered off the road after a problem with her medication. Having no cell phone or means of opening the door, she put her hazard lights on for visibility until help arrived.

Chris, who is also a volunteer fireman, promptly hauled the car to safety, and called an ambulance for the lady, whose injuries were thankfully minor. "God's work," Miracle concluded to *I-TEAM* news anchor Vic Micolucci. "Right place, right time. It was meant to be."

The human mind plans the way, but the Lord directs the steps. (Proverbs 16:9)

Lord, guide me down the right paths today.

An Appointment That Can't Be Missed

On his Facebook page, Deacon Greg Kandra shared a touching story from a site called The Fabulous Fifties. It told of an elderly man rushing to his 8:00 a.m. doctor's appointment because he had another important appointment on his schedule.

When the doctor inquired what it was, the man explained that he goes to the hospital every morning so he can eat breakfast with his wife. The physician asked about her condition, so the elderly man told him she had Alzheimer's disease and had not recognized him for some time.

"The doctor asked why he continues going if she has no idea who he is. The old man replied, 'Because I still know who she is.'"

Alzheimer's and dementia are devastating conditions for both patients and their families. Still, God's love can be made present through the actions of devoted family and friends. If you know anyone dealing with these issues, reach out to offer a helping hand and compassionate heart.

Husbands, love your wives, just as Christ loved the church and gave Himself up for her. (Ephesians 5:25)

Send comfort and strength to families dealing with Alzheimer's and dementia, Divine Healer.

Three Dollars and a Tank Full of Hope

When struggling 75-year-old widow Delores Marotta only had three dollars to pay for gas to get to and from her doctor's appointment, a police officer added 20 dollars to help fill her tank.

Officer Todd Bing had no idea he was going to change a life when he walked into a metro Detroit gas station on August 31, 2018. However, when he overheard Marotta only putting three dollars worth of gas into her tank, he insisted on supplementing the rest and also offered to pump her gas for her.

The 17-year police veteran told *WXYZ-TV* that it was just one citizen helping another: "That interaction...in the moment it had nothing to do with being a police officer...It was just a human thing."

The moment was captured in a photo by the gas station attendant, and it inspired the community to raise money to help Marotta. When reflecting on Officer Bing's small act of kindness, Marotta said, "God must have sent him here for me."

You will be enriched in every way for your great generosity, which will produce thanksgiving to God through us. (2 Corinthians 9:11)

Lord, help me to weave acts of kindness into my daily life.

Catholic School Roots of Deaf Actress

Even though she graduated from Chicago's Holy Trinity School for the Deaf almost 30 years ago, actress Lauren Teruel Ridloff still describes the staff as "family." The actress, known from TV's *The Walking Dead,* visited the school (now called Children of Peace) to talk with current students about her life.

A profile in *The Catholic Spirit* notes that teachers welcomed Lauren and her family when she was there, helping everyone learn to communicate with each other.

Since she describes herself as "painfully shy," Lauren didn't seriously pursue an acting career until 2017, when an unexpected opportunity led her to star in Broadway's *Children of a Lesser God.* She acknowledged that her deafness is a challenge, but also described it as "a gift."

Her message to students was one of encouragement: "Even if we're feeling scared about something, we don't let that stop us. If someone asks us to do something new, we should do it. And if we make a mistake…mistakes are good. When you mess up, you learn something."

I can do all things through Him who strengthens me. (Philippians 4:12)

Help me learn from my mistakes and move forward, Jesus.

I Am God's Storyteller

Jesus may be the world's best storyteller ever, so it's fitting that His followers, who want to reach others with His message and mission, emulate His example. That's the case with Lisa Hendey, who wrote the children's book *I Am God's Storyteller.*

During a *Christopher Closeup* interview, Hendey said that her visits to schools taught her that the next generation needs to understand Scripture's stories and learn that they themselves have a role to play in the storytelling process, be it through words or actions. As she writes, "God sent storytellers before me, to teach me the truth and to show me all the ways that God's stories could be shared. When we tell God's stories, we storytellers help the world around us to know His love."

Hendey's book then touches on the lives of biblical figures, before relating that kids today can be storytellers in their own unique way. The book concludes, "My stories are God's stories, told my way, with the imagination He gave especially to me, and the love He pours into each of us. I am God's storyteller—and you are, too. Let's go share His story of love today."

The style of the story delights the ears of those who read the work. (2 Maccabees 15:39)

Teach me to be Your storyteller, Jesus.

Two Ways of Growing Old

When he died at age 90, Jean Vanier was described by *The New York Times* as a "Savior of People on the Margins." That's because he founded L'Arche, an international group of communities for people with developmental disabilities.

Vanier was also an author and philosopher with powerful insights on God and life. Here is one of his observations about aging: "Old age is the most precious time of life, the one nearest eternity.

"There are two ways of growing old. There are old people who are anxious and bitter, living in the past and illusion, who criticize everything that goes on around them...they are shut away in their sadness and loneliness, shriveled up in themselves.

"But there are also old people with a child's heart, who have used their freedom from function and responsibility to find a new youth. They have the wonder of a child, but the wisdom of maturity as well."

Even though our outer nature is wasting away, our inner nature is being renewed day by day. (2 Corinthians 4:16)

Keep my spirit youthful as I grow older, Jesus.

Laundromat Solves a Problem

Imagine being bullied for not having clean clothes to wear to school. When Akbar Cook, the principal of Newark, New Jersey's West Side High School, discovered this was the reason 85% of his students were being considered chronically absent, he resolved to do something about this massive problem.

For two years, Cook lobbied for help and eventually secured a $20,000 grant from PSE&G. This helped transform the high school football locker room into a free on-campus laundromat with commercial grade machines. After this story initially aired on *CBS2 News* in 2018, additional donations came in to help fund this important initiative.

Cook said, "Confidence is a big thing with everyone...You can get up and go to the teacher's board in front and know no one is going to make fun of stains on your pants... I think this is definitely going to lead to a new generation of empathy."

Cook's students are writing thank you notes to show their appreciation to all who have donated to the laundry program.

So if I, your Lord and Teacher, have washed your feet, you also ought to wash one another's feet. (John 13:14)

God, help me to not judge others in their hour of need.

Telephone "Takes Over" TV Set

Many years ago, the electronics era threw a momentary monkey wrench into a Tulsa couple's marital bliss.

Coming home to find their television blaring, each blamed the other for leaving it on. They were still arguing about it the next morning, when the telephone rang. Then, the TV suddenly switched on.

The couple discovered that the telephone's ring would turn the set on, change channels, adjust the volume, and even turn it off. Telephone repairmen solved the problem by changing the frequency of the phone's ring, which was too closely tuned to the remote control of the set.

Marital problems, like other difficulties in human relations, are not usually so mysterious or solved so readily. Correct small misunderstandings before they get out of hand. Avoid sarcasm like the plague. Go out of your way to pay honest tribute.

Whether in marriage or with friends, such an approach can bring God's blessings in abundance.

Do not find fault before you investigate. (Sirach 11:7)

Spur us to show to our fellow human beings the kind of compassion You have for us, Lord.

The Sheep Hear Her Voice

Technology expert Katie Linendoll travels 300 days a year to get stories featured on the *Today Show, Inside Edition,* the *Weather Channel,* and more. But no matter where she is in the world, she makes it a point to never miss Sunday Mass, even when flocks of sheep are blocking her way.

During a *Christopher Closeup* interview with host Tony Rossi, Katie recalled a trip to the Faroe Islands, a collection of 18 islands, connected by tunnels, between Sweden and Iceland. She said, "It's one of my favorite destinations to detox from technology and appreciate Mother Nature...and God's glory."

The name "Faroe Islands" means "Sheep Islands," which is appropriate. "There are 45,000 people there," Katie said, "but 85,000 sheep!" There is also only one Catholic church, but Katie managed to drive there despite the sheep blocking the roads.

She said, "What's cool about the tradition of the Catholic Church is, no matter where you are and no matter what language it's in, we're all celebrating the same Mass that week...It's been awesome carrying that faith thread through and through."

The Sabbath was made for humankind, and not humankind for the Sabbath. (Mark 2:27)

Help me to keep the Sabbath day holy, Creator.

Three Wooden Crosses

Hardhats, American flags, and handwritten notes lie beneath the three wooden crosses planted in the ground beside Highway 77 and Talton Drive in Chipley, Florida. It's the site where three electrical line workers—Bo Ussery, George Cesil, and Ryan Barrett—were killed in a hit-and-run accident while they worked to restore power after Hurricane Michael.

Writer Sean Dietrich was standing by the crosses when a trucker drove up and commented, "Them linemen were working seventeen-hour days. They came from all over the nation after the storm, worked like dogs. They were good, good men."

"Line workers flooded the town by the multitudes," reported Dietrich. "They swarmed around Chipley like the heavenly host, wearing hardhats."

Dietrich concluded, "I never knew these men, but I know what they stood for, and so do you. They represent the kind I come from, whose collars are blue. They were everything magnificent about our society. In fact, they were the ones who built it. One utility pole at a time."

Render service with enthusiasm, as to the Lord and not to men and women. (Ephesians 6:7)

Lord, may we appreciate the hard work of all laborers.

A Deacon's Love

Deacon Larry Day of Springfield, Ohio, has ministered to many different kinds of people, but one of the most unusual friendships he has struck up is with Josh Estes.

Josh is a convicted murderer and an inmate at an Ohio correctional facility. Years earlier, he was wrapped up in a world of drugs and admitted to killing a man. Josh and Deacon Larry told their story to the *Cincinnati Enquirer.*

Deacon Larry is a former teacher and principal who worked with troubled kids throughout his career. When he became a Catholic deacon, he began working in prisons, which is where he met Josh. The two struck up an unlikely friendship.

Josh calls Deacon Larry two to three times a day, and they talk about everything. Even though Josh still has difficulties in prison, he leans on Deacon Larry. Both men say that God put them into each other's lives, and both are focused on the hope that Josh can turn his life around.

About midnight Paul and Silas were praying and singing hymns to God, and the prisoners were listening to them. (Acts 16:25)

May I remember that nobody is beyond Your redemption, Lord.

Remember to Assist Grace

On a recent September 11th, a friend showed New Yorker Elizabeth Scalia a picture of the gorgeous sky in Manhattan that morning. Scalia's thoughts immediately went back to the sky on that date in 2001, when terror and death struck the city.

Recalling 9/11 on *Aleteia*, Scalia wrote, "Similarly, I cannot look up at the sky and see [a plane's] contrails without remembering how eerily empty, silent and blue were the heavens [that day]…All air traffic had ceased…My husband was stranded in Atlanta, and I was grateful to know it. But the sky was so quiet. The air had no hum.

"Every time [the anniversary] happens, that old sense of helplessness skims over me…and I find myself thinking of those I love. The feeling doesn't last long, but it still makes me aware of the precariousness of life, and prompts me to offer up a prayer, 'Have mercy on us, and on the whole world.'

"It is always a moment of dull grief, and a reminder that life really can be 'nasty, brutish, and short,' and that what peace and beauty we can bring into it assists grace as it may."

Do not close your ear to my cry. (Lamentations 3:56)

May I assist Your grace today and every day, Creator.

Moving Forward After 9/11

On September 11, 2001, Janet Alonso died in the terrorist attacks on the World Trade Center. Her husband Robert would now have to raise their two-year-old daughter Victoria and their baby boy Robby, who had Down syndrome, by himself.

Robert gave up running his family pizza business in order to focus on his children. He told *American Story* author Bob Dotson, "I owe it to my children to be around. If I buried my grief in work, my kids would lose both their parents."

Robert made sure to share experiences of joy with Victoria and Robby, even silly things like jumping on the back of a grocery cart with the kids inside and rolling them through the supermarket parking lot. Robert said, "When my kids smile, the terrorists lose. The people who killed Janet wanted to destroy our happy lives. They lost. We won."

After 9/11, Robert taught his children to treat every moment like an unopened gift. "I don't want to be the rain cloud in my family," he said. "I want to give my kids the incentive to do things and go forward."

He will wipe every tear from their eyes. Death will be no more. (Revelation 21:4)

Help the grieving move through their pain, Redeemer.

Let Us Do Good, Part One

On Sept. 11, 2001, Brooklyn-based firefighter Stephen Siller got the call that a plane had hit the World Trade Center. He drove the truck to the Battery Tunnel to get into Manhattan, only to find the tunnel shut down for security reasons. So Stephen strapped 60 pounds of gear to his back and ran through the tunnel to join rescue efforts at the Trade Center. The husband and father of five was killed when the Towers collapsed.

Stephen's six siblings were determined to keep his memory alive in a way that would help others. In 2002, they created the Stephen Siller Tunnel to Towers Foundation as a New York City-based charity run that retraced Stephen's steps on 9/11. But under the leadership of Stephen's brother, Chairman/CEO Frank Siller, the Foundation has grown into a national force for good.

They build specially adapted smart homes for members of the military who have lost arms and legs, pay off mortgages for families of first responders who have been killed in the line of duty, and pay off mortgages for Gold Star families whose loved ones made the ultimate sacrifice in service to their country.

No one has greater love than this, to lay down one's life for one's friends. (John 15:13)

Bless the victims and survivors of the 9/11 attacks, Jesus.

Let Us Do Good, Part Two

"While we have time, let us do good." Frank Siller heard that quote, attributed to St. Francis of Assisi, quite often from his parents when he was growing up. It serves as the foundation of the work he's done in memory of his late brother, Stephen, who was killed on 9/11.

During an interview on *Christopher Closeup*, Frank recalled that his parents, George and Mae Siller, were devout Catholics who were both a part of the Third Order of St. Francis. "They were such giving people," he said.

"My parents had seven kids. We were very poor, but we were never too poor to do something for our neighbors. I remember one Thanksgiving: my oldest brother, Russ, told [us] that the neighbors didn't have anything for Thanksgiving. [My father] took our turkey dinner and gave it to our neighbors."

Frank also noted that his father used to visit the hospital to talk or pray with the sick. He said, "This is the foundation of our family, of seeing these good, simple works and these acts of kindness and love that we were all brought up with."

We are what He has made us, created in Christ Jesus for good works. (Ephesians 2:10)

While I have time, Jesus, let me do good.

Let Us Do Good, Part Three

Because of his selfless work as Chairman/ CEO of the Stephen Siller Tunnel to Towers Foundation, Frank Siller received the 2019 Christopher Leadership Award. In his acceptance speech, he shared a lesson he learned from his parents.

When Frank celebrated his First Communion, he received many cards with money as gifts. As an eight year old, he was thrilled to have $26 in cash! That night, Frank's parents asked him, "What do you think you should do with the money? We know a very poor family that could use some help."

Knowing how devoted his parents were to helping the poor, Frank felt scared that his parents would ask him to give it all away. But they only asked him to donate $13, which left him ecstatic at the time. But here's the point of the story, as he explained at the Christopher Awards ceremony: "I don't remember what I did with the $13 I kept. I have never forgotten about the $13 that I gave away. And that was the lesson that was taught to me: the lesson of giving and doing for other people."

The righteous give and do not hold back. (Proverbs 21:26)

May I always "give" and "do" for other people, Lord.

Bus Driver Goes Above and Beyond

Natalie Barnes, a bus driver in Milwaukee, Wisconsin, noticed something was wrong with Richard, one of her frequent passengers. In conversation, he revealed that he had just become homeless, Barnes told *CNN*.

She knew she had to do something, so she began by offering him warmth on her bus and food when he was hungry. But she knew something else had to happen, so she reached out to a friend to get Richard into a community shelter.

Barnes was recently honored by her employer, the Transit Authority, for going "above and beyond." She said, "At some point in our lives, everybody needs help. I wanted to do what I could to help Richard in some way."

She didn't just hand Richard off to someone else, though. Throughout the process, Natalie struck up a friendship with him and calls him frequently to see how he's doing. She is happy to report that he's doing well and life is getting better for him.

Is not this the fast...to share your bread with the hungry, and bring the homeless poor into your house? (Isaiah 58:6-7)

Help me be generous to those in need, Lord, and to do what I can to help them, even in a small way.

Alone in the Lunch Room No More

Andrew Kirby of Boiling Springs, South Carolina, was a high school sophomore who had gotten used to eating lunch alone. He was shy, didn't make friends easily, and had some medical challenges. His mother prayed that someone would befriend him.

Her prayers were answered when a group of student council members invited Andrew to join them for lunch each day. The story was recently featured on *CBS This Morning* in a series on small acts of kindness that go a long way.

The student council members had decided that nobody should sit by themselves for lunch. They started inviting anyone who was alone to join them. Teenagers can form cliques and stay away from people who are different, but this group decided to set a new tone for their school, making kindness one of their hallmarks.

"Everyone needs to have someone," one student said in response to the story, "and anyone can be a help with that." The gesture has meant that Andrew has a new group of friends.

When you come together, each one has a hymn, a lesson, a revelation, a tongue, or an interpretation. Let all things be done for building up. (1 Corinthians 14:26)

Let me be a friend to someone who is lonely, Jesus.

No One Dies Alone

In 2001, Nurse Sandra Clarke was working at an Oregon hospital. Her shift was going normally, when one of her patients, an elderly man, asked her to sit with him for a while. Of course she was busy, so she told him she'd come back to sit when she had a minute. When she returned, he had passed away.

Clarke wanted to make sure that would never happen again, so she started "No One Dies Alone," a movement to train volunteers to be with dying people during their final moments. The movement has spread to hospitals around the country.

In a story on *Aleteia*, Georgetown University hospital volunteers describe their experiences with the dying: holding hands, playing music, reading poetry or sacred texts. Each one is different, and each person leaves the world with some company.

"I just think that human presence is so important at the end of someone's life," Beth Orrell, a palliative care nurse, said. "People are not alone when they're born, and they should not be alone when they die."

If we have been united with Him in a death like His, we will...be united with Him in a resurrection like His. (Romans 6:5)

May I be an instrument of Your grace, Lord, to those at the end of their earthly lives.

Second Helpings Offers Recipe for Success

Chef Kathy Jones of Indianapolis has held just about every job in the restaurant business: from dishwasher, to line cook, to chef, to owner. One of her most rewarding roles was that of volunteer, helping train a new batch of chefs through Second Helpings.

Second Helpings is a program for people who are looking to get a new start in life. It is part job-training, part hunger relief. Through the culinary education program, students learn practical kitchen skills. Their lessons each day are to make meals for soup kitchens and residential programs. Their resource is donated surplus and perishable food that might otherwise go to waste.

In 2017, Jones made her volunteer work her full-time job when she was hired as the executive chef for Second Helpings, overseeing all their kitchen work. Speaking to the *Indianapolis Star*, she said, "Transforming lives through the power of food—there's really nothing else like what we do in the country."

Do not turn your face away from anyone who is poor, and the face of God will not be turned away from you. (Tobit 4:7)

Jesus, may I share my joy and good fortune with those in need!

Football Rookie Looks Out For a Friend

After football linebacker Dre Greenlaw was drafted for the San Francisco 49ers, a father thanked the young rookie for protecting his daughter several years ago.

Following the NFL draft in April 2019, Gerry Dales came forward on Twitter to publicly thank Greenlaw for an incident four years earlier, when his daughter was a freshman at the University of Arkansas.

Dales' daughter, who Greenlaw knew from high school, had been drinking at a college party when a young man slipped something in her drink when she wasn't paying attention. This man, unknown to her, was trying to take her out of the bar when Greenlaw intervened. Dales wrote, "[Greenlaw] stopped the guy and said, 'She's not going anywhere.'"

Dales never talked about this story previously because he didn't want to get Greenlaw in trouble for being at that party. But now he said, "Do me a favor. Root for Dre. He's a good kid with a good heart."

Greenlaw, now 21, acknowledged the story and humbly said, "I was just looking out for a friend."

You will be safe with me. (1 Samuel 22:23)

Lord, thank You for protecting me and keeping me safe.

Sanctuary from Stress

Rabbi Abraham Heschel called the Sabbath "a sanctuary in time." In an age when we rush to cram as much activity as possible into every minute, it's especially important to have a time of refuge from constant "doing," to have some time for "being."

A day of "sanctuary" gives us rest emotionally as well as physically. It's a time of healing, a time to spend on our relationship with ourselves, our family and friends, and God.

This time-out can help keep the stress of overfull schedules from damaging our physical, emotional, and spiritual health.

The Sabbath can free us from preoccupations that separate us from God's healing presence, and renew us with peace that only God can give.

If you...call the Sabbath a delight and the holy day of the Lord honorable...you shall take delight in the Lord. (Isaiah 58:13,14)

God, may I set aside moments of silence to seek the refuge of Your loving presence.

Two Ears and One Mouth

There's an old adage: "God gave us two ears and only one mouth, so we can listen twice as much as we speak." However, being a good listener is sometimes easier said than done.

In a post for *Busted Halo,* Elizabeth Manneh discusses ways that we can offer a listening ear to someone who needs to talk about their problems, and how that "can make all the difference to how they feel."

Some ways to improve our listening abilities is to remove distractions, pay attention to your body language, watch your tone of voice, focus on listening, and don't interrupt even if you may disagree with what they are saying.

Asking questions is also a useful tool to help clarify a situation with open-ended inquiries like, "How did that make you feel?" These types of questions help the speaker reflect on his/her own experience.

Depending on the situation, there's always room to pray together, and as a good listener you will help others unburden themselves and find solutions to their own problems.

Happy is the one who finds a friend, and the one who speaks to attentive listeners. (Sirach 25:9)

Jesus, teach me to be a good listener to my friends.

Troubled Girls Find Love

When three teenage girls came to the home of Mrs. Donna Gort many years ago, one was an addict, one was a burglar, and one was a prostitute. A year later, one girl was a university honor student, another was a responsible city hall employee, and the third had graduated from nursing school.

Gort, of Seattle, Washington, had been handling problem girls for more than eight years. "I don't run an institution," explained Gort, a former piano teacher. "And this is not a halfway house or whatever you want to call it. I run a home. We are a family. The girls who come to me need something, someplace, someone stable to anchor to."

Christ's words, "I was a stranger and you welcomed Me," (Matthew 25:36) have as many applications as people have needs. If we haven't found someone to whom we can open our homes—or at least our hearts—perhaps we are not looking hard enough.

Welcome one another, therefore, just as Christ has welcomed you. (Romans 15:7)

Jesus, help us find ways to continue Your concern for those in need.

Bonnie Hunt's Teen Creed

Actress, writer, and director Bonnie Hunt grew up as the sixth of seven children in an Irish Catholic family in Chicago. Right before all the kids turned 13, their mother, Alice, would have them memorize something called "The Teen Creed" to give them guidance on how to live their lives.

While appearing on Phil Keoghan's online talk show, Bonnie said she still follows that creed and recited it in its entirety:

- "Don't let your parents down; they brought you up."
- "Be humble enough to obey; you may give orders someday."
- "Choose companions with care; you become who they are."
- "Choose only a date that would make a good mate."
- "Be master of your habits or they will master you."
- "Don't be a showoff when you drive; drive with safety and arrive."
- "Stand for something or you'll fall for anything."
- "Don't let the crowd pressure you."

Train children in the right way, and when old, they will not stray. (Proverbs 22:6)

Give parents the wisdom to raise good children, Father.

Coffee Shop Grace

Sarah Hart went to a local coffee shop, but the young man who took her order just couldn't get it right. He looked embarrassed and flustered, and she felt sorry for him. After engaging him in small talk, he revealed that he felt lost and didn't know what he wanted out of life.

Recalling the incident on her Facebook page, Sarah told him, "When I was younger, I spent a lot of time trying to kick in doors. It was exhausting. Looking back, the doors I tried to kick in never really opened. Only the ones that God opened for me...seem to have worked out. Maybe don't try so hard, don't beat your head against any walls. Just look for the doors that God is opening for you, and walk through them."

The young man was so appreciative of Sarah's message and revealed he had just started going to church lately. She concluded, "It was such a lovely moment this morning, looking at that young face, seeing myself reflected back, being able to share a little bit of grace with each other."

Let no evil talk come out of your mouths, but only what is useful for building up...so that your words may give grace to those who hear. (Ephesians 4:29)

May I share words of grace with someone today, Lord.

The Hospital Pub

Dementia patients often get agitated in the evenings, a condition known as sundowning. But at Swansea's Cefn Coed Hospital in Wales, that problem has diminished due to a unique experiment: a pub in the dementia ward.

Only non-alcoholic drinks are served in "The Derwen Arms Pub," as it's called. But the socializing the environment allows the 20 male patients to do has been life-changing.

Clinical lead Dawn Griffin explained to *TheAlzheimersSite.com,* "In the evenings some of our gentlemen can get unsettled and agitated. They think they've finished their shift for the day and they are of the generation where they would go to the pub for a pint with their friends after work. We thought—what better way to help them than to get a pub on the ward?"

The pub looks like the real thing, with tables, chairs, coasters, and even plastic darts. "The reaction has been huge," says Griffin. "They're socializing well. They have a day area and they use it, but they often ask when the pub is opening. They can take their relatives and friends there for a pint when they visit."

How very good and pleasant it is when kindred live together in unity! (Psalm 133:1)

Bring dementia patients the community they need, Lord.

How to Build Community, Part One

On the cold, somber day of her brother's funeral, Jenny Anderson felt an immense sense of loss. But she also witnessed a testament to what made her brother's life special—and she decided to make some changes in her own.

The mourners at the Maplewood, New Jersey church included his wife and four daughters, along with hundreds of people whose lives he had touched as a friend, architect, lacrosse coach, mentor, and more.

"In seeing his community," wrote Anderson on *Quartz*, "I became acutely aware of the feeling that I did not have my own. I had friends and a loving family. But...I spent my days focused on optimizing myself: Endlessly working and improving...It was the only way I knew how to be. Compete. Excel. Win."

In being by her brother's side through his cancer battle, Anderson absorbed a new vision of community, grounded in neighbors selflessly giving of their time and talent to care for a family they were not related to. But what are the steps toward building this kind of community? More tomorrow...

Let us consider how to provoke one another to love and good deeds. (Hebrews 10:24)

Help me give selflessly to my neighbor, Messiah.

How to Build Community, Part Two

In seeing her brother's neighbors care for his family through his cancer battle, Jenny Anderson learned that "community is about a series of small choices and everyday actions: how to spend a Saturday, what to do when a neighbor falls ill...Knowing others and being known; investing in somewhere instead of trying to be everywhere. Communities are built, like Legos, one brick at a time."

At the same time, Anderson's research led her to discover that our social networks—the actual human kind, not the social media kind—have decreased by one-third since 1985. We aren't devoting enough attention to developing deep connections with other people, and that is harming our bodies and souls.

A research study in Germany followed a group of people pursuing greater happiness. Some focused on self-improvement, such as making more money, while others simply spent more time with friends and family. In the end, the "friends and family" group achieved more happiness. So how did Anderson translate these findings to her life? More tomorrow...

Turn to me and be gracious to me, for I am lonely and afflicted. (Psalm 25:16)

Help me to make friends and be a friend, Prince of Peace.

How to Build Community, Part Three

Following her brother's funeral, Jenny Anderson returned to her husband and children in London and approached life a little differently. Writing for *Quartz,* she said, "We moved into a new house, and I introduced myself to my neighbors. I decided to act as if we were staying there forever, even though I had no idea how long we were staying. I could no longer afford to always be looking ahead to the next place, or job, or project."

Anderson even quit her job writing for *The New York Times* because she didn't want to be called away from home so frequently. She and her family got to really know the people in their community and developed stronger bonds than they ever had before, bonds that would sustain them through good times and bad.

Anderson concludes that her new approach "has made everything richer. A problem shared is a problem halved, my kids were taught at school. Communities do that too…Keep connecting with people, and in time, you will have a community."

Rejoice with those who rejoice, weep with those who weep. (Romans 12:15)

Fill my life with rich relationships, Jesus.

Monastic Hospitality

Monasteries are known for their hospitality to travelers, but in 1945 a monastery in Bavaria extended that hospitality to help heal the thousands of displaced people who had survived the Nazi concentration camps.

St. Ottilien's was a 100-year-old monastic complex when it was seized by the Germans to serve as a military hospital. In the years after the war, it became a displaced persons camp that welcomed over 5,000 people, many of whom were former Jewish prisoners.

Jewish doctors set up a hospital, a school, and a maternity ward (450 babies were born there). Many others came because they were refugees who had settled in the Soviet Union and were making their way back to their German and western-European homes. St. Ottilien's became known for its good medical care.

On *Aleteia,* a current monk of the Abbey calls those three years "perhaps the most important event in its existence," and a shining example of personal and cultural healing when it was very much needed.

Do not neglect to show hospitality to strangers, for by doing that some have entertained angels without knowing it. (Hebrews 13:2)

Let a generous and hospitable heart guide me today, Lord.

Faith Leads to Well-Being

It may take extra effort to make faith a regular part of your kid's lives, but a 2018 Harvard study demonstrates that the long-term effects are definitely beneficial. As reported by the website *The Stream,* "The researchers followed 5,000 young people for between eight to 14 years, controlling for variables such as maternal health, socioeconomic status, and histories of substance abuse or symptoms of depression."

"Researchers found that people who attended religious services weekly or who practiced prayer or meditation daily in their youth reported having a higher life satisfaction and positivity in their 20s. Individuals were found less likely to smoke, have symptoms of depression, use illicit drugs, or have sexually transmitted infections than people who engaged in less regular spiritual practices."

Ying Chen, the study's first author, said, "Many children are raised religiously, and our study shows that this can powerfully affect their health behaviors, mental health, and overall happiness and well-being."

Remember the Sabbath day, and keep it holy. (Exodus 20:8)

May I be a model of faith to young people, Jesus.

Tyler Trent Made a Difference

Many people throughout the country got to know Tyler Trent through his struggle with cancer. *Indianapolis Star* columnist Gregg Doyel wrote numerous pieces on Tyler: how cancer came into his life at age 15; how he beat it, only to have it return years later; how he prayed that if he was going to have cancer, may God use it to make a difference for others.

God seemed to answer that prayer. Tyler's infectious positivity drew others to him and brought out the best in people. His story spread far and wide. College football coaches, *ESPN* personalities, professional athletes, students, and neighbors all came out to help Tyler, and kept coming back. They were touched by his life, which ended all too soon at age 20 in 2018.

Doyel wrote, "What is it they say? That the Lord works in mysterious ways? Tyler Trent made an impact...If you were one of the hundreds in his army—maybe hundreds of thousands—take a moment. Feel like a hero. Because you made Tyler Trent smile."

The last enemy to be destroyed is death. (1 Corinthians 15:26)

Jesus, may I trust in Your eternal promise always!

A Pep Talk from the Terminator

Born with intellectual challenges, Ephraim Mohlakane of South Africa did poorly in school growing up. As he shared with the website *Humans of New York,* he kept asking God: "Why is this happening to me?" His teachers directed him to learn some handiwork instead, but he felt angry about his situation.

Then, he had a life-changing encounter with Arnold Schwarzenegger, who came to South Africa for an event. Ephraim said, "I told him my entire story, and he said: 'Look here, I am the Terminator, but today I am your friend. Listen to me. You are not strong in academics, but that is just one thing. It's nothing to worry about. You are a very strong man. You can't hate yourself for the rest of your life. It is time for you to move on.' From that moment I began to accept myself."

Ephraim now has a house, a family, a career as a soccer coach, and is involved with Special Olympics. His son, he notes, is very smart: "I tell him: 'Tumi, I never finished school. But God is amazing. He has made you strong where I am weak.'"

[Speak] only what is useful for building up, as there is need, so that your words may give grace to those who hear. (Ephesians 4:29)

May I always offer others encouragement and hope, Lord.

Nine-Year-Old Fights Homelessness

You don't have to be an adult to make a difference. Fourth-grade-student Jahkil Naeem Jackson proved this by starting his own non-profit organization, Project I Am, to help fight homelessness.

Jackson was always drawn to helping the homeless in his Chicago hometown, but wanted to make a bigger impact. "My parents helped me start my own organization, called Project I Am, so that I can collect donations from people who want to help," Jackson wrote for *TheRenewalProject.com*.

Through Project I Am, Jackson distributes "blessing bags" filled with toiletries. He chose toiletries because many people on the streets lack basic necessities, such as toothpaste and a toothbrush, to get them through the day. His goal is to distribute 5,000 bags this year and to expand to other communities.

When Jackson tells his story to kids, he says, "You don't have to wait until you are an adult to become an entrepreneur and changemaker, you can do it now!"

To the present hour we are hungry and thirsty, we are poorly clothed...and homeless. (1 Corinthians 4:11)

Lord, please bless our youth since they are the future.

A Million Dollar Teacher

Franciscan Brother Peter Tabichi teaches high school in a remote African village in Kenya, where drought and hardship are common. A humble and inspiring man, he has given away most of his earnings to the poor. His commitment to helping others recently earned him one of the most prestigious awards in teaching: a one million dollar prize from the Varkey Foundation.

Many of Tabichi's students are orphans or only have one parent. He has inspired many of them to stay in school and go on to college. He told *CBS News,* "At times, whenever I reflect on the challenges they face, I shed tears." Tabichi plans to give away the prize money to the poor and to help improve the school where he teaches.

When Tabichi went to Dubai to accept the award, it was his first time traveling on an airplane. In his acceptance speech at the ceremony, he thanked his father, a primary school teacher, for instilling Christian values in him. The room erupted in applause when Tabichi's father took the stage to hold the award.

The teaching of the wise is a fountain of life. (Proverbs 13:14)

Lord, bless all who taught me and showed me the right paths in life.

Light and Dark

One of the inspirations for singer-songwriter PJ Anderson's album *Light and Dark* came when he stumbled across the Instagram page of acclaimed photographer Eric Brown. There, he found a photo of Brown's third child, a daughter named Pearl Joy, who was born with a rare disease of the nervous system.

Along with the picture was a letter that read, "Dear Doctor, you probably don't remember us, but five years ago you recommended that my wife and I abort our baby. I'm writing to tell you that you were wrong. You said she wouldn't live more than a few seconds, and she just turned five years old."

PJ was moved to tears looking through Brown's page, witnessing the powerful love this family practiced in caring for Pearl Joy. During a *Christopher Closeup* interview, PJ said, "That's what inspired my song 'I Will Sing Forever.' It's about praising God always, not just in good times...Say a prayer for Pearl Joy's family. She passed away a couple of months ago. I can only imagine what the family's going through. They inspired me to realize that you always need to have hope in the Lord."

Let us hold fast to...our hope without wavering, for He who has promised is faithful. (Hebrews 10:23)

Be my light in the darkness, Prince of Peace.

Beyond Good Intentions

Good intentions are no substitute for worthwhile acts, but they can often be the motivating forces that give direction and meaning to our lives. Consider these resolutions by early American theologian Jonathan Edwards:

"Resolved, to live with all my might while I do live.

"Resolved, never to lose one moment of time, to improve it in the most profitable way I can.

"Resolved, never to do anything I should despise or think meanly of in another.

"Resolved, never to do anything out of revenge.

"Resolved, never to do anything which I should be afraid to do if it were the last hour of my life."

God endowed us with the power to know and to love, so that we might influence for the better the people and events we encounter. Resolve, with God's help, to leave the world better for your having been in it. Then, do your best and leave the results in His hands.

Reflect on the statutes of the Lord, and meditate at all times on His commandments. (Sirach 6:37)

Father, keep us mindful of who we are and why we're here.

On Kindness

Is being kind for weak and defenseless people who have few other choices? That's not what Adam Phillips and Barbara Taylor, the authors of *On Kindness,* concluded after researching how kindness has been viewed over the centuries.

The world's religions see kindness and charity as virtues. There are people, however, who believe human beings are—and must only be— self-interested, unless they're saints. But mere mortals know the rewards of kindness, too.

The authors quote a wealthy stockbroker after he started volunteering. He said, "Helping kids just makes me so happy. I feel like a different person."

The lesson? Be kind—despite the pressures of living in a competitive society. Be kind—despite the realities of cruelty and aggression in the world. Be kind—despite the temptation to act in only selfish ways. Be kind—and you will be both sharing and receiving a taste of the divine.

Whoever pursues righteousness and kindness will find life and honor. (Proverbs 21:20)

Grant us the wisdom, Holy Spirit, to appreciate the value of kindness.

The Prayers of a TV Legend

In an article for *Guideposts*, TV host Ed Sullivan recalled being laid off from a newspaper job when he was 18. He wondered how to handle this setback to his journalism career. The rosary he had learned at St. Mary's School in Port Chester, New York, came to mind, so he prayed. Sullivan wrote, "At this point...prayer helped me grow up. I quit feeling sorry for myself."

Soon after, Sullivan was hired by a New York City newspaper, and his goals were back on track. Looking back on those days, he noted that he had been blessed with a wonderful family all his life and that his TV show was like a gift from God.

He concluded, "It is my deepest belief that all of these things have resulted from prayer—not so much my own—but prayers of priests and nuns I have known and with whom I've been privileged to work. And certainly the prayers and intercession of those close to me who have died. So I know about the power of prayer. I know it keeps you steady, unshaken and able to take pain. I know it will guide you to your place—the place that will best help you grow."

God gave the growth. (1 Corinthians 3:6)

Help me to grow in challenging times, Jesus.

The Cuddle Watch

A police department worked a very different yet heartwarming shift by caring for an ailing baby. Axel Winch was born 13 weeks premature with a life-threatening intestinal condition, which made it necessary to airlift him from Grand Junction, Colorado, to a children's hospital in Aurora, over 200 miles away from his home.

"There were many times we didn't think he was going to live," Axel's father, Adam, told the *Today Show.*

After one of Axel's surgeries, Adam and his police officer wife, Melissa, were summoned back home for work. "We were afraid he was going to die while we were gone," Adam recalled.

To ensure Axel wasn't alone, more than 20 officers from the local Aurora precinct volunteered to help one of their own by taking turns reading books, singing songs, and cradling Axel as his health slowly improved. "We were overwhelmed with the support from people we didn't know," Adam said.

Axel is now home, and the Winches will always remember the kindness of those officers who became "the blue family."

Do not be afraid, for I will show you kindness. (2 Samuel 9:7)

Help me, dear Lord, to show kindness to strangers.

An Honest Prayer

Since winning *American Idol* in 2005, country music superstar Carrie Underwood found incredible success, selling 64 million records and counting. Yet she has experienced her share of heartaches, just like anyone else.

She and her husband, hockey star Mike Fisher, already had one son, Isaiah, when Underwood got pregnant again. She revealed to *CBS News* that she miscarried that child, then endured two more miscarriages over the next year.

Underwood had always been afraid to get angry at God because, overall, she had a blessed life. But this time, she indignantly prayed, "Why on Earth do I keep getting pregnant if I can't have a kid?...Either shut the door or let me have a kid."

"For the first time," continued Underwood, "I actually told God how I felt. I feel like we're supposed to do that."

Underwood went on to give birth to her second son, Jacob. She believes that God answered her raw, angry, honest prayer.

> **I say to God, my rock, "Why have you forgotten me?"...Why are you cast down, O my soul... Hope in God; for I shall again praise Him. (Psalm 42:9,11)**

Remind me to be honest with You always, Savior.

The Miracle in Room 106, Part One

After her birth in 1990, Shannon Hickey was diagnosed with a rare and fatal liver disease that would kill her without a liver transplant. Dr. Christoph Broelsch from Germany was working in Chicago, having obtained a government grant to perform living donor liver transplants for the first time in this country.

Shannon's mom, Kelly Ann, was a match for Shannon, so a portion of her liver was cut out and transplanted into her daughter. During this stressful time, Kelly Ann relied on her Catholic faith. She said, "I vowed to God that whatever He chose for Shannon's life, Thy will be done. Whether He chose to leave her with me or take her to heaven, I would praise His name."

Thankfully, Shannon survived and thrived as she was growing up. Her life was filled with the traditional circumstances of young adulthood: college, work, falling in love, and getting married. And in August 2018, Shannon and her husband, Jesse, even welcomed the newborn baby boy they were adopting into their home. It was at that time of joy that Shannon's health took a dark turn. More tomorrow...

When I am afraid, I put my trust in You. (Psalm 56:3)

May I trust in You, Father, in good times and bad.

The Miracle in Room 106, Part Two

Shannon had been on anti-rejection medication all her life, without incident. But in August 2018, her blood work showed she was enduring acute liver rejection. She was admitted into the hospital for a multi-day treatment that would wipe out her entire immune system.

The treatments were going well until September 5th. Shannon woke up in excruciating pain, at first in her head, then moving to her entire body. When Kelly Ann arrived, she was shocked at her daughter's condition and how quickly she was deteriorating. She started posting updates and prayer requests for Shannon's healing on her Facebook page.

Doctors were initially stumped at Shannon's condition, but came to find the cause was a rare form of meningitis brought on by the liver treatment. When Kelly Ann asked doctors if Shannon was dying, they gave her a vague answer and couldn't look her in the eye. Like she had done many years ago, Kelly Ann chose to surrender to God's will, despite the devastating possibility she might lose her daughter. And soon after, everything changed. More tomorrow...

Trust in the Lord with all your heart. (Proverbs 3:5)

Bring comfort to those enduring illness, Jesus.

The Miracle in Room 106, Part Three

A priest named Father Ridley arrived in Shannon's room to check on her, having given her the Anointing of the Sick the day before. Shannon, believing she was dying, managed to whisper to him, "I want to receive the Eucharist."

Kelly Ann said, "He was able to get the Eucharist on her tongue...and I said to her, 'Just let it dissolve.'"

Father Ridley left the room, and within about one minute, what Kelly Ann calls "the miracle in room 106" occurred. Almost instantly, Shannon experienced relief from her pain.

Kelly Ann attributes Shannon's survival to her receiving the Eucharist, as well as the prayers of others. She said, "Those exact moments when this happened is when the rosary was taking place back home, and people everywhere, from all different denominations of faith, were on their knees praying for my daughter...It can't be a coincidence."

In addition, said Kelly Ann, her husband asked doctors if they'd ever seen such a quick turnaround as Shannon had with the meningitis. Their answer: "Never." More tomorrow...

Are any among you sick?...Call for the elders of the church and have them pray over them. (James 5:14)

Thank You for the precious gift of faith, Savior.

The Miracle in Room 106, Part Four

Shannon's health has improved since that fateful day, and her liver is functioning well again. Though she never took life for granted, this experience has changed her perspective.

During a *Christopher Closeup* interview, she said, "It sounds cliché, but I hug people a little longer now. I cherish the small mundane moments. This morning, I was feeding my son and he was laughing at me, and it was such a small moment, but it made me think back to that day... I'm very fortunate."

Both Shannon and Kelly Ann are also in awe of the amount of people who prayed for Shannon's recovery. Kelly Ann noted, "There's no greater gift than when somebody says to you, 'I will pray for you. I will pray for your daughter.' And then they do it! I have at home my prayer board on the fridge. I pray fervently when I put people on this prayer board."

Shannon concludes, "Almost every time I go out, if I run into somebody, they bring up how they pray for me and they ask me how I'm doing, and that they had schools, had children, had people from across the world praying for me on that day, and even still. It blew my mind."

Pray for one another. (James 5:16)

Today, I offer my prayers for someone who is sick, Savior.

A Stranger Saves a Life

Crysti Shirley of Virginia was scrolling through her Facebook feed one day when something stopped her in her tracks. A former co-worker of Crysti's had posted that her cousin, Jim Abed, needed a kidney donation from a blood type O donor, and would likely die without it.

Jim had been on the donor list for two years, and was receiving dialysis several times a week. Though Crysti didn't personally know Jim, she told the *New York Post*, "I knew in my heart that I was meant to give him my kidney. I can't explain it."

After rounds of testing and blood work, Crysti turned out to be a perfect match. The operation went well and both recovered. Jim, a father of two, and his family were full of gratitude.

While Jim's family sees Crysti's action as a blessing, the opposite is true for her. "I am the one who received the blessing," she said. "My hope is that he can go out and live a full, beautiful life. God called me to do this; there is no thanks that's needed."

When was it that we saw You a stranger and welcomed You, or naked and gave You clothing? (Matthew 25:38)

Jesus, when I see someone in need, may I treat him or her like family.

Helping Others Tell Their Story

Sam Anderson of Wheaton, Illinois, is a successful student and a teenage manager of a varsity basketball team. He also has Down syndrome, and his story was recently featured on the *purpose2play* website.

In order to help people better understand those with Down syndrome, Sam started a blog called "In My Own Words." Through interviews, he and his guests share details of their lives with the world.

One of the people he interviewed is his friend Sara Brinkman, who is a hostess at a restaurant and is proud of her independence. The common theme in all of the blog posts is the common humanity that we all share, no matter what challenges people are dealing with.

"I think what [people with Down syndrome] all have in common is their hopes and dreams," Sam said. "The chance to make [them] come true. Down syndrome doesn't make a difference, okay? We make the difference."

See what love the Father has given us, that we should be called children of God. (1 John 3:1)

Thank You, Lord, for showing Your love through the many people You have blessed my life with!

A Lesson in Mourning

In October 2018, an anti-Semitic gunman murdered 11 worshippers at the Tree of Life Synagogue in Pittsburgh. The event prompted *Patheos* blogger Deacon Greg Kandra to recall Jesus' declaration, "Blessed are they who mourn."

Deacon Greg then cited a *New York Times* report about the Jewish burial tradition: "Jews do not mourn alone," the reporter wrote. "During shiva, community members visit the relatives of those who have died, bringing food and standing together for kaddish, the memorial prayer. They sit with them, speak fondly of those who have passed on and comfort those left behind."

Deacon Greg observed, "This suggests that when Jesus spoke of the 'blessed' who mourn, He was speaking of more than sorrow or tears. He was speaking of community. He was talking about those who offer comfort—weeping with those who weep, praying with those who pray, not letting someone mourn alone. To do this is an act of solidarity—a gesture of compassion and love."

Do not avoid those who weep, but mourn with those who mourn. (Sirach 7:34)

Though grieving with others can feel like a burden, Lord, give me the strength to do it with love.

The Thrifty Man's Surprise

Social worker Alan Naiman of Seattle, Washington, was known for his thrifty ways. As reported by the *Associated Press*, he even "patched up his shoes with duct tape." That's why people—even close friends—were so shocked when he left 11 million dollars to children's charities upon his death from cancer at age 63.

Naiman was a former banker who knew how to invest, and had also inherited several million dollars from his parents. One friend, Susan Madsen, noted that he had grown up with a brother who suffered from a developmental disability, which may have influenced his decision to become a social worker focused on helping children.

One of the groups that received part of Naiman's fortune is the Pediatric Interim Care Center, which "cares for babies born to mothers who abused drugs." Barbara Drennen, the charity's founder, said, "I wish very much that I could have met him. I would have loved to have him see the babies he's protecting."

When you give alms, do not let your left hand know what your right hand is doing. (Matthew 6:3)

Remind me, Father, to tend to the needs of the vulnerable and leave this world better than I found it.

A New Kind of Sign Language Interpreter

Roy Allela, an engineer in Kenya, couldn't understand his deaf niece when she used sign language to communicate with him, so he came up with an innovative, groundbreaking idea: he created gloves that translate sign language into audible speech.

The Guardian reports, "The gloves—named Sign-IO—have flex sensors stitched on to each finger. The sensors quantify the bend of the fingers and process the letter being signed. The gloves are paired via Bluetooth to a mobile phone application that Allela also developed, which then vocalizes the letters."

The gloves are still in the testing and development phase, but Allela hopes to make them available to children in Kenya and eventually, around the world. He said, "The general public in Kenya doesn't understand sign language so when [my niece] goes out, she always needs a translator. Picture over the long term that dependency… When it affects you personally, you see how hard people have it. That's why I've strived to develop this project to completion."

Let people learn to devote themselves to good works in order to meet urgent needs. (Titus 3:14)

May people with special needs find bright futures, Lord.

Kolbe House Serves Prisoners

Near Chicago's Cook County Jail and Juvenile Temporary Detention Center stands Kolbe House, a facility that offers hope for rehabilitation and redemption to prisoners. *Franciscan Media* reports, "By offering Masses, religious services, spiritual counseling, and Bible study, workers and volunteers offer a refuge to the incarcerated and a level of mercy to their lives."

Jaime Chavez, age 17, has benefited from Kolbe House's mission. Imprisoned twice for gun possession, he realized that he needed to get his life on the right track. The people of Kolbe House helped Chavez get his G.E.D., tap into his artistic tendencies, and deepen his faith. He said, "They help keep me motivated and give me people to talk to. Also I feel I can't do things wrong because if I do, I'll disappoint them. They care."

Father Arturo Pérez-Rodríguez, who used to work at Kolbe House, said, "I love this because it's direct ministry. It's important to just be with these people without judgment of them. We take these people for who they are and where they are at. We offer a spiritual grounding for their lives."

I have come to call not the righteous but sinners. (Mark 2:17)

May Your Good News reach those in prison, Jesus.

The Benefits of Volunteering

Carolyn Ramey grew up in Harlem and never wanted to live anywhere else. "I am very passionate about who we are and what we do and how that drives a deep-rooted tradition of volunteerism in Harlem," she told the *Manhattan Times*.

Ramey believes volunteering changes people and communities. She says it has two main aspects: "donation of time and engagement." Consider these noted benefits of volunteering:

- It reduces stress.
- It sharpens your social skills.
- It keeps you active.
- It helps you meet new people.
- It gives you a sense of purpose.

There are many organizations that can help you find just the right volunteer activity for you. Look for some in your community.

Like good stewards of the manifold grace of God, serve one another with whatever gift each of you has received. (1 Peter 4:10)

May we strive to be active and dedicated volunteers, Messiah.

Saints Alive!

The story of how the New Orleans Saints got their name is one of the great tales of professional sports. On *Aleteia,* J.P. Mauro recounted how the 1967 merger of two professional football leagues into the NFL created an opportunity for Louisiana to get its first team. Many teams had been named after the heritage of the cities that hosted them, and on November 1st (All Saints Day!), the NFL announced New Orleans would be home to the latest football expansion team.

The city's anthem had long been "When the Saints Go Marching In," a jazz standard and nod to the city's Catholic heritage. In fact, that heritage ran so deep that the team's owners checked with the Archbishop before announcing the name. They were worried some might think it sacrilegious, but their worries were in vain.

The Bishop loved the idea, and even wrote a team prayer that included a plea to "grant our Saints an increase in faith and strength so they will...overcome the Lions, the Bears, the Rams, the Giants, and even those awesome people in Green Bay."

The Spirit intercedes for the saints according to the will of God. (Romans 8:27)

May I find holy inspiration in an unexpected place, Lord.

King of Hearts

It's rare that a song literally saves a life, but that was the case with actress/singer Jen Lilley's debut single "King of Hearts." In fact, she orchestrated it that way because she is a foster parent with a deep passion for children's causes.

Though primarily known as an actress, Lilley had grown up singing in church. When an opportunity to record an album arose in recent years, she decided to pursue it.

As "King of Hearts" was launching, Lilley wanted the proceeds to benefit a worthy cause, so she chose Project Orphans, which was founded by Brittany Rae Stokes, who runs a children's village in Uganda for orphans and kids in foster care.

At first, Lilley wanted to help cover their monthly operating costs, which would help 73 children and 300 families. But then she saw that a boy named John needed heart transplant surgery that would cost $6,500. That seemed like a managcable goal to Lilley, so she invited her fans to buy her single and save a life. And they did. John's operation was successful, and he is grateful to Lilley and her fans for his second chance at life.

Learn to do good; seek justice, rescue the oppressed, defend the orphan. (Isaiah 1:17)

Send me opportunities to do good for others, Holy Spirit.

A Doctor's Grace Towards a Killer

In 2018, a man intent on killing Jews entered the Tree of Life Synagogue in Pittsburgh and murdered 11 people. After police shot the killer in order to apprehend him, his wounds were treated by Dr. Jeffrey Cohen, who was a member of the synagogue's congregation.

Many people on social media felt awed by the grace that Dr. Cohen extended toward a murderer, and admitted they didn't think they could do it themselves. Blogger Elizabeth Scalia offered these thoughts on that topic:

"Grace is available to all of us, and finding oneself the beneficiary of grace has little to do with *worthiness*, and everything to do with one's *willingness*…to co-operate with the Creator who is the author and giver of all graces."

"It is precisely that willingness to pursue Truth and Love that renders one able to co-operate with grace in challenging, unimaginable moments. What Dr. Cohen has modeled for all of us…is the ironic power that comes from making a habit of serving something greater than one's self."

The faithful will abide with Him in love, because grace and mercy are upon His holy ones. (Wisdom 3:9)

Help me to cooperate with Your grace, Yahweh.

Locked In Her Body, Part One

In 2006, Victoria Arlen began experiencing unexplained pain, weight loss, and tiredness. Doctors couldn't figure out what was wrong with the previously energetic fifth grader, so they kept saying, "It's all in her head." As time passed, she lost the ability to walk, control her arms, and swallow food. Again, doctors found no reason for her symptoms, so they moved her to a hospital wing that dealt with psychiatric patients.

There, Victoria was physically and verbally abused by the medical staff who seemed to think that being rough would snap her out of her condition. Through it all, she prayed for healing, but her pain got so unbearable that she believed she was dying. Suddenly, a Bible verse popped into her head: "Be strong and courageous. Do not be afraid; do not be discouraged, for the Lord your God will be with you wherever you go" (Joshua 1:9). Victoria said she felt calmness and the love of God surround her.

She got out of that hospital, but her medical problems remained and she ended up in a different hospital where she fell into a coma for over a year. More of her story tomorrow…

Blessed be...the God...who consoles us in all our affliction. (2 Corinthians 1:3,4)

Instill doctors and nurses with compassion, Messiah.

Locked In Her Body, Part Two

In 2009, after being in a coma for over a year, Victoria Arlen's mind awakened, but her body didn't. She couldn't control anything, but she could hear the grim reports that doctors gave her family every day, assuming she was still in a vegetative state. As difficult as it was to remain hopeful, Victoria focused her mind on her will to live and accomplish great things.

The only outside hope Victoria received at this time came from the visit of a Catholic priest from Africa named Father Bashobora. He was present on her 15th birthday to pray with the family as Victoria endured seizures every few minutes. Father Bashobora kept saying, "In time, she will be healed." They all started to believe him.

Though there was still pain and darkness for Victoria after that visit, she one day received a new sleeping medication that unintentionally stopped her seizures and pain. More importantly, she was able to blink, which allowed her to communicate with her family again. Soon after, she regained the use of parts of her body. The conclusion of her story tomorrow...

Jesus...said, "For mortals it is impossible, but... for God all things are possible." (Mark 10:27)

Bring hope and healing to suffering patients, Jesus.

Locked In Her Body, Part Three

Victoria Arlen slowly regained the use of her body, but was confined to a wheelchair for some time. The sports-loving teen practiced swimming, which led to her winning a gold medal in the 2012 London Paralympics. In 2015, she earned a job as a broadcaster on *ESPN*. In 2016, she learned to walk again. And in 2017, she became a competitor on *Dancing with the Stars*.

Though Victoria moved forward with gratitude for this new chance at life, she had to learn to forgive a major blunder by her doctors in the past. While visiting a specialist in 2013, he reviewed her medical history and quickly deduced that "a simple round of steroids" could have prevented the inflammatory process that nearly killed her.

The realization that all of her troubles could have been avoided knocked the wind out of Victoria, but she chose to focus on the future instead. During a *Christopher Closeup* interview about her memoir *Locked In,* she concluded, "Leaning on the ones I love the most—and knowing that God is bigger [than everything]—is a huge part of what keeps me going."

I, the Lord your God...say to you, "Do not fear, I will help you." (Isaiah 41:13)

Give me the strength to overcome my challenges, Savior.

A WWII Vet's Legacy

Al Mampre of Skokie, Illinois, never cared for the word "hero" in reference to himself, even though he easily exemplified its meaning. A medic with the U.S. Army's Easy Company, he served in Europe during World War II and risked his life many times to save his fellow soldiers.

The *Chicago Sun-Times* recalled that during a firefight with the Nazis in the Netherlands in 1944, Mampre ventured into the open to help save a lieutenant who had been shot. In doing so, Mampre himself was "shot in the calf and groin." He had to give himself a shot of morphine so he wouldn't go into shock. A Dutch civilian helped rescue both men.

Following the war, Mampre was "awarded a Bronze Star and two Purple Hearts for his service." He got married, raised three daughters, and lived an extraordinary ordinary life, often giving speeches to raise money for veterans or police and fire departments. In those speeches, he conveyed a simple message: "Be good, do good." Mampre passed away at age 97 in 2019, but his legacy of being good and doing good live on.

Let us not grow weary in doing what is right, for we will reap at harvest time. (Galatians 6:9)

Inspire me to be good and do good, Father.

An Explosive Return to Faith

Though he grew up in a Christian home, actor Kristoffer Polaha started questioning his faith at age 17. His life was going well, so he decided to test God by giving up prayer for six months and seeing how things went. Those six months turned into six years. Polaha told *The Billy and Justin Show*, "[It was] me sort of wanting to take the place of God in my own heart."

Polaha explored other religions, but eventually came to feel God "knocking on the door of my heart." The actor didn't seriously turn back to his faith, however, until he survived an explosive experience that should have killed him.

He and a friend were standing in front of a building in New York City when the restaurant on the ground floor suddenly blew up. Polaha endured a major head injury, but recalled, "The fire marshal in the emergency room [said], 'You guys should have been decapitated...You should not be here right now, and the fact that you are is a miracle."

From that point on, Polaha surrendered his life to God, believing he'd been given a second chance.

God, who is rich in mercy...made us alive together with Christ. By grace you have been saved. (Ephesians 2:5)

Thank You for the second chances You give me, Father.

Keeping God in the Title

A New York news anchor's decision to leave God in his book may have ruffled a few feathers in the publishing world, but it paid off beyond his wildest imagination.

Anchor John Gray of Albany recalled to *Faithwire* that he wrote a children's book called *God Needed a Puppy,* after his own six-month-old puppy passed away. He wrote the story as therapy, but was encouraged by others to approach publishers about it. Gray's first meeting did not go as planned. The publisher told him that he needed to take God out of the title.

Gray responded that if you take God out of the story, there is no story, so he refused to do so. He self-published the book, expecting to sell a few hundred, but was floored when 8,000 copies flew off the shelves.

Gray self-published again, selling over 14,000 copies, before signing with Paraclete Press, a Christian publisher. Now, this upstate news anchor is as known for his writing—and his faith—as he is for his broadcasts.

Do not be ashamed, then, of the testimony about our Lord. (2 Timothy 1:8)

Give me the courage to stand up for my belief in You, Heavenly Father.

Love Comes From Self-Sacrifice

Our culture has given us the wrong idea of love, writes Christina Antus on *Busted Halo*. Too often we think of someone else completing our needs—or that romantic love will be perfect and make us perfect. That fantasy can come crashing down when faced with the reality of marriage and living with another human being, whose flaws and imperfections have to mesh with your own flaws and imperfections.

After 10 years of marriage, Antus writes that she found love is rooted in giving and self-sacrifice: "Married love is not unlike the love that God has for us. It's a real, genuine, authentic kind of love, and there is a sense of comfort in knowing the person you are with has given up just as much as you for the same reasons as you."

The good news is that the satisfactions of real love are so much more deep and profound than the surface-level happiness we may have been expecting. That's the beauty of a vocation of love well-lived.

**Let all that you do be done in love.
(1 Corinthians 16:14)**

Jesus, help married couples live out their commitment to sacrificial love.

The Spider-Man That Almost Wasn't

"With great power comes great responsibility." That's the motto of the comic book character Spider-Man, who was the brainchild of Stan Lee. When the Marvel Comics writer passed away in 2018 at age 95, tributes noted that he revolutionized the comic book industry by giving his heroes real-world problems and relevant moral issues to deal with. But as *Entertainment Weekly* recalled, his best-known creation, Spider-Man, almost didn't see the light of day.

When Lee came up with the idea in the early 1960s, he pitched it to Marvel's publisher, Martin Goodman, who told him it was "the worst idea he'd ever heard" because "people hate spiders!" When Lee added that he wanted to make Spidey a teen with real problems, Goodman responded, "Ugh! It's obvious you have no conception of what a hero really is."

Lee decided to publish his Spider-Man story anyway in an anthology series that was ending since nobody cared about the contents anymore. After going to print, Spider-Man proved so popular that Goodman told Lee to give the character his own book. "And lo," noted Lee, "a legend was born."

Your work shall be rewarded. (2 Chronicles 15:7)

Give me persistence in pursuing my goals, Father.

Becoming a Saint

In his homily for All Saints Day 2018, Deacon Greg Kandra offered some insightful observations grounded in the Beatitudes. He said, "Each of us has the potential to become a saint. So it's worth asking ourselves: How are we doing? The Gospel gives us a checklist.

"Are we 'poor in spirit'? Do we give up things for ourselves so that we can give more to others? How selflessly do we mourn? How much time do we give to others who are sorrowful, or forgotten, or alone?

"Are we meek? Do we strive, like John the Baptist, to decrease, so that Christ may increase? How zealously do we hunger and thirst for righteousness? Do we stand for justice and what is right? Do we stand beside those who are victims?

"Do we show mercy?...Do we have clean hearts? Or are they cluttered with jealousy or pettiness or hate? Do we strive to make peace?... Finally: are we willing to be persecuted, to suffer, in the name of Christ?

"This is where blessedness begins. This is how holiness takes root. This is how we can become saints."

Contribute to the needs of the saints.
(Romans 12:13)

Guide me in living according to Your will, Jesus.

A Hug is Like Life

Writer Sean Dietrich met Miss Jean Lee at a Methodist church in Enterprise, Florida. Though they didn't know each other well, she gave him the type of hug that his grandmother used to give—and he never forgot it.

When Dietrich heard that Miss Jean Lee was in hospice due to pancreatic cancer, he wrote a tribute to her on Facebook and reflected on the power of hugs: "I believe that a hug is like life. A body lives an entire existence beside the heartbeat of the universe without realizing it. All that ever was, all that ever will be, all that is, all the beauty of life, it's only a few inches from us. All the time. But we are separated by a thin veil.

"A good hug pulls back the veil and whispers things to the human spirit….like: 'You're special to me…' Or: 'Life has been worth living simply because you were in it.' Or: 'I love you.'

"I wish you peace, Miss Jean Lee. I wish for Heaven itself to hold you, squeeze you, look you straight in the eyes, and with all the weight and beauty of Eternity, to tell you…'It's gonna be okay.'"

You are precious in My sight, and honored, and I love you. (Isaiah 43:4)

Embrace Your children when they return to You, Father.

Unchained from Addiction

A child's addiction can test any parent's hope for a better future. That's one reason why Nancy McCann Vericker and her son, JP, wrote *Unchained*, a book about the whole family's experience going through JP's struggles with drugs and alcohol.

Nancy, a former newspaper reporter, tells the story with gripping details. JP's addictions began in his late teens. His parents and siblings all felt helpless as they watched him get worse. It was often isolating, as Nancy writes, as "no one comes to your door with a casserole the day after the police arrive at your house." She spent a lot of her energy trying to protect her family from the judgment of others.

They finally found JP a halfway house and treatment center that helped his sobriety. One counselor, Paul, made a big impact. Nancy told *Catholic New York*, "God put him in our path. His unflinching commitment to give away his gift of recovery to us taught me so much. He taught JP the ropes." Today, JP is living sober and is the co-founder of a substance abuse treatment center. He lives out his message of hope each day.

Endurance produces character, and character produces hope. (Romans 5:4)

My God, may I never give up hope for those who seem lost.

The Power of Positivity

We all know a positive outlook can help throughout life, but new research has shown just what a difference it can make in learning. A Stanford experiment in brain imaging, summarized in an article at *Inc.com*, looked at students, ages seven to ten.

The research showed that liking a particular subject helps the students' brains work better. This was especially true with math, which had the highest level of negative association among the children.

"Attitude is really important," said Dr. Lang Chen, the study's author. "Based on our data, the unique contribution of positive attitude to math achievement is as large as the contribution from IQ."

So take note, parents: the very act of staying positive has a noticeable effect on outcomes, helping change brains for the better. No matter what the difficulty, accentuate the positive!

You have made known to me the ways of life; You will make me full of gladness with Your presence. (Acts 2:28)

Grant me a glad heart, Lord, and may that gladness radiate through me to others!

Blind Player Makes Sports History

Jake Olson was born with a rare form of eye cancer that cost him his vision by age 12. Though blind, he never lost his love for sports, and joined the University of Southern California (USC) football team as a walk-on player in 2015.

When his right eye was removed in 2009, then USC Coach Pete Carroll invited Olson to come and meet the team. He began a friendship with Carroll that resulted in a try-out for the team when he arrived at USC.

Olson was USC's long snapper for years, throwing back the football so that it could be set for the kicker to kick a field goal. Though completely blind, his snaps were perfect. In 2018, he played his last game for USC. His athletic performance and ability to defy the odds of his disability made him an inspiration to people throughout the country.

For his success, Olson gives all the glory to God. He told the *Los Angeles Times,* "There's a beauty in it. If you can't see how God works things out, then I think you're the blind one."

May the God of hope fill you with all joy and peace in believing. (Romans 15:13)

Lord, give me the vision to see how You're working things out in my life.

Project Open Paw

For the past several years, San Francisco resident and doggy daycare worker Paul Crowell had an important self-appointed side job: distributing leftover food to his city's homeless canines. "I became known as the 'doggy food man,'" Crowell told *The Things* writer Mark Lugris.

After the daycare center switched owners, however, giving away leftover dog food became strictly prohibited. So Crowell took matters into his own hands, and created Project Open Paw.

All proceeds from this online nonprofit are used to aid the homeless dogs of San Francisco. To date, Project Open Paw has raised over $98,000. In the near future, Paul hopes to garner enough money to open a shelter for canines whose owners are either temporarily incarcerated or in rehab.

"The dogs give these people a reason to carry on," Crowell concludes. "They help each other live. My goal….has been to keep them together unless there's abuse…to reunite owners with their dogs when they're able to have them again."

The righteous know the needs of their animals. (Proverbs 12:10)

Jesus, may we never underestimate the power and healing of unconditional love.

Spearhead, Part One

In 1944, at age 21, Clarence Smoyer found himself in Nazi-occupied Belgium, serving with the U.S. Army's Third Armored Division on a job that ran counter to his natural, peaceful personality: tank gunner. He was the one who now had to pull the trigger in order to kill another human being.

Far from developing any kind of bloodlust, Clarence's motivation was simply that he wanted to keep every member of his crew alive. That became increasingly difficult when his tank became the Spearhead, the lead tank going into battle.

As recalled on *Christopher Closeup* by author Adam Makos, whose book about Clarence is called *Spearhead,* one of the ways that Clarence dealt with fear was prayer. During a tense situation in the Battle of the Bulge, he started talking to God as if He were sitting next to him in the tank. He would either say to God, "Get me through this night"—or "Thank You for getting me through this day." It was a simple, yet deeply profound way of connecting with his Maker in the worst of circumstances.

More of the story tomorrow...

The Lord used to speak to Moses face to face, as one speaks to a friend. (Exodus 33:11)

Teach me to speak to You as a friend, Jesus.

Spearhead, Part Two

In addition to sharing Clarence Smoyer's experiences with the U.S. Army during World War II, *Spearhead* author Adam Makos also explores the conflict's final days from the perspective of an 18-year-old German tank gunner named Gustav Schaefer, whom he was also able to meet and interview.

During a *Christopher Closeup* interview, Makos said, "Gustav was just a farm kid from northern Germany...I was amazed at how simple his lifestyle was before he joined the military. They didn't have a radio. They didn't have power. They would work the fields in this farm, from sun up until sun down. He basically was so far removed from Nazi Germany."

But in war, you go where you're sent. And Gustav was sent to Cologne, Germany, to face down the American tank squadron, led by Clarence. "It was a suicide mission," explained Makos.

It was in Cologne that Clarence crossed paths with Gustav in a firefight that would haunt them both for years to come—and lead them to meet in person more than 65 years later. That part of the story tomorrow...

Let all the soldiers draw near. (Joel 3:9)

Fill our hearts with peace instead of violence, Lord.

Spearhead, Part Three

In 1945, Clarence Smoyer's tank led the American army through the streets of Cologne, knocking out a German Panzer tank that was guarding Cologne Cathedral. *Spearhead* author Adam Makos said, "In essence, Clarence liberated the symbol of God in the city of Cologne."

It was there that Clarence's tank got into a firefight with German tank gunner Gustav Schaefer. A young German woman named Kathi Esser accidentally "drove through the middle of their gunfire," explained Makos. "These two enemies shot to pieces a civilian car. Eventually, Kathi succumbed to her wounds and died there.

"Her death propelled these two enemies, Clarence and Gustav, to not only seek each other out as old men, but to go back to Cologne in 2013, to reunite on the steps of the Cathedral—and then to go back to the place where they fought to try to find answers. To try to find, how did we shoot this young woman and how can we make amends for it? How can we seek forgiveness from her?"

The conclusion of the story tomorrow...

Out of his anguish he shall see light. (Isaiah 53:11)

Bless the souls of all innocents killed in war, Jesus.

Spearhead, Part Four

Clarence Smoyer and Gustav Schaefer reunited on the steps of Cologne Cathedral in Germany in 2013. They discussed their encounter during the war and realized they would never be able to tell which of their bullets actually killed Kathi Esser. It was a tragedy of war that they couldn't have done anything about.

That meeting was also the start of an unusual but beautiful friendship. *Spearhead* author Adam Makos told The Christophers, "They were men who once fought each other, who once tried to kill each other. But at their core, they were good men and they became friends."

Makos notes how knowing men like Clarence and Gustav has changed him: "These men remind me to look for something bigger, strive for something good, and to be about other people, other than just living for myself...It's important for us to remember as we wait in line at Starbucks or go to a soccer game on a weekend, that 75 years ago, some young guy died in a snowy field in Belgium for us. Or on a street in Cologne in the rubble, bleeding to death with his buddies around him. It's too important to just go about our lives and forget these people."

Pursue peace with everyone. (Hebrews 12:14)

Help us turn enemies into friends, Prince of Peace.

A Humble Marine's Honor

Retired Marine Sgt. Maj. John L. Canley of Oxnard, California, is a decorated Vietnam War veteran. He served 28 years in the Marine Corps, and was awarded numerous medals and commendations for his valor in battle. During one particularly difficult battle, he was credited with saving the lives of 20 of his fellow Marines, having carried these wounded men to safety.

Those who served with Canley thought he deserved the Medal of Honor, the nation's highest military award, for his actions. But time had passed, and the Medal of Honor is given within five years of the extraordinary acts of valor.

After years of pushing for Canley's case, a special exception was made. The now 80-year-old retired sergeant became the 300th Marine to be presented with the medal.

"He is an extraordinarily humble man and he never talks about his role," Congressional Representative Julia Brownley told *ABC News.* "He always talks about his Marines, his Marines that he loved then and he loves now."

God opposes the proud, but gives grace to the humble. (James 4:6)

Help me to be humble, Lord, and serve You and others selflessly.

Johnny-on-the-Spot

Charles Dasch was a hard man to keep down. In 1913, as a teenager in Baltimore, he went to work to support his mother, five sisters and brother. He lost an arm on the job in a piece of machinery he had been assigned to oil. Though given a small cash settlement, Dasch lost his job.

When local authorities threatened to break up the penniless family, the youth went to Annapolis to complain to the governor. The visit gained him publicity, kept the family together, and brought in public donations.

At 21, Dasch rescued a man from a car that had gone off a dock into the water. In Philadelphia in the 1930s, he evacuated dozens of people from a deadly hotel fire in which he was overcome by smoke. Later, he became a crusader for the rights of the elderly in Woodbury, New Jersey, where he ran for public office at age 72.

Do opportunities make people—or do people make opportunities? Charles Dasch would have made his mark no matter where he lived. Ask God to make you a self-starter.

I am confident...that the one who began a good work among you will bring it to completion. (Philippians 1:6)

Jesus, help me to be decisive and proactive in all things.

Stress, Sanity, and Survival

If we learn how to handle stress, it can prolong life and make it a lot more pleasant. Two psychologists, Robert Woolfolk and Frank Richardson, offered tips on handling tension in their book, *Stress, Sanity and Survival:*

- Learn to plan. Disorganization can breed stress.

- Recognize and accept limits. We can never be perfect and often have a sense of failure or inadequacy.

- Be a positive person. Focus on the good qualities in yourself and those around you.

- Learn to tolerate and forgive.

- Avoid unnecessary competition.

- Have fun. Find pastimes that are enjoyable to you.

- Get regular physical exercise and learn how to relax.

- Talk out your troubles. Expressing your bottled-up tension can be incredibly helpful.

Anxiety weighs down the human heart, but a good word cheers it up. (Proverbs 12:25)

Lord, help me to deal with stress in a world that's often filled with it.

Long Name Changed His Life

What's in a name? Plenty, if it happens to be Oliver William Twisleton-Wykeham-Fiennes.

Shortly after World War II, Oliver was a subaltern aboard a British troopship. He was mistakenly awarded a three-berth cabin—one for each of his surnames—so he went out to find other people with whom to share the room.

One of his cabin mates turned out to be an Anglican Franciscan friar. Their conversations changed young Oliver's life. He entered the church, took holy orders, and eventually became the Dean of Lincoln Cathedral in Sydney, Australia.

"The name's a help, really," the soft-spoken English cleric claimed. "Some people think it's a joke and become inquisitive. This means you can talk to people."

Whatever the length or origin of the name we bear, each of us has a role in life that God has assigned to us alone. Let us each live up to that responsibility.

A good name is to be chosen rather than great riches. (Proverbs 22:1)

Help us, Lord, in our struggles to establish ourselves as individuals.

Paying Sam Back

For many years, one of the hottest attractions on late-night radio in the East was a man whose voice was ordinary enough to belong to your Uncle Horace, and whose advice covered everything from marriage problems to home repairs.

The late Bernard Meltzer of *WOR* had a warm, blunt, and spiritual approach to life's problems. Those who called him for advice often waited an hour to get on the air.

Meltzer, who had experience in 12 different fields, said his career at the City College of New York was saved by a $100 book loan he accepted in desperation from an unsuccessful lawyer named Sam. The lawyer told him: "I want no interest. You're not going to pay me back in money. But when anybody needs help, you're going to help him, and you're going to say to yourself, 'I'm paying Sam back.'"

Almost 200,000 people heard Bernard Meltzer sign off each night with: "May the light of the Lord guide you, and keep you in the palm of His hand. God keep you. Good night."

Do not let your hand be stretched out to receive and closed when it is time to give. (Sirach 4:31)

Father, help us to be ready listeners, always willing to help.

Through the Eyes of a Child

Having a child can teach adults to look at their surroundings with a sense of wonder they might have lost through the years. That was certainly true of *ABC News* correspondent Linsey Davis. She admitted on *Christopher Closeup* that the "daily grind of everyday life" left her somewhat jaded and blind to "the rainbow, the sunset, and the grandeur, beauty, and intricacy [of nature]."

One day, when it was snowing heavily, Linsey looked at the streets and lamented how much trouble getting to work would be. Then she observed her young son "holding out his little hand with his gloves on and marveling at each snowflake."

That sight changed Linsey's perspective. She said, "I really did decompress and take the time to talk to him about how no snowflake is alike and they're all different. Just the uniqueness of that and of God's creation. It's so rare, I think, that as adults we take that step back and appreciate life with the eyes of a child, to see life with the same excitement."

**Their children become a blessing.
(Proverbs 37:26)**

When I feel jaded, Holy Spirit, remind me to appreciate the wonders of this world as if I am still a child.

Sportscaster Gives Praise to God

Sportscaster James Brown has been a regular part of the lives of football fans for many years, through his work at *FOX* and *CBS*. But did you know that he is also an ordained minister?

As reported in a recent *Washington Post* profile, Brown grew up in Northeast Washington, D.C., and played basketball for DeMatha Catholic High School. Following college, he was a salesman at Xerox when he took a freelance job as a broadcaster, calling Washington Bullets games.

Though Brown has grown into a major talent, he hasn't let success go to his head. As he arrived at the Acela Express to take him to work, he thanked the men who helped him with his bags by saying, "God bless you, gentlemen." And during the train ride, he meditated quietly on the line from Psalm 33, "We wait in hope for the Lord; He is our help and our shield." Brown notes, "It's how I give thanks and center myself."

Thanksgiving is a core piece of Brown's faith because he knows that both professionally and personally, he's "been blessed over and over again."

I will bless the Lord at all times; His praise shall continually be in my mouth. (Psalm 34:1)

Keep me grounded in thanksgiving, Father.

The 50 State Kindness Challenge

At a fast food restaurant in Hollywood, Father Jim Sichko stands at the drive-thru window buying lunch for everyone who stops by. He has also spent time topping off people's gas tanks at a gas station in Kentucky. Next, he is on his way to Arizona to continue with his mission: spreading kindness across all 50 states in the U.S.

Father Sichko is one of 700 papal missionaries of mercy from around the world, appointed by Pope Francis as part of the "Jubilee of Mercy" that began in December 2015 (but currently has no end date). The pope's simple mandate was, "Go forth and do good deeds."

"My approach," Sichko told the *Associated Press,* "is not so much speaking about the word of God, although I do a lot of that, but showing the presence of God through acts of kindness."

He says the first question people ask is "Why are you doing this?"

Father Sichko's response: "My question is... why not?"

This is the kindness you must do me: at every place to which we come, say of me, He is my brother. (Genesis 20:13)

God, give my love strength to extend across all boundaries.

Let Your Light Shine On

Depression nearly caused young actress Letitia Wright to give up on acting, but it was through her faith in God that she rose out of the darkness and toward her dreams.

When 25-year-old Wright won a BAFTA Rising Star Award in 2019, she took the opportunity to give a voice to those suffering with depression. As reported by *BBC.com,* Wright said during her acceptance speech, "I want to encourage you... anyone going through a hard time...God made you, and you're important."

Backstage, the *Black Panther* star further added that this is a tough industry and she is grateful she had the faith to never give up. Wright's speech was an opportunity to remind anyone dealing with depression to "let their light shine on."

"I was struggling with stuff before that many people in the industry are struggling with and are hiding away from," Wright said, "and that was my opportunity to say, 'I see you and I understand what you're going through.'"

God saw that the light was good; and God separated the light from the darkness. (Genesis 1:4)

Lord, may my light shine on and overpower the darkness.

Befriending the Bully

Texas father Aubrey Fontenot was feeling discouraged. His eight-year-old son Jordan's recent declining progress reports were linked to his being bullied at school. Finally, Aubrey decided to confront the source of the problem, head-on.

In a surprising but generous gesture, Aubrey sat down for an honest heart-to-heart with his son's bully, Tamarion. He discovered that the boy's family had recently become homeless, and the reason Tamarion made fun of Jordan was because he was a frequent victim of bullying himself.

"I just said, 'I'm sorry you had to go through that,'" Fontenot told *Inside Edition*. "I'm sorry my son has to go through this...How about the day you're suspended...you come spend time with me? We're gonna talk...You'll talk to my son.'"

And that is exactly what they did! By the end of this fateful day, which included a shopping trip for new clothes for Tamarion, the two youngsters were friends. Aubrey's sharing of this story on social media prompted the creation of a GoFundMe page for Tamarion's family, which raised over $31,000.

Love your enemies, do good. (Luke 6:35)

Abba, whenever possible, help us make peace with our enemies.

Loaves and Fishes

"Loaves and Fishes" is an organization started by Kathleen DiChiara many years ago to relieve hunger among the unseen poor in the affluent town of Summit, New Jersey. One of those receiving help was a mother who had nothing but a box of cereal to feed her three children for three days. Others were unemployed or elderly people living on a fixed income.

DiChiara got the idea when a parish priest suggested that people give up meat on Wednesdays and Fridays in Lent to protest high meat prices. She took it a step further by asking her friends to use the money saved to provide canned goods to the needy in their own community.

Each week, parishioners brought canned goods to Sunday services. Hundreds of families in Summit and surrounding communities benefited. Many came back a few months later with bags of groceries for other people.

Jesus' multiplication of the loaves and fishes was a mystery of love. We carry on His work when we search out those in need.

Taking the five loaves and the two fish He looked up to Heaven...and gave them to the disciples to set before the crowd. And all ate and were filled. (Luke 9:16-17)

Help me search out those in need, Jesus.

I Serve a Savior

Country music superstar Josh Turner is known for his distinctive baritone voice. But around 26 years ago, in the town of Hannah, South Carolina, he was just a teenager who felt a passion for country music and prayed to God for guidance because he wanted to pursue it as a career.

During a *Christopher Closeup* interview about his album *I Serve a Savior,* he recalled God giving him this answer: "If this is what you want, I'll give it to you as long as you trust Me."

That trust became difficult when Josh developed a lesion on his right vocal cord that caused him to lose his voice. He couldn't understand why God would do this to him.

But, said Josh, "I kept thinking back to [God] saying, 'Hey, just trust Me.' So, that's what I did. I endured the hardship part of it, and I did the work that was required of me, and it actually became a blessing in disguise. Once I went through everything at the Vanderbilt Voice Clinic in Nashville, and the Classical vocal training, and going to Belmont University, I [noticed] that my voice kept getting stronger and richer. Had I not gone through that time, I would never have the voice that I have now."

**When I am afraid, I put my trust in You.
(Psalm 56:3)**

Help me trust Your wisdom for my life, Lord.

A Wish Upon a Star

In November 2018, an 11-year-old girl in foster care saw a star falling from the sky and did what young kids do at that sight: make a wish. In her case, it was to be adopted, along with her six siblings. Happily, that wish came true a few days later.

As reported by *Yahoo,* Terri and Michael Hawthorn of Hot Springs, Arkansas, had been foster parents to many children over several years and even adopted two of them in April 2018. The opportunity then arose to adopt the seven siblings, ranging in age from eight to 15, some of whom had previously lived with them. These brothers and sisters were bounced around the foster care system for years because their parents were drug addicts.

Terri and Michael grew to love them all, so they wanted to make it official. They shared the adoption news with the kids at church on the Sunday before Thanksgiving. The siblings were overjoyed—and so were their new parents! Terri told *WFTV,* "This is a blessing, they are a blessing. Every day these kids wake up and they are giggling and they are happy...Lots of prayer and love is what made this possible."

Whoever welcomes one such child in My name welcomes Me. (Matthew 18:5)

Lead abandoned children to loving homes, Father.

Send in the Clowns

Some people wake up Thanksgiving morning ready to put a smile on people's faces by cooking a scrumptious meal of turkey with all the trimmings. But for the past several years, Rachel Zampino puts a smile on people's faces in a different way: she serves as a clown in the Macy's Thanksgiving Day Parade.

Zampino works as a law clerk in Mineola, New York, but when a friend of hers from Macy's asked if she wanted to join his clown team, she jumped at the chance—and even attended a special school for training.

As reported by *Newsday*, "Zampino learned the tricks of the trade at Macy's Clown U—and hung the diploma on her office wall next to her Harvard University law degree."

Now, she loves interacting with spectators along the parade route. "I always like to pick out somebody who's not smiling or looks disengaged," Zampino said. "I wave or smile at them. To see them pick up and start to glow is a cool feeling."

He lifts up the soul and makes the eyes sparkle; He gives health and life and blessing. (Sirach 34:20)

Move me toward being the kind of person who lifts other's spirits, Holy Spirit.

A Sermon of Gratitude

Pastor Jason Micheli stood on the pulpit of Aldersgate United Methodist Church in Alexandria, Virginia, to deliver the Thanksgiving sermon. It had been a year since he was diagnosed with an incurable form of cancer and had last spoken to the congregation. Micheli's cancer was "controlled," but this husband and father of two young children would need chemo every two months for the remainder of his life.

Micheli told his congregation, "You've fed us and prayed for us and with us. You've helped us with my medical bills and you've sat with me in the hospital." Micheli then noted that it was much easier for him to give others help than to accept it himself. But this experience taught him about gratitude.

Strength and healing, he discovered, came through community. And gratitude is not about "keeping score," but about relationships. As reported in *Guideposts*, Micheli preached, "We can endure all things because you've been with us...It was kind of you to share my nightmare. It was kind of you to make my cancer—our cancer—yours too."

You are those who have stood by Me in My trials. (Luke 22:28)

Lord, help me to face life's many trials with a grateful and humble heart.

Searching for Blessings

"I know I should thank God for my blessings every day, but sometimes I don't feel thankful." So writes author and Patheos blogger Gary Zimak with refreshing honesty. So how does he deal with these moments? With a little help from the short, simple suggestions in an article by Andrew Hess called "100 Remarkable Reasons to Thank God." Here are a few:

- "Thank God for knitting you together in your mother's womb."
- "If you were born to parents who loved you and provided for you, thank God (and thank them)."
- "Thank God for all the times He has protected you when you were unaware."
- "For every automatic bodily process keeping you alive at this very moment, thank God."
- "If you've grown in faith, grace, holiness, joy, love, hope, wisdom or obedience, thank God."
- "If you've never woken up in a war zone, thank God."
- "If you have people with whom you enjoy spending your free time, thank God."

With gratitude in your hearts sing psalms, hymns, and spiritual songs to God. (Colossians 3:16)

May I find something to be grateful for every day, Lord.

After the Fire

During the 1990s, Dawn Foster grew up in a Catholic family in Wales that didn't practice its faith or even think much about God. But her view of religion changed in 2017 after the fire in London's Grenfell Tower killed more than 70 people. She spent hours talking to survivors and noted that churches opened their doors to help the victims.

Writing in *The Guardian*, Foster said, "One evening, speaking to a woman who was close to tears because her friend was missing, she grasped the pendant around my neck—a Miraculous Medal I had been given by a family member—then fixed her eyes on me and asked me to pray for her. I was sorely out of practice but not remotely in a position to say no."

"Offering a prayer for someone seemed materially inconsequential but weighted with significance: it is easy to give money without any thought...but a prayer genuinely prioritizes someone else over your own emotions."

That prayer led Foster to start practicing her faith. By attending church every Sunday, she gained a sense of being part of something greater than herself.

My peace I give to you. (John 14:27)

Help me find peace in You, Jesus.

Teacher Finds Joy in the Classroom

A bulletin board at the front of teacher Grace Chengery's first grade classroom at St. Columba School in Oxon Hill, Maryland, reads, "For the greater glory of God." The bulletin board at the back says, "Go forth and set the world on fire."

In the spring of 2019, the Archdiocese of Washington D.C. presented Grace with a Golden Apple Award, which recognizes a teacher's professionalism, excellence, leadership, and commitment to Catholic values. "Grace brings Jesus to everybody, every day," said one colleague. "In her actions, in her words, she shows nothing but love."

Grace told Washington's *Catholic Standard* newspaper, "Every day I get the joy of bringing my kids around the reading table and teaching them how to read...We also build the foundation of religion in the classroom, so we spend a lot of time talking about being saints and how we are saints in the making...There is a lot of joy in our school. And because we get to celebrate Mass and talk about God, how could there not be joy in what we do?"

Happy are those who find wisdom, and those who get understanding. (Proverbs 3:13)

Lord, guide our educators to teach Your ways.

Advent's Anticipation

To begin Advent with the right mindset, Catholic Charities of Rockville Centre, New York, shared the following reflection: "*Advent* is Latin for 'coming'...From the earliest days of our Church, it was meant to be a time of expectant preparation and waiting. These days, most folks try to avoid waiting at all costs. We yearn to rush right through things...Yet, the Advent wait for the Christ child is precisely what fills our hearts and brings us His peace. This is not something to avoid, but rather to embrace.

"Oftentimes, waiting is made easier when it's done in community with others. Just think, how many lines have been made less tedious by passing time in pleasant conversation with another?... Scripture tells us that even the Magi who looked for the infant king had to patiently search the night skies for weeks to find Him and, when they did, He wasn't on a throne surrounded by wealth. He was in a cave reserved for livestock.

"So this Christmas, may we look up and around like the Magi in search of our Lord. And may you and your loved ones enjoy the wait and find our Savior in the ordinary places all around you."

They were all waiting for Him. (Luke 8:40)

Fill my heart with longing for You, Messiah.

Generosity of the "Everyday Santa"

John Fling of Columbia, South Carolina, passed away in 2007. But during his life he was known as the "Everyday Santa."

Fling used most of the small salary he earned at a car dealership to tend to the needs of many elderly, blind, and disabled people in the city.

In addition to his full-time job, Fling spent up to 40 hours a week serving others. He would buy and deliver groceries to some, and offer money to others. He read mail to the blind and escorted them while they shopped.

His generosity knew no limits. Three different times he signed over the ownership of his own car to someone who desperately needed a means of transportation.

Becoming a Good Samaritan requires sacrifice. But often it's just plain fun. It makes life meaningful to be a kind, giving person day after day. When was the last time you gave up your convenience to help a stranger?

We must support the weak, remembering the words of the Lord Jesus, for He Himself said, "It is more blessed to give than to receive." (Acts 20:35)

May I do my best to help others, Jesus.

Loving the Neighbor You Hate, Part One

When she was anchoring the early morning news at an *ABC* affiliate in Dallas during the early 1980s, Peggy Wehmeyer went to bed at 8:00 p.m. because she had to get up at 2:30 a.m. But there was one thing standing between her and a good night's sleep: her neighbor's dog, a Yorkshire terrier that would bark loudly outside every evening.

Wehmeyer's hatred for the boisterous canine and its owner grew every night. Finally, Wehmeyer and her husband filed a noise complaint with the city, which led to bad blood with the woman who owned the dog. The case was scheduled to go to court on December 24th.

When Wehmeyer's in-laws arrived for a visit a few days before Christmas, she asked their opinion. Writing in the *Washington Post,* Wehmeyer recalled her father-in-law saying, "If you're going to be a follower of Jesus, you'll love your enemy, not sue her." Her father-in-law was a former prisoner of war in Japan who had forgiven his captors, so she took his words seriously. And she knew what she had to do next. That part of the story tomorrow...

Love your enemies. (Matthew 5:44)

Teach me to be a better follower of Yours, Jesus.

Loving the Neighbor You Hate, Part Two

Taking to heart her father-in-law's advice to forgive the neighbor with the loudly barking dog, Peggy Wehmeyer reluctantly walked over to her house and knocked on the door. The woman, who Wehmeyer dubs "Laura," answered the door with a resentful look on her face and asked, "What do you want?"

Wehmeyer answered, "I came to apologize. I'm sorry I've ramped up this conflict by taking you to court on Christmas Eve. I don't want to fight anymore. If there's anything I can do to be a better neighbor, I hope you'll let me know."

Initially, Wehmeyer felt humiliated saying these words. "But as I watched the surprise register on my neighbor's face," she wrote in the *Washington Post,* "something else happened in me. I felt lighter, freer, released from an ugly burden. As our brief exchange ended, I glanced past her shoulder into her cluttered living room where a toddler sat coloring. My rage inexplicably gave way to compassion."

That compassion grew even more when Laura knocked on Wehmeyer's door a few weeks later asking for a favor. That part of the story tomorrow…

**Whenever you stand praying, forgive.
(Mark 11:25)**

Give me the humility to do Your will, Father.

Loving the Neighbor You Hate, Part Three

Laura arrived at Peggy Wehmeyer's door, saying that she had run out of grocery money for herself and her daughter, Kassie. She asked Peggy if she could borrow a few dollars to tide them over. Though Peggy was surprised by the request, she lent Laura $20—and received it back a few days later.

More importantly, the two women began talking more frequently—and the dog even stopped barking! "I came to know Laura as a bright and kind woman with a warm smile," wrote Peggy. "Over time, I learned that she had been deeply wounded and that she struggled with mental illness, much like my own mother. She told me she had one friend, and it was me."

Peggy and Laura lived next door to each other for seven years, until they moved to different parts of town and eventually lost touch. But in 2019, Peggy received a message from Kassie notifying her that Laura was near death in the hospital. Peggy asked if she could visit her, and Kassie responded, "Yes, please come. You were her only friend. It would mean a lot."

The conclusion of the story tomorrow...

When...people please the Lord, He causes even their enemies to be at peace with them. (Proverbs 16:7)

Open my heart to new friendships, Savior.

Loving the Neighbor You Hate, Part Four

When Peggy Wehmeyer arrived at the hospital, Kassie revealed that Laura had attempted suicide due to her depression. Laura was unconscious, but Peggy told her, "Laura, it's Peggy, your friend, and I'm here. You're not alone. I love you. God loves you." Peggy then read Laura some Bible verses.

Writing in the *Washington Post*, Peggy said, "As she died, Laura handed me a bittersweet gift. Years before we met, my mother, who also battled depression, had taken her life in the same way...I couldn't get to her in time to say goodbye. I never got to stroke my mother's hair or remind her that she was loved. Now, a woman I once called my enemy was freeing me from that long-held regret and sorrow.

"Laura died that night. I'll never forget her, nor the friendship that taught me that it's likely to take much more than a better political candidate, cable news show or party platform to reverse the tide of hatred and revenge that is tearing this country apart. Maybe it will have to start with us, walking across the driveways that divide us and knocking on a door."

Blessed are the merciful, for they will receive mercy. (Matthew 5:7)

Prince of Peace, may we never underestimate the importance of human connections.

An Unusual First Date

Some couples go out for "dinner and a movie" on their first date, but Brad Bond asked his then-girlfriend Jessica to do something a little different. Since it was December, they went shopping for children's gifts that they could donate to their local Toys for Tots Christmas campaign.

As Brad told Orlando, Florida's *WESH-TV*, his parents had always made Christmas special for him, so he wanted to bring joy to kids who might not otherwise receive presents for the holiday.

The charitable outing became an annual tradition for Brad and Jessica when they celebrated the anniversary of their first date. And in 2018, on their December wedding day, they asked all their guests to join them at a nearby store to buy gifts to donate to Toys for Tots.

Eric LaRoche, Brad's best man, said, "It's a great benefit for all the kids. There are so many that are in need." Brad added, "I have the most amazing wife on the planet, so if we (are) able to give back and share our blessing with others, then what better thing can we do on our wedding day?"

God loves a cheerful giver. (2 Corinthians 9:7)

May marriages be grounded in selflessness, love, and generosity, Jesus.

Moses' Christmas Gifts

It's common for pedestrians to give money to homeless people on the street, especially during the Christmas season. But in 2018 in Phoenix, Arizona, a homeless man named Moses Elder was the one giving away $100 bills to strangers.

As reported by Steve Hartman of *CBS News,* the idea was hatched by "Secret Santa, the anonymous, wealthy businessman who every year goes around the country handing out $100 bills to random strangers." He wanted to "dispel the myth that the homeless just take," so he gave Elder $3,000 to distribute as he saw fit.

One of the recipients was father of seven Danny McCoy, who had dropped some loose change in Elder's cup. A homeless mother of five and a man from church were also on the receiving end of Elder's kindness. And Secret Santa made sure that Elder was well taken care of, too.

Elder noted the joy he received from giving away all that money. He added, "This here is a new beginning for me. Today we changed a lot of people's lives. But I believe my life was changed the most."

Be rich in good works. (1 Timothy 6:18)

Instill me with a generous heart, Jesus.

The Christmas Cradle

Christopher Award-winning author Meadow Rue Merrill is a mother of five, and she laments the fact that Christmas has gotten so commercialized. As a way for children to maintain the joy of the holiday while still centering it on Jesus, she wrote an illustrated book called *The Christmas Cradle*.

It tells the story of a girl named Molly and her family who are visiting her Aunt Jenny to celebrate the holiday. Molly comes across a Christmas cradle in a box, and asks her aunt its purpose.

Aunt Jenny explains, "Growing up, we played a game to share God's love with others. Each December, we sang carols, delivered meals, and visited people who were lonely. Then we wrote each act of love on a card and put it in the cradle as a gift for Jesus. On Christmas morning, we read the cards and prayed for each person we'd served."

In writing the book, Merrill said she contemplated the questions, "How do we give a gift to Jesus, who has everything? How do we honor Him on this day? I feel like we can do that best by giving gifts to other people in His name."

Serve one another with whatever gift each of you has received. (1 Peter 4:10)

Help me perform many acts of love this Christmas, Jesus.

What Would Mary Do?

People can seem a little self-obsessed nowadays, with our endless selfies and social media posts. But during the season of Advent, the Church asks us to look at ourselves in a way that isn't about vanity, in a way that's honest and can change us for the better. In his book *Daily Devotions for Advent,* Deacon Greg Kandra offers reflections that help readers do just that.

One of those reflections looks at Mary, the Mother of Jesus, who gave of herself joyfully and selflessly. During a *Christopher Closeup* interview, Deacon Greg observed: "Mary is such a great example for all of us! So often we ask ourselves, 'What would Jesus do? WWJD?' I challenge people [in homilies], 'Ask yourself, WWMD? What would Mary do?'

"She accepted everything that God asked her to do, and did it unquestioningly, with so much trust, love and fidelity. I think that is part of our great challenge, particularly in the age that we live in now: to trust God, and to not be suspicious of Him, and to feel like whatever happens, God is going to get me through this. Certainly, Mary did that with courage, conviction, and complete trust. If we can live our lives like that, what a joy."

My spirit rejoices in God my Savior. (Luke 1:47)

Guide me closer to your son, Mary.

The Red Cardinal's Gift

On the back cover of Matt Maher's album *The Advent of Christmas,* the singer-songwriter expresses an unusual sentiment of gratitude: "Thanks to the red cardinal that kept showing up during the making of this record."

Matt lost his father in 2017, so he had to navigate feelings of sorrow while making an album about a season of joy. Some of the tracks include a trace of melancholy, though, such as the song "When I Think of Christmas," which includes the lyric "There are faces I miss, the ones not with us."

That was one of the two songs for which the cardinal showed up. Having grown up in Newfoundland, Maher had never seen many cardinals, so he Googled the words "red cardinal Christian symbolism."

Maher told The Christophers, "It said that if you keep seeing a red cardinal, it's a sign that someone you love is praying for you. And immediately, I thought, 'Dad!'...My dad loved Christmas...and loved melancholic Christmas songs...He was Irish, and the Irish love a good cry. So as soon as I saw that cardinal, I just knew my dad is praying for me with this record."

Blessed are those who mourn, for they will be comforted. (Matthew 5:4)

Bring comfort to the grieving this Christmas, Savior, and remind us that love never dies.

The Advent of Christmas

Singer-songwriter Matt Maher hopes that his album *The Advent of Christmas* helps listeners who are dealing with anxiety to rediscover feelings of hope and peace. During a *Christopher Closeup* interview, he shared a quote he once heard on that very topic: "If you're up all night because you're worried, you know how to meditate; you just need to change the subject."

Advent, he pointed out, can move us beyond that anxiety. It's a season of anticipation in which we're called to reflect on "the deeper things you're longing for in life. We celebrate the birth of Jesus at the darkest time of the year...to remind people that it's okay to have expectation and hope for God to show up in dark times. Because that's what He was born to do."

Each of us can reflect that light to others and help make this the world God intended it to be. It's an idea Maher addresses on the track "Glory (Let There Be Peace)." He said, "Peace in the world today [is] not going to start on some ethereal plane and just descend upon everybody. It's going to start in the individual human hearts asking for it. Every great spiritual moment in... Christianity starts with one person."

**Let them seek peace and pursue it.
(1 Peter 3:11)**

Lord, make me an instrument of Your peace.

Between Dark and Light

An ancient parable goes like this: A rabbi once asked his students how they could tell when the night had ended and the day was dawning. One student responded: "Could it be when you can see an animal in the distance and can tell whether it is a sheep or a dog?"

The rabbi said, "No."

Another asked: "Could it be when you look at a tree in the distance and can tell whether it is a fig tree or a peach tree?" Again the rabbi shook his head no.

"Well, then, when?" demanded the students.

The rabbi responded: "It is when you look on the face of any man and see that he is your brother. Because if you cannot do this, then no matter what time it is, it is still night."

Each of us can be a light in the darkness, bringing the warmth and peace of God's love to our brothers and sisters. We only need the eyes to see that we are the light of the world.

For with You is the fountain of life; in Your light we see light. (Psalm 36:9)

Creator, set me afire with the light of Your grace.

When You See Unicorn Slippers...

Bridget Spillane and her two sons had often driven down Woodbine Avenue in Northport, New York, but Christmas night 2018 was the first time they'd seen little pink unicorn slippers lying in the street. They got out of their car and found several other items, too, that looked like they were supposed to be Christmas presents.

As reported by Jenna DeAngelis on *CBS2 News,* Spillane took the packages to the local police station, then posted a message on Facebook stating that anyone who lost some gifts should contact the Northport Village Police Department. Her post went viral and within one hour, Cathy Montague arrived to reclaim the presents.

Montague related that her children and grandchildren were visiting from California, when the trunk of their car somehow opened up and the packages fell out. As a result of the Spillanes initiative and kindness, the Montague family went to bed "with big smiles" that night.

Do not withhold good from those to whom it is due, when it is in your power to do it. (Proverbs 3:27)

May kindness and initiative guide my actions, Lord, even when it means extra time and effort.

A Christmas Lesson

Writing in *Guideposts,* author Norman Vincent Peale recalled a Christmas in the early 1900s that taught him about not judging people by appearances. "When I was seven or so," he said, "we lived in Cincinnati, close to the tracks where the streetcars screeched around corners. A special car came along to grease the rails, and we children, I'm sorry to say, made fun of the grimy old guy who ran it." They shouted "Greasy!" at him whenever he came by.

A few days before Christmas, Peale's father, a minister, asked Norman to come along with him on one of his hospital calls. "Someone you will recognize isn't feeling well," he said.

Upon entering the hospital room, Norman was shocked to see "Greasy" laying there: "My father introduced him by his real name, just as he would the finest gentleman, and when he shook my hand, it didn't feel greasy at all. 'I hope you grow up to be a fine man like your father,' he exclaimed."

When they left, Norman's father reminded him that their sick friend wasn't Greasy: "He's a child of God."

In Christ Jesus you are all children of God through faith. (Galatians 3:26)

Christ, may I see Your face in everyone I meet.

Everyone Has a Backstory

Jesse Carpenter lived on the streets of Washington for 22 years. After he froze to death one December day, it was discovered that he had been decorated for heroism during World War II for having made three trips to a forward area to rescue wounded comrades.

But after his discharge, Carpenter couldn't cope with civilian life. He developed a drinking problem. Still, there was poignant evidence that he never stopped being a caring individual.

His body was found at the feet of his street companion—a disabled man whom he pushed around the city in a wheelchair.

It's unfair to stereotype the homeless. Each story is different. They are people with human emotions, problems, and needs. Judge not. And remember, your smile might be the only one they see that day, so offer it willingly to everyone you meet.

Do not judge, so that you may not be judged. (Matthew 7:1)

Jesus, I do not want to be judgmental. Help me.

The Way We Love Our Children

Since 1955, California's Disneyland has held a candlelight Christmas-themed celebration featuring 700 musicians and singers, and a celebrity guest. As reported by *Aleteia,* "The show intersperses the telling of the biblical Christmas story between some of the most popular Christmas carols."

In 2018, actor Chris Pratt read from the gospel of Luke, then added his own comments, saying: "Being a parent has really changed my life in so many ways. And one of those ways is to understand, truly, the love that a father could have for a child."

"The way we love our children, the more we love our children, the more we will understand the capacity for our Father in heaven to love us. Each and every one of us is a precious creation, and He just marvels in the ways that we can try to please Him. That should give us a great deal of comfort."

"This holiday season, let us embrace every one of our tomorrows with hope and love. And through this holiday spirit, may we continue to spread peace and good will throughout the world. Thank you, and Merry Christmas!"

See what love the Father has given us, that we should be called children of God. (1 John 3:1)

Help me to accept and share Your divine love, Father.

A Simple Sign of Love

Shortly after finishing dinner, Katie Powell Bell rushed to put on makeup for a get-together she was attending, while also dressing her young daughter. The dirty dishes, she decided, would have to wait until she came home.

Later that evening, when she returned, she was happily surprised to find that the kitchen was "sparkling clean." Her husband had washed everything in her absence.

Writing on the *Today Show's* Community blog, Bell noted that she and her spouse aren't perfect and have let each other down numerous times. "We don't always get it right," Bell noted. "But, a lot of days, we do."

She continued, "We tackle life as a team because that's what being married is all about: stepping up when your partner really needs you... offering support, reassurance, and validation when life gets busy and you need to be reminded what a blessing marriage really is. It's real life, not a rom-com. It's a partnership, not a contest. It's forever and always; a daily choice to love and cherish. And if, like me, you are really lucky...it's your husband secretly cleaning the kitchen just because he loves you."

**The heart of her husband trusts in her.
(Proverbs 31:11)**

May loving actions strengthen marriages, God.

The Greatest Christmas Gift

Just before Thanksgiving in 1918, the Fleury family of Woodhaven, New York, received a heartbreaking telegram from the War Department: their son, Private Fred Fleury, had been killed in action during a World War I battle in France.

Also devastated by this news was another soldier, Private Frank Nauth, who had been a childhood friend of Fred's. As reported by the *Ridgewood Times,* "They served together in the same unit in France and were at each other's side when fragments of the same shell struck them both."

Nauth suffered a serious leg wound and was sent to a hospital in Bath, England, where he continued to grieve over the loss of his friend. That's why he was so shocked when he ran into Fleury at the hospital!

Fleury had not been killed after all, just injured. The report had been a mistake. Fleury's family in New York got word two weeks later that he was still alive. They all rejoiced at the greatest Christmas gift they ever received.

The people who survived the sword found grace in the wilderness. (Jeremiah 31:2)

Lord, bring comfort to the families of our military men and women who have lost their lives in battle.

Buon Natale!

Writer and chef Caroline Chirichella grew up in New York, where she enjoyed visiting the "beautifully insane" streets of Manhattan during the Christmas season. But at age 24, she decided to move to a small village in Italy, called Guardia Sanframondi, "to live life at a slower pace, more quietly, and at a much lower cost," she wrote in New York's *Daily News*.

The Italians, she discovered, had their own beautiful Christmas traditions. A marching band made its way through the town playing carols; villagers took part in a competition to build their own manger scenes; and everyone, even strangers, greeted each other on the streets to say, "Buon Natale!"

Chirichella observed that almost everyone in town knows each other, and short shopping excursions can take hours because people invite you into their homes for "panettone." Though she still treasures her New York Christmases, she concludes, "I've learned to go with the flow and see what comes my way. I've learned to walk at a slower pace and take the time to see and hear what's around me. That's part of the magic. And that's what's really important in life."

**Wisdom makes one's face shine.
(Ecclesiastes 8:1)**

Help me to appreciate what's important in life, Jesus.

Santa Colonel, Part One

It was 1955, and the U.S. was on edge about the Cold War with Russia escalating into a real conflict. Col. Harry Shoup of the Continental Air Defense Command had a red phone in his Colorado Springs office to alert him in case of an attack. But the phone number was a secret. Only a four star general at the Pentagon and Shoup himself had the number.

One December, the red phone rang. Shoup was shocked when a child's voice on the other end asked, "Is this Santa Claus?" As reported by *NPR*, the no-nonsense military man initially got annoyed because he thought someone was playing a practical joke on him. But he quickly realized the caller was serious, so he played along, pretending to be Santa. Then he asked to speak to the child's mother.

She explained that she had gotten the number from a Sears ad, encouraging kids to call Santa. Apparently, the newspaper had printed one of the digits incorrectly. Now, the Air Defense Command was getting inundated with calls from children. But this mistake led to a beloved tradition that continues to this day. That part of the story tomorrow...

God has brought laughter for me. (Genesis 21:6)

Help me find humor in awkward situations, Jesus.

Santa Colonel, Part Two

Though the Santa phone calls to the Air Defense Command office eventually died down, the men who worked there joked about it often. Since they had a big glass board on which they tracked all planes coming into the U.S. and Canada, they decided to draw Santa and his reindeer on it on Christmas Eve 1955.

When Col. Shoup saw the drawing, he got an idea. He called a local radio station and told them the Command Center was tracking Santa in his trip across the world. The media loved it—and so did children. Shoup became known as "Santa Colonel," and the tracking became an annual tradition, now led by NORAD, the North American Aerospace Defense Command.

In an interview with *NPR*, Col. Shoup's three children—Terri, Rick, and Pam—recalled this aspect of their father's life. Terri said, "Later in life he got letters from all over the world, people saying, 'Thank you, Colonel'...And in his 90s, he would carry those letters around with him in a briefcase that had a lock on it like it was top-secret information. He was an important guy, but this is the thing he's known for." Rick added, "It's probably the thing he was proudest of, too."

A cheerful heart is a good medicine. (Proverbs 17:22)

Teach me to bring joy to a child, Savior.

A Christmas Across Borders

In Nogales, Mexico, an eight-year-old girl named Dayami wrote a letter to Santa Claus, asking for art supplies, a doll, a dollhouse, and a few more things. She attached the note to a balloon and let it float away, hoping it would find its way to Kris Kringle.

Several days later, 20 miles away in Patagonia, Arizona, Randy Heiss was out walking his dog when he saw the remains of the balloon, along with the letter. As reported by *NBC News*, Randy and his wife wanted to fulfill Dayami's Christmas wishes, so they contacted *Radio XENY* in Nogales to ask if they could find the girl. One hour after the station posted the message on its Facebook page, the girl was located.

The Heisses traveled to Mexico to personally deliver their gifts to Dayami and her sister. "Love has no borders," said Randy. Seeing the children's happy faces brought the Heisses "healing joy" because their only son had died nine years prior. Randy said, "We don't have grandchildren in our future, so getting to share Christmas with kids was something that's been missing in our lives."

The measure you give will be the measure you get back. (Luke 6:38)

May generosity lead me to "healing joy," Messiah.

A Bus Driving Santa Claus

When Curtis Jenkins took a job as a school bus driver for Lake Highlands Elementary School in Dallas, Texas, he didn't plan on following in the footsteps of Santa Claus, too. But Jenkins' kind and giving nature led him to live out the spirit of Christmas in a special way.

As he got to know the kids on his bus, he would ask them what they wanted for Christmas, all the while keeping a list of what they said. Then, using mostly his own money with a little help from a few community members, Jenkins bought and wrapped presents for more than 50 children. On December 22nd, he handed them out on the bus to a group of delighted students.

Jenkins told *Good Morning America* that his motivation was to "magnify loving and caring" because "kids these days need to see positivity."

To further his mission of promoting kindness, Jenkins created a nonprofit called the Magnify, Caring and Change Foundation. He concludes, "If you show a lot of kids a lot of love, they will do the same."

Whoever is kind to the poor lends to the Lord, and will be repaid in full. (Proverbs 19:17)

Teach me to be kind and generous, Jesus.

A Christmas Mercy

On Christmas Eve, Melanie Wilson was finishing her shift at a retail store when she discovered a young man had been shoving items into his pants pockets and sweatshirt. She asked if she could help him with anything, hoping that would deter him from shoplifting. But he just looked distraught and quickly left.

Wilson followed him into the parking lot, confronted him about the stolen items, and said she wouldn't call the police if he simply returned them. He agreed, so they re-entered the store where he gave her back toys, candy, and decorations.

Wilson asked the man, whose name was Shawn, if he stole these things for his family. He teared up and told her they were for his two children and nephew. He had no money, but wanted to give them a nice Christmas. Touched by his plight, Wilson rang up the items at the register (they came to $75) and paid for them herself. Shawn was profoundly thankful.

Wilson said, "[God] works in the most amazing ways. He has touched me today. I'm not even a real religious person, but you can feel it in your heart...Merry Christmas."

Whoever gives to the poor will lack nothing. (Proverbs 28:27)

Inspire me to offer someone a second chance, Messiah.

Silent Night

On Christmas Eve 1818, in Oberndorf, Austria's St. Nicholas Church, the beloved hymn "Silent Night" was performed for the first time. As Thomas McDonald recounted in the *National Catholic Register,* Father Josef Mohr, the church's assistant pastor, wrote the lyrics, while Franz Gruber, its organist and choir director, composed the melody.

The song's message of God's love and peace grew out of an era in which Austria had endured years of war and unrest. "And in the midst of this chaos and transformation," said McDonald, "Father Mohr wrote about 'heavenly peace.'"

The human heart's longing for peace continued to make the song resonate, especially during times of strife. McDonald noted, "Almost 100 years after the song's composition, war once again ravaged Europe, but at midnight on Christmas Eve 1914, the guns fell silent. In Flanders, along the front, men could be heard on both sides singing 'Silent Night' in their own languages. Those languages continue to multiply... bringing the simple and profound message around the world: Christ the Savior is born."

To you is born this day in the city of David a Savior, who is the Messiah, the Lord. (Luke 2:11)

May Your heavenly peace shine in my heart, Jesus.

The Line Between Heaven and Earth

We sometimes make distinctions between "the sacred" and "the worldly," but Father Michael Simone makes the point that "the birth of Jesus revealed that any part of creation could be a suitable dwelling place for the Almighty."

Writing in *America,* Father Simone continues, "On the night of Jesus' birth, the line between heaven and earth is blurred. Not only do angels appear to shepherds, but they appear to shepherds who are going about their normal duties.

"These are not individuals on a vision quest or undergoing some kind of mystical initiation or heavenly ascent. These are shepherds on the job, doing what they normally do, but on that night, they perceived the glory of God and heard the angels' anthem. [Luke's] account of the mingling of heaven and earth at the birth of Christ...directs later generations of disciples to pay attention to the grace all around them.

"Jesus' birth reminds us that any part of creation can communicate God's presence. If we live with that expectation, we, too, will hear angels sing even as we toil."

Our help is in the name of the Lord, who made heaven and earth. (Psalm 124:8)

May I find signs of Your grace all around me, Jesus.

Christmas in the Sky

Pierce Vaughan was happy to have graduated from flight attendant school and gotten a job with Delta Airlines. The only downside was that 2018 would mark her first Christmas separated from her parents because she had to work.

Then, her dad, Hal, came up with an unusual idea: he would use his airline benefits to get free tickets on all the flights Pierce was scheduled to work on Christmas Day and the day after. This way, they could spend the holiday together, after all.

The story won the world's attention because Hal started chatting with Mike Levy, a passenger sitting next to him on one of the flights. Levy was so impressed at the lengths this loving father went through to spend Christmas with his daughter that he wrote about it on Facebook—and the story went viral.

What made the Vaughan's Christmas adventure even more special is that Hal had broken his neck earlier in the year and didn't know whether he would ever walk again. He recovered with intense physical therapy and created a beautiful Christmas memory with his daughter.

He will turn the hearts of parents to their children. (Malachi 4:6)

Strengthen the bonds of love between parents and children, Lord.

God, Give Me a Sign

Singer Michael Ketterer rose to fame as a finalist on *America's Got Talent,* but his personal story is also worthy of attention. With his wife, Ivey, he has adopted five boys from foster care. Their story was recently told in *Lightworkers* news.

After their daughter was born, medical complications ruled out any further pregnancies for the Ketterers. They still wanted to expand their family, though, so they adopted three rambunctious brothers. Later, when the opportunity presented itself to adopt a boy with cerebral palsy, they said yes. This adoption was harder than the others. The medical appointments and the boy's needs were taking their toll. Michael recalls praying, "God, if this boy is my son and should stay with me, send me a sign."

The next moment, Michael looked up to see a billboard with a father running a marathon, pushing his disabled son in a wheelchair. Then it clicked. "No matter how messy your life may be," said Michael, "God still wants to be a champion for you." Michael knew that God had purposefully placed this boy, and the others, in his family.

Be a father to orphans...You will then be like a son of the Most High. (Sirach 4:10)

May I never fear opening my heart to someone in need, Lord.

Coffee with a Cause

"Be kind and drink great coffee." This is the motto of the recently established Burly Man Coffee, a Christian-based subscription company in South Florida which is also passionate about helping people, specifically single mothers.

Jeremy Wiles, one of Burly Man Coffee's co-founders, told *Fox News* reporter Caleb Parke, "If you look at what's going on in some of the most impoverished parts of our country, there's poverty—but what's at the root of that is fatherlessness."

One of the short-term goals for Burly Man Coffee is to give away 100 cars to single mothers in need. There has already been one amazing success story.

Celeste Bokstrom, a single mom and caretaker of her autistic 16-year-old son, Logan, had been without a car for four years. After two years, she had finally saved up enough to purchase a used vehicle, only to have it stolen. Enter Burly Man Coffee Company.

"I had faith and believed that God knew my struggles," Bokstrom exclaimed, "but I never expected this. Receiving a car has changed my world...I am so grateful."

Do not neglect to do good. (Hebrews 13:16)

Heavenly King, open our hands and hearts to those in need.

A Short History of the Calendar

The word "calendar" comes from the Latin "calendarium," meaning an interest or account book. Julius Caesar decreed that the calendar year match the solar year—365 days, with an extra day every fourth year.

To correct errors in the Julian calendar, Pope Gregory XIII ordered 10 days dropped and the new year to begin on January 1st instead of March 25th. He also decreed that each year divisible by four should be a "leap" year, except the years numbering the centuries which should have extra days only when divisible by four hundred.

Calendars can number our days. But they cannot guarantee that we will put them to good use. More of us should set aside a few minutes each day for prayerful reflection and to allow God to speak to us in silence. This practice would help us record more accomplishments before the final accounting.

Teach us to count our days that we may gain a wise heart. (Psalm 90:12)

Help us, Holy Spirit, to make the most of the time that has been given to us.

A Rabbi's Resolutions for All

Rabbi David Wolpe of Sinai Temple in Los Angeles shared some suggestions for New Year's resolutions on his Facebook page. They include:

- "To laugh often, but in amusement, not in derision.

- "To pray often, but with appreciation, not avarice.

- "To lift my eyes from screens and remind myself of the variety, beauty, occasional savagery and sublimity of God's created world.

- "To try listening without simultaneously preparing a response.

- "To believe that opinions other than my own... deserve the dignity of serious appraisal.

- "To recognize that as a fortunate person, I cannot permit myself the luxury of exhausting my compassion for others.

- "To push myself—and the world—a little closer, in whatever way I am able, toward betterment as I understand God would have it.

- "To forgive myself and others for the shortcomings in realizing these goals, without abandoning or belittling them."

I resolved to live according to wisdom, and I was zealous for the good. (Sirach 51:18)

Teach me to walk always in Your ways, Father.

A Deacon's Resolutions for All

"Exercise and lose weight. Save money. Travel."

Deacon Greg Kandra noted that a survey showed those were people's top resolutions for two years in a row. So on his blog, he suggested making alternate resolutions inspired by Mary, the mother of Jesus. Deacon Greg wrote:

"First, let us resolve to be open to miracles and to listen to angels, wherever and however we may find them. Let's be prepared to expect the unexpected—and to welcome what God brings us as a gift of grace...

"Resolve to serve, and to do it for others with haste, as Mary served her cousin Elizabeth. Let us resolve to magnify God, so our souls and our lives and everything we are can beautifully and boldly proclaim the greatness of the Lord. Let us resolve to live our lives in a way that honors and celebrates His work in the world...

"In times of anxiety and trial may we, like Mary and Joseph, resolve to still seek Jesus when we fear we have lost Him—and trust that God will help us to find Him."

His mother said to the servants, "Do whatever He tells you." (John 2:5)

Lead me to be more like Your mother, Jesus.

Also Available

We hope that you have enjoyed *Three Minutes a Day, Volume 54*. These other Christopher offerings may interest you:

- **News Notes** are published 10 times a year on a variety of topics of current interest. Single copies are free; quantity orders available.

- **Appointment Calendars** are suitable for wall or desk and provide an inspirational message for each day of the year.

- **Annual Poster Contest for High School Students** and **Video Contest for College Students**

- **Syndicated "Light One Candle" newspaper columns**

- **Website—www.christophers.org**—has *Christopher Closeup* radio programs; links to our blog, Facebook and Twitter pages; a monthly *What's New* update; and much more.

For more information about The Christophers or to receive News Notes, please contact us:

> The Christophers
> 5 Hanover Square
> New York, NY 10004
> Phone: 212-759-4050/888-298-4050
> E-mail: mail@christophers.org
> Website: www.christophers.org

The Christophers is a non-profit media organization founded in 1945 by Father James Keller, M.M. We share the message of personal responsibility and service to God and humanity with people of all faiths and no particular faith. Gifts are welcome and tax-deductible. Our legal title for wills is The Christophers, Inc.